INDIA BOOKVARSITY

LOTUS CHOICES

Editor: Mahendra Kulasrestha

Classics Revived
for an
Ultramodern World

The Golden Book of JAINISM

Humanity's Oldest Religion of Non-Violence

Acharanga Sutra
Uttaradhyayana Sutra
Sutrakritanga
Kalpa Sutra

Lotus PRESS
4735/22, Prakash Deep Building,
Ansari Road, Darya Ganj,
New Delhi- 110002

THE GOLDEN BOOK OF JAINISM

Selected Sutras, with Life of Tirthankara Mahavira, translated into easy-to-understand English by the renowned scholar

HERMANN JACOBI

Lotus Press : Publishers & Distributors
Unit No. 220, 2nd Floor, 4735/22, Prakash Deep Building,
Ansari Road, Darya Ganj, New Delhi- 110002
Ph.: 41325510, 23280047, 98118-38000
• E-mail : lotuspress1984@gmail.com
www.lotuspress.co.in

Source:
Sacred Books of the East
Edited by F. Max Muller
and published by
Clarendon Press, Oxford, UK
in the 1880s

The Golden Book of Jainism

ISBN: 81-8382-014-X (H/B)

Printed & Published by : **Lotus Press Publisher & Distributors,** New Delhi-02

Editorspeak

No God, Only Soul

The Jaina philosophy and practice is perhaps the most unique system of ancient world philosophies, which in its metaphysics as well as the monastic order easily surpasses all scholarship and behavioural imagination. It is one religion that admits no intelligent Creator who could be credited with the creation of life and the universe—and what is significant is that, unlike the Buddha, it does not prefer to keep quiet about the subject, but goes rather deeply into its analysis, and states its logic quite emphatically. The last short chapter deals with it, and in a world, which, with the exception of China and Japan, is deeply embedded in the easy idea of God—or Creator—to the forceful exclusion of any other idea, even the theory of Evolution—which generates querulous situations even in the progressive Americas—this should provide a new dimension for thought and debates in modern times.

According to Jainism, Reality is uncreated and eternal. Every object possesses infinite characters both in regard to what it is and what it is not. It has its modes and qualities through which persists the essential substance through all the times. This basic substance is permanent while its modes etc. emerge as well as disappear. Both permanence and change are facts of existence. The soul and its consciousness are eternal, but is subjected to pain and pleasure, superimposed by modes like the body, all of which keep changing.

The substances are real, and are six in numbers, broadly divided into living and non-living. The soul is a living unit of consciousness, and are infinite in number. These may be free or in bondage, the latter may possess only one or more sense organs, the former being associated with earth, water, fire, wind, etc., and the latter being different according to the number of sense organs they possess. These classifications and names etc. of these are amazingly detailed in Jaina scriptures.

The elaborate presentations of every given subject is another special feature of Jaina doctrines, to be found in no other system of the world. Those related to cosmology, universe, its inhabitants, the middle and nether worlds, the world of gods, the history of the world, its periods and eras, its great men, even the world-periods and holy men of the future, anything and everything about life that one can imagine of, is most astounding and engrossing. The doctrine of Karma is equally fantastic, most meticulously worked out about the journey of the soul from its lowest state to liberation.

The Nayavada and Syadvada are two other unique features of Jainism, their very own singular contributions to world-logic systems. The former is an instrument of analysis which, by a most judicious search and balance of viewpoints, presents perhaps the best approach to reality, which also saves humanity from all kinds of extremism, dogmatism and fanaticism, a rare virtue in view especially of the modern times.

Syadvada, or the logic of 'somehow', emphasises the conditional or relative character of every life-situation. It regards objectivity as complex, knowledge limited, speech imperfect, and therefore, believes that nothing can be described as plain 'yes' or 'no'. It formulates the answers in seven ways: (1) Somehow A is B; (2) Somehow A is not B; (3) Somehow A is indescribable; (4) Somehow A is B and is also not B; (5) Somehow A is B and is also indescribable; (6) Somehow A is not B and is also indescribable; and (7) Somehow A is B and also is not B, and is also indescribable.

Jainism is thus an ocean of thought and I am sometimes surprised that it has not yet received its due in world philosophy. Its conjectures, as well as practices, may or may not be right, but it does provide a landscape of philosophical deliberations which cannot and should not be avoided or ignored. The present editor has derived the utmost pleasure and satisfaction out of the labour on this work.

Hermann Jacobi

Jainism in Perspective

The origin and development of the Jaina sect is a subject on which some scholars think it safe to speak with a sceptical caution, though this seems little warranted; for a large and ancient literature has been made accessible, and furnishes ample materials for the early history of the sect. Nor is the nature of these materials such as to make us distrust them. The sacred books of the Jainas are old, avowedly older than the Sanskrit literature which we are accustomed to call classical. Regarding their antiquity, many of those books can vie with the oldest books of the Buddhists. The character of the Jaina literature differs little from the Buddhistical. How is it then that so many writers are inclined to accord a different age and origin to the Jaina sect from what can be deduced from their own literature? The obvious reason is the similarity, real or apparent, which scholars have discovered between Jainism and Buddhism. Two sects which have so much in common could not, it is thought, have been independent from each other, but one sect must needs have grown out of, or branched off from the other. This a priori opinion has prejudiced the discernment of many critics.

The Jainas, both Shvetambaras and Digambaras, state that Mahavira was the son of king Siddhartha of Kundapura or Kundagrama. Kundagrama is called in the *Acharanga Sutra* a 'sannivesa', a term which the commentator interprets as denoting a halting-place of caravans or processions. It must therefore have been an insignificant place, of which tradition has only recorded that it lay in Videha.

In the *Mahavagga* of the Buddhists we read that Buddha, while sojourning at Kotiggama, was visited by the courtesan Ambapali and the Lichchhavis of the neighbouring capital Vesali. From Kotiggama he went to where the Natikas lived.

There he lodged in the Natika Brickhall, in the neighbourhood of which place the courtesan Ambapali possessed a park, Ambapalivana, which she bequeathed on Buddha and the community. From there he went to Vesali, where he converted the general-in-chief of the Lichchhavis, a lay-disciple of the Nirgranthas or Jaina monks. It is highly probable that the Kotiggama of the Buddhists is identical with the Kundagrama of the Jainas. Apart from the similarity of the names the mentioning of the Natikas, apparently identical with the Jnatrika Kshatriyas to whose clan Mahavira belonged, and of Siha, the Jaina, point to the same direction. Kundagrama, therefore, was probably one of the suburbs of Vesali, the capital of Videha. This conjecture is borne out by the name Vesalie, i.e., Vaisalika, given to Mahavira in the *Sutrakritanga*.

If then Kundagrama was scarcely more than an outlying village of Vaisali, it is evident that the sovereign of that village could at best have been only a petty chief. Still he may have enjoyed a greater influence than many of his fellow-chiefs, for he is recorded to have been highly connected by marriage. His wife Trisala was sister to Chetaka, king of Vaisali. She is called Vaidehi or Videhadatta, because she belonged to the reigning line of Videha. The Jainas cherished the memory of the maternal uncle and patron of their prophet, to whose influence we must attribute the fact, that Vaisali used to be a stronghold of Jainism, while being looked upon by the Buddhists as a seminary of heresies and dissent.

Through his mother Mahavira was related to the ruling dynasty in Magadha; for Chetaka's daughter Chellana was married to Seniya Bimbhisara or Bimbisara, king of Magadha, and residing in Rajagriha. He is praised by the Jainas and Buddhists, as the friend and patron of both Mahavira and Buddha.

Vardhamana was, like his father, a Kasyapa. He seems to have lived in the house of his parents till they died, and his elder brother, Nandivardhana, succeeded to what principality they had. Then, at the age of twenty-eight, he, with the consent of those in power, entered the spiritual career. For twelve years he led a life of austerities, visiting even the wild tribes of the country called Radha. After the first year he went about naked. From the end of these twelve years of preparatory self-mortification dates Vardhamana's Kevaliship. Since that time he was recognised as omniscient, as a prophet of the Jainas, or a Tirthankara, and had the titles Jina, Mahavira, etc. The last thirty years of his life he passed in teaching his religious system and organising his order of ascetics, which was patronised or at least countenanced chiefly by those princes with whom he was related through his mother.

In the towns which lay in these parts he spent almost all the rainy seasons during his spiritual career, though he extended his travels as far west and north as Sravasti and the foot of the Himalaya. The names of his chief disciples, the eleven Ganadharas or apostles of the Jainas, as detailed in the *Kalpa Sutra* (List of Sthaviras), are given without any variation by both divisions of the church, the Shvetambaras and Digambaras. Of the details of Mahavira's life, mentioned in the canonical books, his rivalry with, and victory over Gosala, the son of Makkhali, and lastly, the place of his death, the small town Pava, deserve to be noticed. Nor are we by any means forced to rely on the tradition of the Jainas only, since for some particulars we have the testimony of the Buddhists also, in whose writings Mahavira is mentioned under his well-known name Nataputta, as the head of the Nirgranthas or Jaina monks and a rival of Buddha. Mahavira being a contemporary of Buddha, they both had the same contemporaries, viz., Bimbisara and his sons, Abhayakumara and Ajatasatru, the Lichchhavis and Mallas, Gosala Makkhaliputra, whom we meet with in the sacred books of either sect.

Comparing this outline of Mahavira's life with that of Buddha's, we can detect little or nothing in the former which can be suspected as having been formed after the latter by tradition. The general resemblance between the lives of both is due to their being lives of ascetics, which from the nature of the things must present some uniformity.

We shall now put side by side the principal events of Buddha's and Mahavira's lives, in order to demonstrate their difference. Buddha was born in Kapilavastu, Mahavira in a village near Vaisali; Buddha's mother died after his birth, Mahavira's parents lived to see him a grown-up man; Buddha turned ascetic during the lifetime and against the will of his father, Mahavira did so after the death of his parents and with the consent of those in power; Buddha led a life of austerities for six years, Mahavira for twelve; Buddha thought these years wasted time, and that all his penances were useless for attaining his end, Mahavira was convinced of the necessity of his penances, and persevered in some of them even after becoming a Tirthankara. All the disciples of Buddha bear other names than those of Mahavira. To finish this enumeration of differences, Buddha died in Kusinagara, whereas Mahavira died in Pava, avowedly before the former.

Both sects give the same titles or epithets to their prophets: Jina, Arhat, Mahavira, Sarvajna, Sugata, Tathagata, Siddha, Buddha, Sambuddha, Parinivrita, Mukta, etc. All these words occur more or less frequently in the writings of both sects; but there is this difference, that with the exception of Jina, and perhaps Sramana, the preference is given to some set of titles by one sect, and to another set by the rival sect; e.g., Buddha, Tathagata, Sugata, and Sambuddha are common titles of Sakyamuni, and are only occasionally used as epithets of Mahavira. The case is exactly reverse with regard to Vira and Mahavira, the usual titles of Vardhamana.

There was and is at all times a number of honorific adjectives and substantives applicable to persons of exalted virtue. These words were used as epithets in their original meaning by all sects; but some were selected as titles for their prophets, a choice in which they were directed either by the fitness of the word itself, or by the fact that such or such a word was already appropriated by heterodox sects as a title for their highest authority. Thus the etymological meaning of Tirthankara is founder of a religion, prophet, and accordingly, this title was adopted by the Jainas and other sects, whereas the Buddhists did not adopt it in this sense, but in that of an heterodox or heretical teacher.

Where we have to look for the originals of the monastic orders of the Jainas and Buddhists? The Brahminic ascetic was their model, from which they borrowed many important practices and institutions of ascetic life. The Buddhists had no reason not to borrow from the Brahmins, because they greatly respected the latter for the sake of their intellectual and moral superiority. Hence the Jainas and Buddhists use the word Brahmin as an honorific title, applying it even to persons who did not belong to the caste of Brahmins.

It may be remarked that the monastical order of the Jainas and Buddhists though copied from the Brahmins were chiefly and originally intended for Kshatriyas. Buddha addressed himself in the first line to noble and rich men. He, in his first sermon at Benares, speaks of his religion as that for the sake of which sons of noble families leave the house and enter the state of houselessness. That the Jainas too gave the Kshatriyas the preference over the Brahmins is proved by that curious legend about the transfer of the embryo of Mahavira from the womb of the Brahmini Devananda to that of the Kshatriyani Trisala, it being alleged that a Brahmini or another woman of low family was not worthy to give birth to a Tirthankara.

It is probable that Brahminic ascetics did not regard fellow-ascetics of other castes as quite their equals, though they were just as orthodox as themselves. For in later times the opinion prevailed that only Brahmins were entitled to enter the fourth Asrama. It became, in later times, the custom that a Brahmin, as a rule passed through four, a nobleman through three, a citizen through two, a Sudra through one of the four Asramas.

Neither the Jaina legends about their last prophet, nor the ascetic life ordained for Jaina monks, nor any other religious practices adhered to by the faithful warrant our assuming that the Jaina sect has developed, in one way or other, out of the Buddhistical church. The difference of both creeds as regards the principal tenets is such as not to admit a common origin. Whatever Buddha may have taught and thought about the state of Nirvana, whether he went the length to identify it with absolute non-existence, or imagined it to be a sort of existence different from all we know or can conceive, it is beyond doubt, and a striking feature of Buddha's philosophy, that he combated the Brahminic theory of the Atman, as being the absolute and permanent soul, according to the pantheist as well as the monadic point of view. But the Jainas fully concur in the Brahminic theory of the Atman, with only this difference, that they ascribe to the Atmans a limited space, while the Brahmins of the Sankhya, Nyaya, and Vaishesika schools contend that the Atmans are co-extensive with the universe.

On the other hand, the Buddhistical theory of the five Skandhas with their numerous sub-divisions have no counterpart in the psychology of the Jainas. **A characteristic dogma of the Jainas which pervades their whole philosophical system and code of morals, is the hylozoistic theory that not only animals and plants, but also the smallest particles of the elements, earth, fire, water, and wind, are endowed with souls (*Jiva*).** No such dogma, on the other hand, is contained in the philosophy of the Buddhists. To Indian philosophers the various degrees of knowledge up to omniscience are matters of great moment.

The Jainas have a theory of their own on this head, and a terminology which differs from that of the Brahminic philosophers and of the Buddhists. Right knowledge, they say, is fivefold: (1) Mati, right perception; (2) Sruta, clear knowledge based on Mati; (3) Avadhi, a sort of supernatural knowledge; (4) Manahparyaya, clear knowledge of the thoughts of others; and (5) Kevala, the highest degree of knowledge, consisting in omniscience. This psychological theory is a fundamental one of the Jainas, as it is always before the mind of the authors of the sacred books when describing the spiritual career of the saints. We search in vain for something analogous in the Buddhist scriptures. We could multiply the instances of difference between the fundamental tenets of both sects.

Such tenets as the Jainas share with the Buddhists, both sects have in common with the Brahminic philosophers, e.g., the belief in the regeneration of souls, the theory of the Karman, or merit and demerit resulting from former actions, which must take effect in this or another birth, the belief that by perfect knowledge and good conduct man can avoid the necessity of being born again and again, etc. Even the theory that from time immemorial prophets, Buddhas or Tirthankaras, have proclaimed the same dogmas and renewed the sinking faith, has its Brahminic counterpart in the Avataras of Vishnu. Besides, such a theory is a necessary consequence both of the Buddhistical and Jaina creeds.

For what Buddha or Mahavira had revealed was, of course, regarded by the followers of either as truth and the only truth; this truth must have existed from the beginning of time, like the Veda of the Brahmins; but could the truth have remained unknown during the infinite space of time elapsed before the appearance of the prophet? No, would answer the pious believer in Buddhism or Jainism, that was impossible; but the true faith was revealed in different periods by numberless prophets, and so it will be in the time to come. The theory of former prophets seems, therefore, to be a natural consequence of both religions; besides, it was not wholly unfounded on facts, at least as regards the Jainas. For the Nirgranthas are never spoken of in the Buddhist writings as a newly risen sect, nor Nataputta as their founder. Accordingly, the Nirgranthas were probably an old sect at the time of Buddha, and Nataputta only the reformer of the Jaina church, which may have been founded by the twenty-third Tirthankara Parsva.

The detailed lists of teachers handed down in the several Gachchhas, and those incorporated in their sacred books, show that the Jainas did possess an interest in the history of their church. I do not deny that a list of teachers may be invented, or an incomplete one filled up; the necessity of proving itself to be legitimately descended from a recognised authority may induce a sect to invent the names of a line of teachers. But what could have caused the Jainas to fabricate such a detailed list of teachers, Ganas, and Sakhas as that in the *Kalpa Sutra*? Of most of the details the Jainas of later times knew nothing beyond what they found in the *Kalpa Sutra* itself,—and that is unfortunately very little,—nor did they pretend to anything more. For all practical purposes the short list of Sthaviras, as it stands in the *Kalpa Sutra*, would have been sufficient; the preservation of the detailed list, containing so many bare names, proves that they must have had an interest for the members of the early church, though the more accurate knowledge of the times and events chronicled in that list was lost after some centuries.

The redaction of the Jaina canon or the Siddhanta took place, according to the unanimous tradition, in the council of Valabhi, under the presidency of Devarddhi. The date of this event, 454 (or 467) A.D., is incorporated in the *Kalpa Sutra*. Devarddhi Ganin, says the tradition, perceiving the Siddhanta in danger of becoming extinct, caused it to be written in books. Before that time teachers made no use of written books when teaching the Siddhanta to novices, but after that time they did use books.

Devarddhi's position relative to the sacred literature of the Jainas appears to us in a different light from what it is generally believed to have been. He probably arranged the already existing MSS. in a canon, taking down from the mouth of learned theologians only such works of which MSS. were not available. Devarddhi's edition of the Siddhanta is only a redaction of the sacred books which existed before his time in nearly the same form. Any single passage in a sacred text may have been introduced by the editor, but the bulk of the Siddhanta is certainly not of his making.

The origin of the extant Jaina literature cannot be placed earlier than about 300 B.C., or two centuries after the origin of the sect. But we are not from this fact obliged to assume that the Jainas in the time intermediate between their last prophet and the composition of their canon had to rely on nothing more solid than a religious and legendary tradition, never brought into a fixed form. We are told by the Shvetambaras, as well as the Digambaras, that besides the Angas, there existed other and probably older works, called Purvas, of which there were originally fourteen. The knowledge of these Purvas was gradually lost, till at last it became totally extinct. The tradition of the Svetambaras about the fourteen Purvas is this: the fourteen Purvas had been incorporated in the twelfth Anga, the Drishtivada, which was lost some time ago. A detailed table of contents of it, and consequently of the Purvas, has survived in the fourth Anga, the *Samavayanga*, and in the *Nandi Sutra*.

There are no grounds for suspecting the correctness of so general and old a tradition as that about the Purvas. For the Angas do not derive their authority from the Purvas, but are believed to be coeval with the creation of the world. The name itself testifies to the fact that the Purvas were superseded by a new canon, for 'purva' means former, earlier; and it is assuredly not by accident that the knowledge of the Purvas is said to have commenced to fade away at the same time when the Angas were collected by the Sangha of Pataliputra. For after Bhadrabahu, only ten out of the fourteen Purvas were known.

As regards the cause of the abolition of the old canon and the composition of a new one, we are left to conjecture and only as such I shall give my opinion. We know that the Drishtivada, which included the fourteen Purvas, dealt chiefly with the Drishtis or philosophical opinions of the Jainas and other sects. It may be thence inferred that the Purvas related controversies held between Mahavira and rival teachers. The title 'pravada', which is added to the name of each Purva, seems to affirm this view. Besides, if Mahavira was not the founder of a new sect, but the reformer of an old one, it is very likely that he should vigorously have combated the opinions of his opponents, and defended those he had accepted or improved. Now if the discourses of Mahavira, remembered and handed down by his disciples, were chiefly controversies, they must have lost their interest when the opponents of Mahavira had died and the sects headed by them had become extinct.

After the splitting of the church in two sects, the philosophical system of the Jainas remained stationary, since it is nearly the same with both sects. As regards ethics, both sects differ more. But as the extant canon of the Shvetambaras is not falling into neglect, though many practices enjoined in it have long since been abandoned, it is not more probable that they should have been more sensible on the same score at the time when the Purvas formed their canon. They disappeared, not by an intentional neglect, but because the new canon set into clearer light the Jaina doctrines, and put them forward more systematically than had been done in the controversial literature of the Purvas.

Our discussion proves that the development of the Jaina church has not been, at any time, violently interrupted by some very extraordinary events; that we can follow this development from its true beginning through its different stages, and that Jainism is as much independent from other sects, especially from Buddhism, as can be expected from any sect.

Contents

1. Lord Mahavira and His Five Great Vows 19
2. Acharanga Sutra:
   - Knowing the Basics 36
   - Conquest of the World 46
   - The Path of Righteousness 54
   - Essence of the World 58
   - Liberation 65
3. Uttaradhyayana Sutra:
   - On Living Beings and Things Without Life 75
   - The Jaina Creed 88
4. Sutrakritanga:
   - The Conduct 119
5. Life, Food, Liberation 139
6. Kalpa Sutra:
   - Lives of Tirthankaras 200
7. There Is No God (Based on Adi Purana) 244

1

Lord Mahavira and His Five Great Vows

In that period, in that age lived the Venerable Ascetic Mahavira, the five most important moments of whose life happened when the moon was in conjunction with the asterism Uttaraphalguni. In Uttaraphalguni he descended from heaven, and having descended, he entered the womb of Devananda; in Uttaraphalguni he was removed from the womb of Devananda to the womb of Trishala; in Uttaraphalguni he was born; in Uttaraphalguni tearing out his hair, he left the house, and entered the state of houselessness; in Uttaraphalguni he obtained the highest knowledge and intuition, called Kevala, which is infinite, supreme, unobstructed, unimpeded, complete, and perfect. But in Svati the Venerable One obtained final liberation.

When in this Avasarpini era, the Sushama-sushama period, the Sushama period, the Sushamaduhshama period, and much time of the Duhshamasushama period had elapsed, seventy-five years nine and a half months of it being left; in the fourth month of summer, in the eighth fortnight, in the light fortnight of Ashadha, on its sixth day, while the moon was in conjunction with Uttaraphalguni, the Venerable Ascetic Mahavira descended from the great Vimana, the all-victorious and all-prosperous Pushpottara, which is like the lotus amongst the best and highest flowers, and like the Svastika and Vardhamanaka amongst the celestial regions, where he had lived for twenty Sagaropamas till the termination of his allotted length of life, divine nature and existence among gods.

Here, forsooth, in the continent of Jambudvipa, in Bharatavarsha, in the southern part of it, in the southern brahmanical part of the place Kundapura, he took the form of an embryo in the womb of Devananda, of the Jalandharayana gotra, wife of the Brahmin Rishabhadatta, of the gotra of Kodala, taking the form of a lion. The knowledge of the Venerable Ascetic Mahavira was threefold: he knew that he was to descend; he knew that he had descended; he knew not when he was descending. For that time has been declared to be infinitesimally small.

Then in the third month of the rainy season, the fifth fortnight, the dark fortnight of Ashvina, on its thirteenth day, while the moon was in conjunction with Uttaraphalguni, after the lapse of eighty-two days, on the eighty-third day current, the compassionate god Indra, reflecting on what was the established custom with regard to the birth of Tirthankaras, removed the embryo from the southern brahmanical part of the place Kundapura to the northern Ksahtriya part of the same place, rejecting the unclean matter, and retaining the clean matter, lodged the fetus in the womb of Trishala of the Vasishtha gotra, wife of the Kshatriya Siddhartha, of the Kashyapa gotra, of the clan of the Jnatris, and lodged the fetus of the Kshatriyani Trishala in the womb of Devananda of the Jalandharayana gotra, wife of the Brahmin Rishabhadatta, of the gotra of Kodala, in the southern brahmanical part of the place Kundapuri. The knowledge of the Venerable Ascetic Mahavira was threefold: he knew that he was to be removed; he knew that he was removed; he also knew when he was being removed.

In that period, in that age, once upon a time, after the lapse of nine complete months and seven and a half days, in the first month of summer, in the second fortnight, the dark fortnight of Chaitra, on its thirteenth day, while the moon was in conjunction with Uttaraphalguni, the Kshatriyani Trishala, perfectly healthy herself, gave birth to a perfectly healthy boy, the Venerable Ascetic Mahavira.

In that night in which the Kshatriyani Trishala, perfectly healthy herself, gave birth to a perfectly healthy boy, the

Venerable Ascetic Mahavira, there was one great divine, godly lustre originated by descending and ascending gods and goddesses of the four orders of Bhavanapatis, Vyantaras, Jyotishkas, and Vimanavasins; and in the conflux of gods the bustle of gods amounted to confusion.

In that night, the gods and goddesses rained down one great shower of nectar, sandal powder, flowers, gold, and pearls.

In that night the gods and goddesses (of the above-mentioned four orders) performed the customary ceremonies of auspiciousness and honour, and his anointment as a Tirthankara.

Upwards from the time when the Venerable Mahavira was placed in the womb of the Kshatriyani Trishala, that family's treasure of gold, silver, riches, corn, jewels, pearls, shells, precious stones, and corals increased. When the parents of the Venerable Ascetic Mahavira had become aware of this, after the lapse of the tenth day, and the performance of the purification, they prepared much food, drink, sweets, and spices; and having invited a host of friends, near and remote relatives, they distributed, portioned out bestowed the above-mentioned materials to Shramanas, Brahmins, paupers, beggars, eunuchs, etc., and distributed gifts to those who wanted to make presents; then they gave a dinner to the host of friends, near and remote relatives, and after dinner they announced the name of the child to their guests: 'Since the prince was placed in the womb of the Kshatriyani Trishala this family's treasure of gold, silver, riches, corn, jewels, pearls, shells, precious stones, and corals increased; therefore the prince shall be called Vardhamana.

The Venerable Ascetic Mahavira was attended by five nurses: a wet-nurse, a nurse to clean him, one to dress him, one to play with him, one to carry him; being transferred from the lap of one nurse to that of another, he grew up on that beautiful ground, paved with mosaic of precious stones, like a Champaka tree growing in the glen of a mountain.

Then the Venerable Ascetic Mahavira, after his intellect had developed and the childhood had passed away, lived in the enjoyment of the allowed, noble, fivefold joys and pleasures: consisting in sound, touch, taste, colour, and smell.

The Venerable Ascetic Mahavira belonged to the Kashyapa gotra. His three names have thus been recorded by tradition: by his parents he was called Vardhamana, because he is devoid of love and hate.; he is called Shramana, i.e., Ascetic, because he sustains dreadful dangers and fears, the noble nakedness, and the miseries of the world; the name Venerable Ascetic Mahavira has been given to him by the gods.

The Venerable Ascetic Mahavira's father belonged to the Kashyapa gotra; he had three names: Siddhartha, Shreyamsa, and Jasamsa. His mother belonged to the Vasishtha gotra, and had three names: Trishala, Videhadatta, and Priyakarini. His paternal uncle Suparshva belonged to the Kashyapa gotra. His eldest brother, Nandivardhana, and his eldest sister, Sudarshana, belonged both to the Kashyapa gotra. His wife Yashoda belonged to the Kaundinya gotra. His daughter, who belonged to the Kashyapa gotra, had two names: Anojja and Priyadarshana. His granddaughter, who belonged to the Kaushika gotra, had two names: Sheshavati and Yashovati.

The Venerable Ascetic Mahavira's parents were worshippers of Parshva and followers of the Shramanas. During many years they were followers of the Shramanas and for the sake of protecting the six classes of lives they observed, blamed, repented, confessed, and did penance according to their sins. On a bed of Kusha-grass they rejected all food, and their bodies dried up by the last mortification of the flesh, which is to end in death. Thus they died in the proper month, and, leaving their bodies, were born as gods in Adhbuta Kalpa. Thence descending after the termination of their allotted length of life, they will, in Mahavideha, with their departing breath, reach absolute perfection, wisdom, liberation, final Nirvana, and the end of all misery.

In that period, in that age the Venerable Ascetic

Mahavira, a Jnatri Kshatriya, Jnatriputra, a Videha, son of Videhadatta, a native of Videha, a prince of Videha, lived thirty years amongst the householders under the name of Videha.

After his parents had gone to the worlds of the gods and he had fulfilled his promise, he gave up his gold and silver, his troops and chariots, and distributed, portioned out, and gave away his valuable treasure consisting of riches, corn, gold, pearls, etc. and distributed among those who wanted to make presents to others. Thus he gave away during a whole year. In the first month of winter, in the first fortnight, in the dark fortnight of Margashiras, on its tenth day, while the moon was in conjunction with Uttaraphalguni, he made up his mind to retire from the world.

A year before the best of Jinas will retire from the world, they continue to give away their property, from the rising of the sun.

One crore and eight lacs of gold is his gifts at the rising of the sun, as if it were his morning meal.

Three hundred and eighty-eight crores and eighty lacs were given in one year.

The Kundaladharas of Vaishramana, the Laukantika and Maharddhika gods in the fifteen Karmabhumis wake the Tirthankara.

In Brahma Kalpa and in the line of Krishnas, the Laukantika Vimanas are eightfold and infinite in number.

These orders of gods wake the best of Jinas, the Venerable Vira: 'Arhat! propagate the religion which is a blessing to all creatures in the world!'

When the gods and goddesses. of the four orders of Bhavanapatis, Vyantaras, Jyotishkas, and Vimanavasins had become aware of the Venerable Ascetic Mahavira's intention to retire from the world, they assumed their proper form, dress, and ensigns, ascended with their proper pomp and splendour, together with their whole retinue, their own vehicles and chariots, and rejecting all gross matter, retained only the subtle matter. Then they rose and with that excellent, quick, swift, rapid, divine motion of the gods they came down again crossing numberless continents and oceans till they arrived in Jambudvipa at the northern Kshatriya part of the place Kundapura; in the north-eastern quarter of it they suddenly halted.

Shakra, the leader and king of the gods, quietly and slowly stopped his vehicle and chariot, quitely and slowly descended from it and went apart. There he underwent a great transformation, and produced by magic a great, beautiful, lovely, fine-shaped divine pavilion, which was ornamented with many designs in precious stones, gold, and pearls. In the middle part of that divine pavilion he produced one great throne of the same description, with a footstool.

Then he went where the Venerable Ascetic Mahavira was, and thrice circumambulating him from left to right, he praised and worshipped him. Leading him to the divine pavilion, he softly placed him with the face towards the east on the throne, anointed him with hundredfold and thousandfold refined oil, with perfumes and decoctions, bathed him with pure water, and rubbed him with beautifying cool sandal, laid on a piece of cloth worth a lac. He clad him in a pair of robes so light that the smallest breath would carry them away; they were manufactured in a famous city, praised by clever artists, soft as the fume of horses, interwoven with gold by skilful masters, and ornamented with designs of flamingos.

Then the god decked him with necklaces of many and fewer strings, with one hanging down over his breast and one consisting of one row cf pearls, with a garland, a golden string, a turban, a diadem, wreaths of precious stones, and decorated him with garlands, ribbons, scarves, and sashes like the Kalpavriksha.

The god then, for a second time, underwent a great transformation, and produced by magic the great palanquin, called Chandraprabha, which a thousand men carry. This palanquin was adorned with pictures of wolves, bulls, horses, men, dolphins, birds, monkeys, elephants, antelopes, sarabhas, yacks, tigers, lions, creeping plants, and a train of couples of Vidyadharas; it had a halo of thousands of rays; it was decorated with thousands of brilliant glittering rupees; its lustre was mild and bright; the eyes could not bear its light; it shone with heaps and masses of pearls; it was hung with strings and ribbons, and with golden excellent necklaces, extremely beautiful; its was embellished with designs of lotuses and many other plants; its cupola was adorned with many precious stones of five colours, with bells and flags; it was conspicuous, lovely, beautiful, splendid, magnificent.

This palanquin was brought for the best of Jinas, who is free from old age and death; it was hung with wreaths and garlands of divine flowers, grown in water or on dry ground.

In the middle of the palanquin was a costly throne covered with a divine cloth, precious stones and silver, with a footstool, for the best of Jinas.

He wore on his head a chaplet and a diadem, his body was shining, and he was adorned with many ornaments; he had put on a robe of muslin worth a lac.

After a fast of three days, with a glorious resolution he ascended the supreme palanquin, purifying all by his light.

He sat on his throne, and Shakra and Ishana, on both sides, fanned him with chowries, the handles of which were inlaid with jewels and precious stones.

In front it was uplifted by men, covered with joyful horripilation; behind the gods carried it: the Suras and Asuras, the Garudas and the chiefs of Nagas.

The Suras carried it on the eastern side, and the Asuras on the southern one; on the western side the Garudas carried it, and the Nagas on the northern side.

As a grove in blossom, or a lotus-covered lake in autumn looks beautiful with a mass of flowers, so did then the firmament with hosts of gods.

As a grove of Siddhartha, of Karnikara or of Champaka looks beautiful with a mass of flowers, so did the firmament with hosts of gods.

In the skies and on earth the sound of musical instruments produced by hundreds of thousands of excellent drums, kettle-drums, cymbals, and conches was extremely pleasant.

Then the gods ordered many hundreds of actors to perform a very rich concert of four kinds of instruments: stringed instruments and drums, cymbals and wind-instruments.

At that period, in that age, in the first month of winter, in the first fortnight, the dark fortnight of Margashiras, on its tenth day, called Suvrata, in the Muhurta called Vijaya, while the moon was in conjunction with the asterism Uttaraphalguni, when the shadow had turned towards the east, and the first Paurushi was over, after fasting three days without taking water, having put on the one garment, the Venerable Ascetic Mahavira, in his palanquin Chandraprabha, which only a thousand men can carry, with a train of gods, men, and Asuras left the northern Kshatriya part of the place Kundapura by the high way for the park Jnatri Khanda. There, just at the beginning of night, he caused the palanquin Chandraprabha to stop quietly on a slightly raised untouched ground, quitely descended from it, sat quitely down on a throne with the face towards the east, and took off all his ornaments and finery.

The god Vaishravana, prostrating himself, caught up the finery and ornaments of the Venerable Ascetic Mahavira in a cloth of flamingo-pattern. Mahavira then plucked out with his right and left hands on the right and left sides of his head his hair in five handfuls. But Sakra, the leader and king of the gods, falling down before the feet of the Venerable Ascetic Mahavira, caught up the hair in a cup of diamond, and requesting his permission, brought them to the Milk Ocean.

After the Venerable Ascetic Mahavira had plucked out his hair in five handfuls, he paid obeisance to all liberated spirits, and vowing to do no sinful act, he adopted the holy conduct. At that moment the whole assembly of men and gods stood motionless, like the figures on a picture.

At the command of Shakra, the clamour of men and gods, and the sound of musical instruments suddenly ceased, when Mahavira chose the holy conduct.

Day and night following that conduct which is a blessing to all animated and living beings, the zealous gods listen to him with joyful horripilation.

When the Venerable Ascetic Mahavira had adopted the holy conduct which produced that state of soul in which the reward of former actions is temporarily counteracted, he reached the knowledge called Manahparyaya, by which he knew the thoughts of all sentient beings, with five organs, which are not defective, and possess a developed intellect, living in the two and a half continents and the two oceans. Then he formed the following resolution: I shall for twelve years neglect my body and abandon the care of it; I shall with equanimity bear, undergo, and suffer all calamities arising from divine powers, men or animals.

The Venerable Ascetic Mahavira having formed this resolution, and neglecting his body, arrived in the village Kummara when only one Muhurta of the day remained. Neglecting his body, the Venerable Ascetic Mahavira meditated on his Self, in blameless lodgings, in blameless wandering, in restraint, kindness, avoidance of sinful influence, chaste life, in patience, freedom from passion, contentment; control, circumspectness, practising religious postures and acts; walking the path of Nirvana and liberation, which is the fruit of good conduct. Living thus he with equanimity bore, endured, sustained, and suffered all calamities arising from divine powers, men, and animals, with undisturbed and unafflicted mind, careful of body, speech, and mind.

The Venerable Ascetic Mahavira passed twelve years in this way of life; during the thirteenth year in the second month of summer, in the fourth forthnight, the light fortnight of Vaishakha, on its tenth day, called Suvrata, in the Muhurta called Vijaya, while the moon was in conjunction with the asterism Uttaraphalguni, when the shadow had turned towards the east, and the first wake was over, outside of the town Jrimbhikagrama, on the northern bank of the river Rijupalika, in the field of the householder Samaga, in a north-eastern direction from an old temple, not far from a Sal tree, in a squatting position with joined heels exposing himself to the heat of the sun, with the knees high and the head low, in deep meditation in the midst of abstract meditation, he reached Nirvana, the complate and full, the unobstructed, unimpeded, infinite and supreme, best knowledge and intuition, called Kevala.

When the Venerable One had become an Arhat and Jina, he was a Kevalin, omniscient and comprehending all objects, he knew all conditions of the world, of gods, men, and demons; whence they come, where they go, whether they are born as men or animals, or become gods or hell-beings; their food, drink, doings, desires, open and secret deeds, their conversation and gossip, and the thoughts of their minds; he saw and knew all conditions in the whole world of all living beings.

On the day when the Venerable Ascetic Mahavira reached the Kevala, the gods of the four orders of Bhavanapatis, Vyantaras, Jyotishkas, and Vimanavasins descended from, and ascended to heaven.

Then when the Venerable Ascetic Mahavira had reached the highest knowledge and intuition, he reflected on himself and the world: first he taught the law to the gods, afterwards to men.

The Venerable Ascetic Mahavira endowed with the highest knowledge and intuition taught the five great vows, with their clauses, the six classes of lives to the Shramanas and Nirgranthas, to Gautama, etc.

The first great vow

The first great vow, runs thus:

I renounce all killing of living beings, whether subtle or

gross, whether movable or immovable. Nor shall I myself kill living beings nor cause others to do it, nor consent to it. As long as I live, I confess and blame, repent and exempt myself of these sins, in the thrice threefold way, i.e., acting, commanding, consenting, either in the past or the present or the future.

There are five clauses.

The first clause runs thus:

A Nirgrantha is careful in his walk, not careless. The Kevalin assigns as the reason, that a Nirgrantha, careless in his walk, might with his feet hurt or displace or injure or kill living beings. Hence a Nirgrantha is careful in his walk, not careless in his walk.

This is the first clause.

Now follows the second clause:

A Nirgantha searches into his mind. If his mind is sinful, blamable, intent on works, acting on impulses, produces cutting and splitting (or division and dissension), quarrels, faults, and pains, injures living beings, or kills creatures, he should not employ such a mind in action; but if, on the contrary, it is not sinful, then he may put it in action.

This is the second clause.

Now follows the third clause:

A Nirgrantha searches into his speech; if his speech is sinful, blamable, etc., kills creatures, he should not utter that speech. But if, on the contrary, it is not sinful, then he may utter it.

This is the third clause.

Now follows the fourth clause:

A Nirgrantha is careful in laying down his utensils of begging, he is not careless in it. The Kevalin says: A Nirgrantha who is careless in laying down his utensils of begging, might hurt or displace or injure or kill all sorts of living beings. Hence a Nirgrantha is careful in laying down his utensils of begging, he is not careless in it.

This is the fourth clause.

Now follows the fith clause:

A Nirgrantha eats and drinks after inspecting his food and drink; he does not eat and drink without inspecting his food and drink. The Kevalin says: If a Nirgrantha would eat and drink without inspecting his food and drink, he might hurt and displace or injure or kill all sorts of livng beings. Hence a Nirgrantha eats and drinks after inspecting his food and drink, not without doing so.

This is the fifth clause.

In this way the great vow is correctly practised, followed, executed, explained, established, effected according to the precept.

This is, the first great vow: Abstinence from killing any living beings.

The second great vow

The second great vow runs thus:

I renounce all vices of lying speech arising from anger or greed or fear or mirth. I shall neither myself speak lies, nor cause others to speak lies, As long as I liue, I confess and blame, repent and exempt myself of these sins in the thrice threefold way, in mind, speech, and body.

There are five clauses.

A Nirgrangtha speaks after deliberation, not without deliberation. The Kevalin says: Without deliberation a Nirgrantha might utter a falsehood in his speech. A Nirgrantha speaks after deliberation, not without delibertion.

This the first clause.

Now follows the second clause:

A Nirgrantha comprehends and renounces anger, he is

not angry. The Kevalin says: A Nirgrantha who is moved by anger, and is angry, might utter a falsehood in his speech.

This is the second clause.

Now follows the third clause:

A Nirgrantha comprehends and renounces greed; he is not greedy. The Kevalin says: A Nirgrantha who is moved by greed, and is greedy, might utter a falsehood in his speech.

This is the third clause.

Now follows the fourth clause:

A Nirgrantha comprehends and renounces fear; he is afraid. The Kevalin says: A Nirgrantha who is moved by fear, and is afraid, might utter a falsehood in his speech.

This is the fourth clause.

Now follows the fifth clause:

A Nirgrantha comprehends and renounces mirth; he is not mirthful. The Kevalin says: A Nirgrantha who is moved by mirth, and is mirthful, might utter a falehood in his speech.

This the fifth clause.

In this way the great vow is correctly practised, followed, executed, explained, established, effected according to practice.

This is, the second great vow.

The third great vow

The third great vow runs thus:

I renounce all taking of anything not given, either in a village or a town or a wood, either of little or much, of small or great, of living or lifeless things. I shall neither take myself what is not given, nor cause others to take it, nor consent to their taking it. As long as I live, I confess and blame, repent and exempt myself of these sins, in the thrice threefold way in mind, speech and body.

There are five clauses:

The first clause runs thus:

A Nirgrantha begs after deliberation, for a limited ground, not without deliberation. The Kevalin says: If a Nirgrantha begs without deliberation for a limited ground, he might take what is not given.

This is the first clause.

Now follows the second clause:

A Nirgrantha consumes his food and drink with permission of his superior, not without his permission. The Kevalin says: If a Nirgrantha consumes his food and drink without the superior's permisison, he might eat what is not given.

This is the second clause.

Now follows the third clause:

A Nirgrantha who has taken possession of some ground, should always take possession of a limited part of it and for a fixed time. The Kevalin says: If a Nirgrantha who has taken possession of some ground, should take possession of an unlimited part of it and for an unfixed time, he might take what is not given.

This is the third clause.

Now follows the fourth clause:

A Nirgrantha who has taken possession of some ground, should constantly have his grant renewed. The Kevalin says: If a Nirgrantha has not constantly his grant renewed, he might take possession of what is not given.

This is the fourth clause.

Now follows the fifth clause:

A Nirgrantha begs for a limited ground for his co-religionists after deliberation, not withut deliberation. The Kevalin says: If a Nirgrantha should beg without deliberation, he might take possession of what is not given.

This is the fifth clause.

This is the third great vow.

The fourth great vow

The fourth great vow runs thus:

I renounce all sexual pleasures, either with gods or men or animals. I shall not give way to sensuality. As long as I live, I confess and blame, repent and exempt myself.

There are five clauses:

The first clause runs thus:

A Nirgrantha does not continually discuss topics relating to women. The Kevalin says: If a Nirgrantha discusses such topics, he might fall from the law declared by the Kevalin, because of the destruction or disturbance of his peace.

This is the first clause.

Now follows the second clause:

A Nirgrantha does not regard and contemplate the lovely forms of women. The Kevalin says: If a Nirgrantha regards and contemplates the lovely forms of women, he might fall from the law declared by the Kevalin.

This is the second clause.

Now follows the third clause:

A Nirgrantha does not recall to his mind the pleasures and amusements he formerly had with women. The Kevalin says: If a Nirgrantha recalls to his mind the pleasures and amusements he formerly had with women, he might fall from the law declared by the Kevalin.

This is the third clause.

Now follows the fourth clause:

A Nirgrantha does not eat and drink too much, nor does he drink liquors or eat highly-seasoned dishes. The Kevalin says: If a Nirgrantha did eat and drink too much, or did drink liquors and eat highly seasoned dishes, he might fall from the law declared by the Kevalin.

This is the fourth clause.

Now follows the fifth clause:

A Nirgrantha does not occupy a bed or couch affected by women, animals, or eunuchs. The Kevalin says: If a Nirgrantha did occupy a bed or couch affected by women, animals, or eunuchs, he might fall from the law declared by the Kevalin.

That is the fifth clause.

This is, the fourth great vow.

The fifth great vow

The fifth great vow runs thus:

I renounce all attachments, whether little or much, small or great, living or lifeless; neither shall I myself form such attachments, nor cause others to do so, nor consent to their doing so. As long as I live, I confess and blame, repent and exempt myself.

There are five clauses:

The first clause runs thus:

If a creature with ears hears agreeable and disagreeable sounds, it should not be attached to, nor delighted with, nor desiring of, nor infatuated by, nor covetous of, nor disturbed by the agreeable or disagreeable sounds. The Kevalin says: If a Nirgrantha is thus affected by the pleasant or unpleasant sounds, he might fall from the law declared by the Kevalin.

If it is impossible not to hear sounds which reach the ear, the mendicant should avoid love or hate, originated by them. A creature with ears hears agreeable and disagreeable sounds.

This is the first clause.

Now follows the second clause:

If a creature with eyes sees agreeable and disagreeable forms or colours, it should not be attached, to them. If a

Nirgrantha is thus affected by the pleasant or unpleasant forms, he might fall from the law declared by the Kevalin.

This is the second clause.

Now follows the third clause:

If a creature with an organ of smell smells agreeable or disagreeable smells, it should not be attached to them. So he falls from the law declared by the Kevalin.

This is the third clause.

Now follows the fourth clause:

If a creature with a tongue tastes agreeable or disagreeable tastes, it should not be attached, to them. So he falls from the law declared by the Kevalin.

This is the fourth clause.

Now follows the fifth clause:

If a creature with an organ of feeling feels agreeable or disagreeable touches, it should not be attached to them. So he falls from the law declared by the Kevalin.

This is the fifth clause.

In this way the great vow is correctly practised, followed, executed, explained, established, effected, according to the precept.

He who is well provided with these great vows and their twenty-five clauses is really Houseless, if he, according to the sacred lore, the precepts, and the way correctly practises, follows, executes, explains, establishes, and, according to the precept, effects them.

2

Acharanga Sutra

Knowing the Basics

O long-lived Jambusvamin! I Sudharman have heard the following discourse from the venerable Mahavira: Here many do not remember whether they have descended in an eastern direction when they were born in this world, or in a southern, or in a western, or in a northern direction, or in the direction from above, or in the direction from below, or in a direction intermediate between the cardinal points, or in a direction intermediate between these and the cardinal points. Similarly, some do not know whether their soul is born again and again or not; nor what they were formerly, nor what they will become after having died and left this world.

Now this is what one should know, either by one's own knowledge or through the instruction of a Tirthankara, or having heard it from others: that he descended in an eastern direction, or in any other direction. Similarly, some know that their soul is born again and again, that it arrives in this or that direction, whatever direction that may be. He believes in soul, believes in the world, believes in reward, believes in action acknowledged to be our own doing in such judgements as these: 'I did it;' 'I shall cause another to do it;' 'I shall allow another to do it.' In the world, these are all the causes of sin, which must be comprehended and renounced.

A man that does not comprehend and renounce the causes of sin, descends in a cardinal or intermediate direction, wanders to all cardinal or intermediate directions, is born again and again in manifold births, experiences all painful feelings. About this the Revered One has taught the truth of comprehension and renunciation. for the sake of the splendour, honour, and glory of this life, for the sake of birth, death, and final liberation, for the removal of pain, all these causes of sin are at work, which are to be comprehended and renounced in this world. He who, in the world, comprehends and renounces these causes of sin, is called a reward-knowing sage. Thus I say.

The Living World is Full of Pain

The living world is afflicted, miserable, difficult to instruct, and without discrimination. In this world full of pain, suffering by their different acts, see the benighted ones cause great pain. See! there are beings individually embodied in earth; not one all-soul. See! there are men who control themselves, whilst others only pretend to be houseless (i.e. monks, such as the Bauddhas, whose conduct differs not from that of householders), because one destroys this earth-body by bad and injurious doings, and many other beings, besides, which he hurts by means of earth, through his doing acts relating to earth.

About this the Revered One has taught the truth: for the sake of the splendour, honour, and glory of this life, for the sake of birth, death, and final liberation, for the removal of pain, man acts sinfully towards earth, or causes others to act so, or allows others to act so. This deprives him of happiness and perfect wisdom. About this he is informed when he has understood or heard, either from the Revered One or from the monks, the faith to be coveted.

There are some who, of a truth, know this, i.e., injuring, to be the bondage, the delusion, the death, the hell. For this a man is longing when he destroys this earth-body by bad, injurious doings, and many other beings, besides, which he huyts by means of earth, through his doing acts relating to earth. Thus I say.

As somebody may cut or strike a blind man who cannot see the wound, as somebody may cut or strike the foot, the ankle, the knee, the thigh, the hip, the navel, the belly, the flank, the back, the bosom, the heart, the breast, the neck, the arm, the finger, the nail, the eye, the brow, the forehead, the head, as some kill openly, as some extirpate secretly, thus the earth-bodies are cut, struck, and killed though their feeling is not manifest.

He who injures these earth-bodies does not comprehend and renounce the sinful acts; he who does not injure these, comprehends and renounces the sinful acts. Knowing them, a wise man should not act sinfully towards earth, nor cause others to act so, nor allow others to act so. He who knows these causes of sin relating to earth, is called a reward-knowing sage. Thus I say.

Injure Not the Water-Bodies

Thus I say: He who acts rightly, who does pious work, who practises no deceit, is called houseless. One should, conquering the world, persevere in that vigour of faith which one had on the entrance in the order; the heroes of faith, humbly bent, should retain their belief in the illustrious road to final liberation and in the world of water-bodies; having rightly comprehended them through the instruction of Mahavira, they should retain that which causes no danger, i.e., self-control. Thus I say. A man should not himself deny the world of water-bodies, nor should he deny the self. He who denies the world of water-bodies, denies the self; and he who denies the self, denies the world of water-bodies.

See! there are men who control themselves; others pretend only to be houseless; for one destroys this water-body by bad, injurious doings, and many other beings, besides, which he hurts by means of water, through his doing acts relating to water. About this the Revered One has taught the truth: for the sake of the splendour, honour, and glory of this life, for the sake of birth, death, and final liberation, for the removal of pain, man acts sinfully towards water, or causes others to act so, or allows others to act so.

This deprives him of happiness and perfect wisdom. About this he is informed when he has understood and heard from the Revered One, or from the monks, the faith to be coveted. There are some who, of a truth, know this, i.e., injuring, to be the bondage, the delusion, the death, the hell. For this a man is longing when he destoroys this water-body by bad and injurious doings, and many other beings, besides, which he hurts by means of water, through his doing acts relating to water. Thus I say.

There are beings living in water, many lives; of a truth, to the monks water has been declared to be living matter. See! considering the injuries done to water-bodies, those acts which are injuries, but must be done before the use of water, e.g., straining, have been distinctly declared. Moreover, he who uses water which is not strained takes away what has not been given, i.e., the bodies of water-lives. A Bauddha will object: 'We have permission, we have permission to drink it, or to take it for toilet purposes.' Thus they destroy by various injuries the water-bodies. But in this their doctrine is of no authority.

He who injures these water-bodies does not comprehend and renounce the sinful acts; he who does not injure these, comprehends and renounces the sinful acts. Knowing them, a wise man should not act sinfully towards water, nor cause others to act so, nor allow others to act so. He who knows these causes of sin relating to water, is called a reward-knowing sage. Thus I say.

Injure Not the Fire-Bodies

Thus I say: A man should not of his own accord, deny the world of fire-bodies, nor should he deny the self. He who denies the world of fire-bodies, denies the self; and he who denies the self, denies the world of fire-bodies. He who knows that, viz., fire, through which injury is done to the long-living bodies, i.e., plants, knows also that which does no injury, i.e, control; and he who knows that which does no injury, knows also that through which no injury is done to the long-living bodies. This has been seen by the heroes of faith who conquered ignorance; for they control themselves, always exert themselves, always mind their duty.

He who is unmindful of duty, and desiring of the qualities, i.e., of the pleasure and profit which may be derived from the elements, is called the torment of living beings. Knowing this, a wise man resolves: 'Now I shall do no more what I used to do wantonly before.' See! there are men who control themselves; others pretend only to be houseless; for one destroys this fire-body by bad and injurious doings, and many other beings, besides, which he hurts by means of fire, through his doing acts relating to fire. About this the Revered One has taught the truth: for the sake of the splendour, honour, and glory of this life, for the sake of birth, death, and final liberation, for the removal of pain, man acts sinfully towards fire, or causes others to act so, or allows others to act so.

This deprives him of happiness and perfect wisdom. About this he is informed when he has understood, or heard from the Revered One or from the monks, the faith to be coveted. There are some who, of a truth, know this, i.e., injuring, to be the bondage, the delusion, the death, the hell. For this a man is longing, when he destroys this fire-body by bad and injurious doings, and many other beings, besides, which he hurts by means of fire, through his doing acts relating to fire. Thus I say.

There are beings living on the earth, living in grass, living on leaves, living in wood, living in cowdung, living in dust-heaps, jumping beings, which coming near fire fall into it. Some, certainly, touched by fire, shrivel up; those which shrivel up there, lose their sense there; those which lose their sense there, die there.

He who injures these fire-bodies does not comprehend and renounce the sinful acts; he who does not injure these, comprehends and renounces the sinful acts. Knowing them, a wise man should not act sinfully towards fire, nor cause others to act so, nor allow others to act so. He who knows the causes of sin relating to fire, is called a reward-knowing sage. Thus I say.

Injure Not the Plants

'I shall not do acts relating to plants after having entered the order, having recognised the truth about these acts, and having conceived that which is free from danger, i.e., control.'

He who does not acts relating to plants, has ceased from works; he who has ceased from them is called 'houseless.' Quality is the whirlpool and the whirlpool is quality. Looking up, down, aside, eastward, he sees colours, hearing he hears sounds; longing upwards, down, aside, eastward, he becomes attached to colours and sounds. That is called the world; not guarded against it, not obeying the law of the Tirthankaras, relishing the qualities, conducting himself wrongly, he will wantonly live in a hosue, i.e., belong to the world.

See! there are men who control themselves; others pretend only to be houseless, for one destroys this body of a plant by bad and injurious doings, and many other beings, besides, which he hurts by means of plants, through his doing acts relating to plants. About this the Revered One has taught the truth: for the sake of the splendour, honour, and glory of this life, for the sake of birth, death, and final liberation, for the removal of pain, man acts sinfully towards plants, or causes others to act so, or allows others to act so.

This deprives him of happiness and perfect wisdom. About this he is informed when he has understood, or heard from the Revered One or from the monks, the faith to be coveted. There are some who, of a truth, know this, i.e., injuring, to be the bondge, the delusion, the death, the hell. For this a man is longing when he destroys this body of a plant by bad and injurious doings, and many other beings, besides, which he hurts by means of plants, through his doing acts relating to plants. Thus I say.

As the nature of this, i.e., men is to be born and to grow old, so is the nature of that, i.e., plants to be born and to grow old; as this has reason, so that has reason; as this falls sick when cut, so that falls sick when cut; as this needs food, so that needs food; as this will decay, so that will decay; as this is not eternal, so that is not eternal; as this takes increments, so that takes increment; as this is changing, so that is changing. He who injures these plants does not comprehend and renounce the sinful acts; he who does not injure these, comprehends and renounces the sinful acts. Knowing them, a wise man should not act sinfully towards plants, nor cause others to act so, nor allow others to act so. He who knows these causes of sin relating to plants, is called a reward-knowing sage. Thus I say.

Injure Not the Animate Beings

Thus I say: There are beings called the animate, viz., those who are produced from eggs (birds, etc.), from a fetus as elephants, etc., from a fetus with an enveloping membrane as cows, buffaloes, etc., from fluids as worms, etc., from sweat as bugs, lice, etc., by coagulation as locusts ants, etc., from sprouts as butterflies, wagtails, etc., by regeneration as men, gods, hell-beings. This is called the Samsara for the slow, for the ignorant.

Having well considered it, having well looked at it, I say thus: all beings, those with two, three, four senses, plants, those with five senses, and the rest of creation, experience individually pleasure or displeasure, pain, great terror, and unhappiness. Beings are filled with alarm from all directions and in all directions. See! there the benighted ones cause great pain. See! there are beings individually embodies.

See! there are men who control themselves; others pretend only to be houseless, for one destroys this body of an animal by bad and injurious doings, and many other beings, besides, which he hurts by means of animals, through his doing acts relating to animals. About this the Revered One has taught the truth: for the sake of the splendour, honour, and glory of this life, for the sake of birth, death, and final liberation, for the removal of pain, man acts sinfully towards animals, or causes others to act so, or allows others to act so.

This deprives him of happiness and perfect wisdom. About this he is informed, when he has understood, or heard from the Revered One or from the monks, the faith to be coveted. There are some who, of a truth, know this, i.e, injuring, to be the bondage, the delusion, the death, the hell. For this a man is longing, when he injures this body of an animal by bad and injurious doings, and many other beings, besides, which he hurts by means of animals, through acts relating to animals. Thus I say.

Some slay animals for sacrificial purposes, some kill animals for the sake of their skin, some kill them for the sake of their flesh, some kill them for the sake of their blood; thus for the sake of their heart, their bile, the feathers of their tail, their tail, their big or small horns, their teeth, their tusks, their nails, their sinews, their bones; with a purpose or without a purpose. Some kill animals because they have been wounded by them, or are wounded, or will be wounded.

He who injures these animals does not comprehend and renounce the sinful acts; he who does not injure these, comprehends and renounces the sinful acts. Knowing them, a wise man should not act sinfully towards animals, nor cause others to act so, nor allow others to act so. He who knows these causes of sin relating to animals, is called a reward-knowing sage. Thus I say.

Injure Not the Wind-Bodies

He who is averse from all actions relating to wind, knows affliction. Knowing what is bad, he who knows it with regard to himself, knows it with regard to the world outside; and he who knows it with regard to the world outside, knows it with regard to himself: this reciprocity between himself and others one should mind. Those who are appeased, who are free from passion, do not desire to live.

See! there are men who control themselves; others pretend only to be houseless, for one destroys this wind-body by bad and injurious doings, and many other beings, besides, which he hurts by means of wind, through his doing acts relating to wind. About this the Revered One has taught the truth: for the sake of the splendour, honour, and glory of this life, for the sake of birth, death, and final liberation, for the removal of pain, man acts sinfully towards wind, or causes others to act so, or allows others to act so.

This deprives him of happiness and perfect wisdom. About this he is informed when he has understood, or heard from the Revered One or from the monks, the faith to be coveted. There are some who, of a truth, know this to be the bondage, the delusion, the death, the hell. For this a man is longing when he destroys this wind-body by bad and injurious acts, and many other beings, besides, which he hurts by means of wind, through his doing acts relating to wind. Thus I say.

There are jumping beings which, coming near wind, fall into it. Some certainly, touched by wind, shrivel up; those which shrivel up there, lose their sense there; those which lose there sense there, die there.

He who injures these wind-bodies does not comprehend and renounce the sinful acts; he who does not injure these, comprehends and renounces the sinful acts. Knowing them, a wise man should not act sinfully towards wind, nor cause others to act so, nor allow others to act so. He who knows these causes of sin relating to wind, is called a reward-knowing sage. Thus I say.

Be aware that about this wind-body too those are involved in sin who delight not in the right conduct, and, though doing acts, talk about religious discipline, who conducting themselves according to their own will, pursuing sensual pleasures, and engaging in acts, are addicted to worldliness. He who has the true knowledge about all things, will commit no sinful act, nor cause others to do so. Knowing them, **a wise man should not act sinfully towards the aggregate of six kinds of lives, nor cause others to act so, nor allow others to act so. He who knows these causes of sin relating to the aggregate of the six kinds of lives, is called a reward-knowing sage**. Thus I say.

Conquest of the World

Quality is the seat of the root, and the seat of the root is quality. He who longs for the qualities, is overcome by great pain, and he is careless. For he thinks I have to provide for a mother, for a father, for a sister, for a wife, for sons, for daughters, for a daughter-in-law, for my friends, for near and remote relations, for my acquaintances, for different kinds of property, profit, meals, and clothes. Longing for these objects, people are careless, suffer day and night, work in the right and the wrong time, desire wealth and treasures, commit injuries and violent acts, direct the mind, again and again, upon these injurious doings.

Doing so, the life of some mortals which by destiny would have been long is shortened. For when with the deterioration of the perceptions of the ear, eye, organs of smelling, tasting, touching, a man becomes aware of the decline of life, they after a time produce dotage. Or his kinsmen with whom he lives together will, after a time, first grumble at him, and he will afterwards grumble at them. They cannot help thee or protect thee, nor canst thou help them or protect them. He is not fit for hilarity, playing, pleasure, show. Therefore, ah! proceeding to pilgrimage, and thinking that the present moment is favourable for such intentions, he should be steadfast and not, even for an hour, carelessly conduct himself. His youth, his age, his life fade way.

A man who carelessly conducts himself, who killing, cutting, striking, destroying, chasing away, frightening living beings resolves to do what has not been done by any one—

him his relations with whom he lived together, will first cherish, and he will afterwards cherish them. But they cannot help thee or protect thee, nor canst thou help them or protect them.

Or he heaps up treasures for the benefit of some spendthrifts, by pinching himself. Then, after a time, he falls in sickness; those with whom he lives together will first leave him, and he will afterwards leave them. They cannot help thee or protect thee, nor canst thou help them or protect them.

Knowing pain and pleasure in all their variety, and seeing his life not yet decline, a wise man should know that to be the proper moment for entering a religious life; while the perceptions of his ear, eye, organs of smelling, tasting, touching are not yet deteriorated, while all these perceptions are not yet deteriorated, man should prosecute the real end of his soul. Thus I say.

Control is the Key

A wise man should remove any aversion to control; he will be liberated in the proper time. Some, following wrong instructions, turn away from control. They are dull, wrapped in delusion. While they imitate the life of monks, saying, 'We shal be free from attachment,' they enjoy the pleasures that offer themselves. Through wrong instruction the would-be sages trouble themselves for the pleasures; thus they sink deeper and deeper in delusion, and cannot get to this, nor to the opposite shore.

Those who are freed from attachment to the world and its pleasures, reach the opposite shore. Subduing desire by desirelessness, he does not enjoy the pleasures that offer themselves. Desireless, giving up the world, and ceasing to act, he knows, and sees, and has no wishes because of his discernment; he is called houseless.

But on the contrary, he suffers day and night, works in the right and the wrong time, desires wealth and treasures, commits injuries and violent acts, again and again directs his mind upon these injurious doings,; for his own sake, to support or to be supported by his relations, friends, the ancestors, gods, the king, thieves, guests, paupers, Shramanas.

Thus violence is done by these various acts, deliberately, out of fear, because they think, it is for the expiration of sins, or for some other hope. Knowing this, a wise man should neither himself commit violence by such acts, nor order others to commit violence by such acts, nor consent to the violence done by somebody else.

This road to happiness has been declared by the noble ones, that a clever man should not be defiled by sin. Thus I say.

Neither Glad Nor Angry

'Frequently I have been born in a high family, frequently in a low one; I am not mean, nor noble, nor do I desire social preferment.' Thus reflecting, who would brag about his family or about his glory, or for what should he long?

Therefore, a wise man should neither be glad nor angry about his lot: thou shouldst know and consider the happiness of living creatures. Carefully conducting himself, he should mind this: blindness, deafness, dumbness, one-eyedness, hunchbackedness, blackness, variety of colour he will always experience; because of his carelessness he is born in many births, he experiences various feelings.

Not enlightened about the cause of these ills he is afflicted by them, always turning round in the whirl of birth and death. Life is dear to many who own fields and houses. Having acquired dyed and coloured clothes, jewels, earrings, gold, and women, they become attached to these things. And a fool who longs for life, and is worldly-minded, laments that for these worldly goods penance, self-restraint, and control do not avail, will ignorantly come to grief.

Those who are of a steady conduct do not desire this wealth. Knowing birth and death, one should firmly walk the path, i.e., right conduct, and not wait for old age to commence a religious life.

For there is nothing inaccessible for death. All beings are fond of life, like pleasure, hate, pain, shun destruction, like life, long to live. To all life is dear.

Having acquired, employing bipeds and quadrupeds, gathering riches in the three ways, whatever his portion will be, small or great, he wil desire to enjoy it. Then at one time, his manifold savings are a large treasure. Then at another time, his heirs divide it, or those who are without a living steal it, or the king takes it away, or it is ruined in some way or other, or it is consumed by the conflagration of the house. Thus a fool doing cruel deeds which benefit another, will ignorantly come thereby to grief.

This certainly has been declared by the sage. They do not cross the flood, nor can they cross it; they do not go to the next shore, nor can they go to it; they do not go to the opposite shore, nor can they go to it.

And though hearing the doctrine, he does not stand in the right place; but the clever one who adopts the true faith, stands in the right place, i.e., control.

He who sees by himself, needs no instruction. But the miserable, afflicted fool who delights in pleasures, and whose miseries do not cease, is turned round in the whirl of pains. Thus I say.

Neither Hope Nor Desire

Then, after a time, he falls in sickness: those with whom he lives together, first grumble at him, and he afterwards grumbles at them. But they cannot help thee or protect thee, nor canst thou help them or protect them.

Knowing pleasure and pain separately, they trouble themselves about the enjoyment of the external objects. For some men in this world have such a character that they will desire to enjoy their portion, whether it be large or small. Then, at one time, it will be sufficiently large, with many resources. Then, at another time, his heirs divide it, or those who have no living steal it, or the king takes it away, or it is ruined in some way or other, or it is consumed by the conflagration of the house. Thus a fool, doing cruel acts, comes ignorantly to grief.

Wisely reject hope and desire, and extracting that thorn, i.e., pleasure, thou shouldst act rightly. People who are enveloped by delusion do not understand this: he who gathers wealth will, perhaps, not have the benefit of it.

The world is greatly troubled by women. They, men, forsooth say, 'These are the vessels of happiness.' But this leads them to pain, to delusion, to death, to hell, to birth as hell-beings or brute beasts. The fool never knows the law.

Thus spake the hero: 'Be careful against this great delusion; the clever one should have done with carelessness by considering death in tranquillity, and that, the nature of which is decay, viz., the body; these pleasures, look! will not statisfy thee. Therefore, have done with them! Sage, look! this is the great danger, it should overcome none whomsoever. He is called a hero who is not vexed by the hardships caused by control. He should not be angry because the householder gives him little. If turned off, he should go. Thou shouldst conform to the conduct of the sage.' Thus I say.

Accept Nothing Unclean

That for pleasure the wants of the world should be supplied by bad injurious doings: for one's own sons, daughters, daughters-in-law, kinsmen, nurses, kings, male and female slaves, male and female servants, for the sake of hospitality, of supper and breakfast, the accumulation of wealth is effected.

This is here for the enjoyment of some men. But a wise man exerting himself, houseless, noble, of noble intellect, of noble perception recognises the proper moment for all actions. He should not accept, nor cause others to accept, or permit them to accept anything unlean. Free from uncleanliness he should wander about.

Being not seen in buying and selling, he should not buy,

nor cause others to buy, nor consent to the buying of others. This mendicant who knows the time, the strength of himself, the measure of all things, the practice, the occasion for begging, etc., the conduct, the religious precepts, the true condition of the donor or hearer, who disowns all things not requisite for religious purposes, who is under no obligations, he proceeds securely on the road to final liberation after having cut off both love and hate.

Clothes, alms-bowls, blankets, brooms, property, straw mats, with regard to these things he should know what is unclean. When he receives food he should know the quantity required. This has been declared by the Revered One: he should not rejoice in the receipt of a gift, nor be sorry when he gets nothing. Having got much, one should not store it away; one should abstain from things not requisite for religious purposes. With a mind different from that of common people a seer abandons these things. This is the road taught by the noble ones, well acquainted with which one should not be defiled by sin. Thus I say.

Pleasures are difficult to reject, life is difficult to prolong. That man, certainly, who loves pleasures, is afflicted by their loss, is sorry in his heart, leaves his usual ways, is troubled, suffers pain. The farsighted one who knows the world, knows its inferior part, hell, its upper part, heaven, its side-long part the state of brute beasts. He who knows the relation of human affairs, that he who desires for the world is always turned round in the Samsara, is called among mortals a hero, who liberates those who are fettered.

As the interior of the body is loathsome, so is the exterior; as the exterior, so is the interior. In the interior of the body he perceived the foul interior humours, he observes their several courses or eruptions. A well-informed man knowing and renouncing the body and pleasures, should not eat his saliva; he should not oppose himself to the current of knowledge. Certainly, that man who engages in wordly affairs, who practises many tricks, who is bewildered by his own doings, acts again and again on that desire which increases his unrighteousness. Hence the above has been said for the increase of this life. A man addicted to pleasures acts as if immortal, and puts great faith in pleasure; but when he perceives that this body sustains pains, he cries in his ignorance. Therefore, keep in your mind what I say.

A heretic professes to cure the love of pleasure while he kills, cuts, strikes, destroys, chases away, resolves to do what has not been done before. To whom he applies the cure—enough of that fool's affection; or he who has the cure applied, is a fool. This does not apply to the houseless. Thus I say.

Treat Yourself Roughly

He who perfectly understands what has been said in the preceding lesson and follows the faith to be coveted, should therefore do no sinful act, nor cause others to do one. Perchance he meditates a sin by an act against only one of the six aggregates of lives; but he will be guilty of sin against every one of the six. Desiring happiness and bewailing much, he comes ignorantly to grief through his own misfortune. Through his own carelessness every one produces that phase of life in which the vital spirits are pained. Observing the pain of mundane existence, one should not act with violence. This is called the true knowledge and renunciation. He who ceasing from acts relinquishes the idea of property, relinquishes property itself. That sage has seen the path to final liberation for whom there exists no property. Knowing this, a wise man, who knows the world and has cast off the idea of the world, should prudently conquer the obstructions to righteousness. Thus I say.

The hero does not tolerate discontent,
The hero does not tolerate lust.
Because the hero is not careless.
The hero is not attached to the objects of the senses.

Being indifferent against sounds and the other perceptions, detest the comfort of this life.

A sage adopting a life of wisdom, should treat his gross body roughly.

The heroes who have right intuition, use mean and rough food.

Such a man is said to have crossed the flood of life, to be a sage, to have passed over the Samsara, to be liberated, to have ceased from all activity. Thus I say.

A sage is called unfit who does not follow the law and fails in his office. But on the contrary, he is praised as a hero, he overcomes the connection with the world, he is called the guide of the right way. What has been declared to be here the unhappiness of mortals, of that unhappiness the clever ones propound the knowledge.

Thus understanding and renouncing acts, a man who recognises the truth, delights in nothing else; and he who delights only in the truth, recognises nothing else. As the law has been revealed for the full one, so for the empty one; as for the empty one, so for the full one. But he to whom the faith is preached will perhaps disrespectfully beat the preacher. Yet know, there is no good in this indiscriminate preaching. but ascertain before what sort of man he is, and whom he worships. He is called a hero who liberates the bound, above, below, and in the sideward directions. He always conforms to all knowledge and renunciation; the hero is not polluted by the sin of killing. He is a wise man who perfectly knows the non-killing, who searches after the liberation of the bound. The clever one is neither bound nor liberated; he should do or leave undone what the hero does or does not do; he should not do what the hero leaves undone:

Knowing and renouncing murder of any kind and worldly ideas in all respects.

He who sees himself, needs no instruction. But the miserable and afflicted fool who delights in pleasures and whose miseries do not cease, is turned round in the whirl of pains. Thus I say.

The Path of Righteousness

The Arhats and Bhagavats of the past, present, and future, all say thus, speak thus, declare thus, explain thus: all breathing, existing, living, sentient creatures should not be slain, nor treated with violence, nor abused, nor tormented, nor driven away.

This is the pure, unchangeable, eternal law, which the clever ones, who understand the world, have declared: among the zealous and the not zealous, among the faithful and the not faithful, among the not cruel and the cruel, among those who have worldly weakness and those who have not, among those who like social bonds and those who do not: 'that is the truth, that is so, that is proclaimed in this creed.'

Having adopted the law, one should not hide it, nor forsake it. Correctly understanding the law, one should arrive at indifference for the impressions of the senses, and 'not act on the motives of the world.' 'He who is not of this mind, how should he come to the other?'

What has been said here, has been seen by the omniscient ones, heard by the believers, acknowledged by the faithful, and thoroughly understood by them. Those who acquiesce and indulge in worldly pleasure, are born again and again. 'Day and night exerting thyself, steadfast, always having ready wisdom, perceive that the careless stand outside of salvation; if careful, thou wilt always conquer. Thus I say.

Pain Is Not Pleasant to Anyone

There are as many Asravas as there are Parisravas, and

there are as many Parisravas and there are Asravas. There are as many Anasravas as there are Aparisravas, and there are as many Aparisravas as there are Anasravas. He who well understands these words and regards the world according to the instruction and understands, that which has been distinctly declared, that wise man proclaims the truth here to men, who still belong to the Samsara, who are awakened, and have reached discrimination.

'Those also who are afflicted and careless' will be instructed. I say this as a truth. There is nothing secure from the mouth of death. Those who are led by their desires, who are the tabernacle of fraud, 'who seized by Time dwell in the heap of Karman,' are born again and again. Many who are again and again immersed in delusion, will often renew their acquaintance with the places of pain; they experience the pains inherent in regeneration. He who often does cruel acts, often undergoes punishment in hell, etc. He who seldom does cruel acts, seldom undergoes punishment.

Some say thus, also the wise ones; the wise ones say thus, also some others. Many and several in this world, Brahmins or Shramanas, raise this discussion: We have seen, heard, acknowledged, thoroughly understood, in the upper, nether, and sidelong directions, and in all ways examined it: all sorts of livng beings may be slain, or treated with violence, or abused, or tormented, or driven away. Know about this: there is no wrong in it.

That is a doctrine of the unworthy. But those who are teachers, have said: You have wrongly seen, wrongly heard, wrongly acknowledged, wrongly understood, in the upper, nether, and sidelong directions, in all ways wrongly examined it, when you say thus, speak thus, declare thus, explain thus: All sorts of living beings may be slain, or treated with violence, or abused, or tormented, or driven away. Know about this: There is no wrong in it. That is a doctrine of the unworthy.

But we say thus, speak thus, declare thus, explain thus: All sorts of living beings should not be slain, nor treated with violence, nor abused, nor tormented, nor driven away. Know

©about this, there is no wrong in it. This is the doctrine of the teachers.

First the persuasion of every one should be ascertained, and then we will ask them severally: Ye professors! is pain pleasant to you, or unpleasant? If they give the right answer, reply: For all sorts of living beings pain is unpleasant, disagreeable, and greatly feared. Thus I say.

Abstain from Cruelty

Reflect and observe that whether you go to this world or to that beyond, in the whole world those who are discerning beings, who abstain from cruelty, relinquish Karman. They are flesh-subduing, called duty-knowing, upright men, aware that pain results from actions. Thus say those who have right intuition.

All the professors, conversant with pain, preach renunciation. Thus thoroughly knowing Karman, observing the commandment, wise, unattached to the world, recognising thy Self as one, subdue the body, chastise thyself, weaken thyself: 'just as fire consumes old wood!' Thus with a composed mind, unattached, 'unhesitatingly avoid wrath!' Considering the shortness of life 'know pain, or what will come;' one shall feel the several feelings; and perceive the world suffering under them.

Those who are free from sinful acts are called Anidana. Hence a very wise man should not be inflamed by wrath. Thus I say.

Subdue Blood and Flesh

One should mortify one's flesh in a low, high, and highest degree, quitting one's former connections, and entering tranquillity. Therefore, a hero is careful, a person of pith, guarded, endowed with knowledge, etc., and always restrained. Difficult to go is the road of the heroes, who go whence there is no return, final liberation. Subdue blood and flesh.

That man is called a worthy one, a hero, one to be followed, who living in chastity guarding his eyes shakes off the aggregate.

He who desires the current of Karman, is a fool who has not cut off the fetters of, nor conquered the connection with, the world. For such as dwell in darkness, and are without knowledge, there is no success in faith. Thus I say.

'Whence should he have it, who does not get it early, late, or in the middle of life?' But the discerning one is awakened, and ceases to act. See that it is good to be so! Cutting off that 'whence bondage, cruel death, and dreadful pain,' 'and the desire for external objects flow, he who among mortals knows freedom from acts,' 'seeing that acts will bear fruit, the knower of the sacred lore, parts from Karman.'

There are those who have established themselves in the truth, who were, are, or will be heroes, endowed with knowledge, always exerting themselves, full of equanimity, valuing the world as it deserves in the east, west, south, north. We shall tell the knowledge of them who were heroes, endowed with knowledge, always exerting themselves, full of equanimity, valuing the world as it deserves.

Is there any worldly weakness in the Seer? There exists none, there is none. Thus I say.

Essence of the World

Many entertain cruel thoughts against the world with a motive or without one; they entertain cruel thoughts against the six classes of living beings. To him pleasures are dear. Therefore he is near death. Because he is near death, he is far from liberation. But he who is neither near death nor far from liberation, considers the life of a slow and ignorant fool as similar to a dew drop trembling on the sharp point of the blade of Kusha grass which falls down when shaken by the wind.

A fool, doing cruel acts, comes thereby ignorantly to grief. 'Through delusion he is born, dies, etc.' Being conversant with the deliberation about this delusion, one is conversant with the Samsara; being not conversant with that deliberation, one is not conversant with the Samsara. He who is clever, should not seek after sexual intercourse. But having done so, it would be a second folly of the weak-minded not to own it. Repenting and excluding from the mind the begotten pleasures, one should instruct others to follow the commandment. Thus I say.

See! many who desire colours, are led around in the Samsara, they experience here again and again feelings, i.e., punishment. Many live by injurious deeds against the world, they live by injurious deeds against these living beings. Also the fool, suffering for his passions, delights in bad acts here, mistaking that for salvation which is none. Many heretics lead the life of a hermit in order to avoid worldly sorrows and pains.

Such a man has much wrath, much pride, much conceit, much greed; he delights in many works, acts frequently like a stage-player or a rogue, forms many plans, gives way to his impulses, is influenced by his acts though he pretends to be awakened: thinking that nobody will see him. Through the influence of ignorance and carelessness the fool never knows the law. Men! unhappy creatures, world-wise are those who, not freeing themselves from ignorance, talk about final liberation: they turn round and round in the whirlpool of births. Thus I say.

Free Yourself from Bonds

Many do not live by injurious deeds against the world, they do not live by injurious deeds against these living beings. Ceasing from them, making an end of them, he perceives: this is a favourable opportunity; he who searches for the right moment for this body should never be careless. This is the road taught by the noble ones.

When he has become zealous for the law, he should never be careless, knowing pain and pleasure in their various forms. Men acts here on their own motives; it has been declared that they suffer for their own sins. Neither killing nor lying, he should patiently bear all unpleasant feelings when affected by them. That man is called a true monk.

Those who are not given to sinful acts are nevertheless attacked by calamities; but then the steadfast will bear them. He has to bear them afterwards as he has done before his conversion. The body is of a fragile, decaying nature, it is unstable, transient, uneternal, increasing and decreasing, of a changeable nature. Perceive this as its true character. For him who well understands this, who delights in the unique refuge, for the liberated and inactive there is no passage from birth to birth. Thus I say.

Many are attached to something in the world— be it little or much, small or great, sentient or nonsentient—they are attached to it here amongst these householders. Thus some incur great danger. For him who contemplates the course of the world and does not acknowledge these attachments there is no such danger. Knowing that that which is well understood if well practised, man! with thy eyes on the highest good, be victorious in control. Among such men only is real Brahmanhood. Thus I say.

I have heard this, and it is in my innermost heart; and the freedom from bonds is in your innermost heart. He who has ceased to have worldly attachments, the houseless, suffers with patience a long time.

The careless stand outside, the careful lead a religious life.

Maintain rightly this state of a sage. Thus I say.

Cease from Acts for Liberation

Many are not attached to something in this world, they are not attached to it among these householders. He is a wise man who has heard and understood the word of the learned ones. Without partiality the law has been declared by the noble ones. As I have destroyed here the connection with the world, so is the connection elsewhere difficult to destroy.

Therefore I say: One should not abandon firmness. Some who early exert themselves, do not afterwards slide back; some who early exert themselves, afterwards slide back; those who do not early exert themseleves, can of course not silde back. That man also is of this description, who knowing the world as worthless nevertheless follows its ways. 'Knowing this, it has been declard by sage.' Here the follower of the commandent, the wise, the passionless, he who exerts himself before morning and after evening, always contemplating virtue, and hearing the merit of it will became free from love and delusion. Fight with this your body! why should you fight with anything else?

Difficult to attain is this human body which is worth the fight. For the clever ones have praised the discernment of wisdom; the fool who falls from it, is liable to birth, etc. In this religion (of the Jainas) the case of the fool's fall has been declared to depend on colour and killing. But a sage who walks the beaten track to liberation, regards the wold in a different way. 'Knowing thus the nature of acts in all regards, he does not kill,' he controls himself, he is not overbearing.

Comprehending that pleasure and pain are individual, advising kindness, he will not engage in any work in the whole world: keeping before him the one great aim, liberation, and not turning aside, 'living humbly, unatached to any creature.' The rich in control who with a mind endowed with all penetration recognises that a bad deed should not be done, will not go after it. What you acknowledge as righteousness, that you acknowledge as sagedom; what you acknowledge as sagedom, that you acknowledge as righteousness.

It is inconsistent with weak, sinning, sensual, ill-conducted house-inhabiting men. 'A sage, acquiring sagedom, should subdue his body.' 'The heroes who look at everything with indifference, use mean and rough food, etc.' Such a man is said to have crossed the flood of life, to be a sage, to have passed over the Samsara, to be liberated, to have ceased from acts. Thus I say.

No Women for Monks

For a monk who has not yet reached discrimination, it is bad going and difficult proceeding when he wanders alone from village to village. Some men when going wrong will become angry when exhorted with speech. And a man with wary pride is embarrassed with great delusion. There are many obstacles which are very difficult to overcome for the ignorant and the blinded. Let that not be your case! That is the doctrine of the clever one, Mahavira. Adopting the acharya's views, imitating his indifference for the outer world, making him the guide and adviser in all one's matters, sharing his abode, living carefully, acting according to his mind, examining one's way, not coming too near the acharya, minding living beings, one should go on one's business.

A monk should according to the acharya's order go and return, contract or stretch his limbs, thoroughly clean what ought to be cleaned. Sometimes, though a monk be endowed with virtue and walks in righteousness, living beings, coming in contact with his body, will be killed. If this happens through mere carelessness then he will get his punishment in this life; but if it was done contrary to the rules, he should repent of it and do penance for it. Thus he who knows the sacred lore, recommends penance combined with carefulness.

When a monk with fully developed intuition and knowledge, calm, guarded, endowed with knowledge, always restrained, perceives a woman tempting him, he should consider within himself: what will this person do? The greatest temptation in this world are women. This has been declared by the sage.

When strongly vexed by the influence of the senses, he should eat bad foodf, mortify himself, stand upright, wander from village to village, take no food at all, withdraw his mind from women. First troubles, then pleasures; first pleasures, then troubles: thus they are the cause of quarrels. Considering this and well understanding it, one should teach oneself not to cultivate sensuality. Thus I say. He should not speak of women, nor look at them, nor converse with them, nor claim them as his own, nor do their work. Careful in his speech and guarding his mind, he should always avoid sin. He should maintain this sagedom. Thus I say.

Find Out the Truth

Thus I say: a lake is full of water, it is in an even plain, it is free from dust, it harbours many fish. Look! the teacher stands in the stream of knowledge and is guarded in all directions. Look! there are great seers in the world, wise, awakened, free from acts. Perceive the truth: from a desire of a pious end they chose a religious life. Thus I say.

He whose mind is always wavering, does not reach Samadhi. Some, bound by worldly ties, are followers, i.e., understand the truth; some who are not bound, are followers. How should he not despond who amongst followers is a non-follower? 'But that is truth beyond doubt, what has been declared by the Jinas.'

Whatever a faithful, well-disposed man, on entering the

order, thought to be true, that may afterwards appear to him true; what he thought to be true, that may afterwards appear to him untrue; what he thought to be untrue, that may afterwards appear to him true. What he thinks to be true, that may, on consideration, appear to him true, whether it be true or untrue. What he thinks to be untrue, that may, on consideration, appear to him untrue, whether it be true or untrue. But he who reflects should say unto him who does not reflect: Consider it to be true. Thus the connection, i.e., the continuity of sins is broken.

Regard this as the course of the zealous one, who stands in obedience to the spiritual guide. In this point do not show yourself a fool!

As it would be unto thee, so it is with him whom thou intendest to kill. As it would be unto thee, so it is with him whom thou intendest to tyrannise over. As it would be unto thee, so it is with him whom thou intendest to torment. In the same way, it is with him whom thou intendest to punish, and to drive away. The righteous man who lives up to these sentiments, does therefore neither kill nor cause others to kill living beings. He should not intentionally cause the same punishment for himself.

The Self is the knower or experiencer, and the knower is the Self. That through which one knows, is the Self. With regard to this to know the Self is established. Such is he who maintains the right doctrine of Self. This subject has truly been explained. Thus I say.

The Liberated

Some not instructed in the true law make only a show of good conduct; some, though instructed, have no good conduct. Let that not be your case! That is the doctrine of the clever one. Adopting the acharya's views, imitating his indifference for the outer world, making him the guide and adviser in all one's matters, sharing his abode, conquering sinfulness, one sees the truth; unconquered one should be one's own master, having no reliance on anything in the world. He who is great and withdraws his mind from the outer world, should learn the teaching of the Tirthankaras through the teaching of the acharya; by his own innate knowledge, or through the instruction of the highest, or having heard it from others.

A wise man should not break the commandment. Examining all wrong doctrines from all sides and in all respects, one should clearly understand and reject them. 'Knowing the delight of this world, circumspect and restrained, one should lead the life of an ascetic.' Desiring liberation, a hero should, through the sacred lore, ever be victorious. Thus I say.

The current of sin is said to come from above, from below, and from the sides; these have been declared to be the currents through which, look, there is sinfulness.

'Examining the whirlpool, a man, versed in the sacred lore, should keep off from it.' Leaving the world to avert the current of sin, such a great man, free from acts, knows and sees the truth; examining pleasures he does not desire them. Knowing whence we come and whither we go, he leaves the road to birth and death, rejoicing in the glorious liberation. 'All sounds recoil thence, where speculation has no room,' nor does the mind penetrate there. The saint knows well that which is without support.

The liberated is not long nor small nor round nor triangular nor quadrangular nor circular; he is not black nor blue nor red nor green nor white; neither of good nor bad smell; not bitter nor pungent nor astringent nor sweet; neither rough nor soft; neither heavy nor light; neither cold nor hot; neither harsh nor smooth; he is without body, without resurrection, without contact of matter, he is not feminine nor masculine nor neuter; he perceives, he knows, but there is no analogy whereby to know the nature of the liberated soul; its essence is without form; there is no condition of the unconditioned. There is no sound, no colour, no smell, no taste, no touch—nothing of that kind. Thus I say.

Liberation

I say: To friendly or hostile heretics one should not give food, drink, dainties and spices, clothes, alms-bowls, and brooms; nor exhort these persons to give such things, nor do them service, always showing the highest respect. Thus I say.

A heretic may say: Know this for certain: having or not having received food, etc., down to brooms, having or not having eaten, come to our house, even turning from your way or passing other houses; we shall supply your wants. Confessing an individual creed, coming and going, he may give, or exhort to give, or do service, but one should not accept anything from him, showing not the slightest respect. Thus I say.

Some here are not well instructed as regards the subject of conduct; for desirous of acts, they say: 'Kill creatures;' they themselves kill or consent to the killing of others; or they take what has not been given; or they pronounce opinions, e.g., the world exists, the world does not exist, the world is unchangeable, the world is ever changing; the world has a beginning, the world has no beginning; the world has an end, the world has no end; or with regard to the self and actions: this is well done, this is badly done; this is merit, this is demerit; he is a good man, he is not a good man; there is beatitude, there is no beatitude; there is a hell, there is no hell.

When they thus differ in their opinions and profess their individual persuasion, know that this is all without reason. Thus they are not well taught, not well instructed in the religion such as it has been declared by the Revered One, who knows and sees with quick discernment. One should either instruct the opponent in the true faith or observe abstinence as regards speech. Thus I say.

In all other religious sects, sins are admitted; but to avoid them is called my distinction. For ye who live in a village or in the forest, or not in a village and not in the forest, know the law as it has been declared. 'By the Brahmin, the wise Mahavira, three vows have been enjoined.' Noble and tranquil men who are enlightened and exert themselves in these precepts, are called free from sinful acts.

Knowing and renouncing severally and singly the actions against living beings, in the regions above, below, and on the surface, everywhere and in all ways—a wise man neither gives pain to these bodies, nor orders others to do so, nor assents to their doing so. Nay, we abhor those who give pain to these bodies. Knowing this, a wise man should not cause this or any other pain to any creatures. Thus I say.

For the Mendicant

A mendicant may exert himself, or stand or sit or lie in a burying-place or in an empty house or in a mountain cave or in a potter's workshop. A householder may approach a mendicant who stays in any of these places, and say unto him: O longlived Shramana! I shall give you what I have bought or stolen or taken, though it was not to be taken, nor given, but was taken by force, viz., food, drink, dainties and spices, clothes, an alms-bowl, a plaid, a broom—by acting sinfully against all sorts of living beings; or I shall prepare you snug lodgings; eat the offered food, dwell in the prepared house.

O long-lived Shramana! A mendicant should thus refuse a householder of good sense and ripe age: O long-lived householder! I do not approve of thy words, I do not accept thy words, that, for my sake, thou givest unto me what thou hast bought or stolen or taken, though it was not to be taken, nor given, but was taken by force, viz., food, drink, dainties and spices, clothes, an alms-bowl, a plaid, a broom—by acting sinfully against all sorts of living beings; or that thou preparest pleasant lodgings for me. O long-lived householder! I have given up this, because it is not to be done. A householder, without betraying his intention, may approach him who stays in some one of the above-mentioned places, and give unto him what has been taken, or prepare pleasant lodgings, and accommodate the mendicant with food and lodging. A mendicant should know it by his own innate intelligence, or through the instruction of the Tirthnkaras, or having heard it from others: This householder, forsooth, for my sake injures all sorts of living beings, to give me food, clothes, or to prepare pleasant lodgings. A mendicant should well observe and understand this, that he may order the householder not to show such obsequiousness. Thus I say.

Those who having, with or without the mendicant's knowledge, brought together fetters, become angry on the monk's refusal and will strike him, saying: Beat, kill, cut, burn, roast, tear, rob, despatch, torture him! But the hero, come to such a lot, will bravely bear it, or tell him the code of conduct, considering that he is of a different habit; or by guarding his speech he should in due order examine the subject, guarding himself.

This has been declared by the awakened ones: The faithful should not give to dissenters food, clothes, nor should they exhort them to give, nor do them service, always showing the highest respect. Thus I say.

Know the law declared by the wise Brahmin: one should give to one of the same faith food, clothes, and one should exhort him to give or do him service, always showing the highest respect. Thus I say.

Some are awakened as middle-aged men and exert themselves well, having, as clever men, heard and received the word of the learned. The noble ones have impartially preached the law. Those who are awakened, should not wish for pleasure, nor do harm, nor desire any forbidden things.

A person who is without desires and does no harm unto any living beings in the whole world, is called by me 'unfettered.'

One free from passions understands perfectly the bright one, knowing birth in the upper and nether regions.

Bodies increase through nourishment, they are frail in hardships.' See some whose organs are failing, give way to weakness.

A person who has no desires, cherishes pity. He who understands the doctrine of sin, is a mendicant who knows the time, the strength, the measure, the occasion, the conduct, the religious precept; he disowns all things not requisite for religious purposes, in time exerts himself, is under no obligations; he proceeds securely on the road to final liberation after having cut off both love and hate.

A householder approaching a mendicant whose limbs tremble for cold, may say:

O long-lived Shramana! are you not subject to the influences of your senses?

O long-lived householder! I am not subject to the influences of my senses. But I cannot sustain the feeling of cold. Yet it does not become me to kindle or light a fire, that I may warm or heat myself; nor to procure that comfort through the order of others.

Perhaps after the mendicant has spoken thus, the other kindles or lights a fire that he may warm or heat himself. But the mendicant should well observe and understand this, that he may order him to show no such obsequiousness. Thus I say.

A mendicant who is fitted out with three robes, two linen under garments and one woollen upper garment, and a bowl as fourth article, will not think: I shall beg for a fourth robe. He should beg for clothes which he wants, and which are permitted by the religious code; he should wear the clothes in the same state in which they are given him; he should neither wash nor dye them, nor should he wear washed or dyed clothes, nor should he hide his garments when passing through other villages, being careless of dress. This is the whole duty of one who wears clothes. But know further, that, after winter is gone and the hot season has come, one should leave off the used-up garment of the three, being clad with an upper and under garment, or with the undermost garment, or with one gown, or with no clothes—aspiring to freedom from bonds. Penance suits him. Knowing what the Revered One has declared, one should thoroughly and in all respects conform to it.

When it occurs to a blessed mendicant that he suffers pain, and cannot bear the influence of cold, he should not try to obviate these trials, but stand fast in his own self which is endowed with all knowledge. 'For it is better for an ascetic that he should take poison.' Even thus he will in due time put an end to existence. This way to escape trials has been adopted by many who were free from delusion; it is good, wholesome, proper, beatifying, meritorious. Thus I say.

A mendicant who is fitted out with two robes, and a bowl as third article, will not think: I shall beg for a third robe. He should beg for robes which are allowed to be begged for; he should wear the clothes, etc. This is the whole outfit of one who wears clothes. But know further, that after the winter is gone and the hot season has come, one should leave off the used-up garments; having left off the used-up garments, one should be clad with the undermost garment, with a gown, or with no clothes at all—aspiring to freedom from bonds. Penance suits him. Knowing what the Revered One has declared, one should thoroughly and in all respects conform to it.

When the thought occurs to a mendicant that through illness he is too weak, and not able to beg from house to house—and on his thus complaining a householder brings food, etc., obtained without injuring life, and gives it to him—then he should, after deliberation, say: O long-lived householder! it does not become me to eat or drink this food, etc., or accept anything else of the same kind.

A mendicant who has resolved, that he will, when sick,

accept the assistance of fellow-ascetics in good health, when they offer assistance without being asked, and that vice versa he, when in health, will give assistance to sick fellow-ascetics, offering it without being asked—he should not deviate from his resolution though he die for want of help.

Taking the vow to beg food, etc., for another who is sick, and to eat when sick what is brought by another; taking the vow to beg, etc., and not to eat what is brought; taking the vow not to beg, etc., but to eat what is brought; taking the vow neither to beg, etc., nor to eat what is brought—one should adhere to that vow. Practising thus the law as it has been declared, one becomes tranquil, averted from sin, guarded against the allurements of the senses. Even thus though sick he will in due time put an end to existence by rejecting food and drink. This method has been adopted by many who were free from delusion; it is good, wholesome, proper, beatifying, meritorious. Thus I say.

A mendicant who is fitted out with one robe, and a bowl as second article, will not think: I shall beg for a second robe. He should beg for such a robe only as is allowed to be begged for, and he should wear it in the same state as he receives it.

But when the hot season has come, one should leave off the used-up clothes; one should be clad with one or no garment—aspiring to freedom from bonds.

When the thought occurs to a mendicant: 'I am myself, alone; I have nobody belonging to me, nor do I belong to anybody', then he should thoroughly know himself as standing alone—aspiring to freedom from bonds. Penance suits him. Knowing what the Revered One has declared, one should thoroughly and in all respects conform to it.

A male or female mendicant eating food, etc., should not shift the morsel from the left jaw to the right jaw, nor from the right jaw to the left jaw, to get a fuller taste of it, not caring for the taste of it—aspiring to freedom from bonds. Penance suits him. Knowing what the Revered One has declared, one should thoroughly and in all respects conform to it.

If this thought occurs to a monk: 'I am sick and not able, at this time, to regularly mortify the flesh,' that monk should regularly reduce his food; regularly reducing his food, and diminishing his sins, 'he should take proper care of his body, being immovable like a beam; exerting himself he dissolves his body.'

Entering a village, or a scot-free town, or a town with an earth-wall, or a town with a small wall, or an isolated town, or a large town, or a sea-town, or a mine, or a hermitage, or the halting-places of processions, or caravans, or a capital—a monk should beg for straw; having begged for straw he should retire with it to a secluded spot. After having repeatedly examined and cleaned the ground, where there are no eggs, nor living beings, nor seeds, nor sprouts, nor dew, nor water, nor ants, nor mildew, nor waterdrops, nor mud, nor cobwebs— he should spread the straw on it. Then he should there and then effect the religious death called Itvara (starving oneself).

This is the truth: speaking truth, free from passion, crossing the Samsara, abating irresoluteness, knowing all truth and not being known, leaving this frail body, overcoming all sorts of pains and troubles through trust in this religion, he accomplishes this fearful religious death. Even thus he will in due time put an end to existence. This has been adopted by many who were free from delusion; it is good, wholesome, proper, beatifying, meritorious. Thus I say.

The Naked Monk

To a naked monk the thought occurs: I can bear the pricking of grass, the influence of cold and heat, the stinging of flies and mosquitos; these and other various painful feelings I can sustain, but I cannot leave off the covering of the privities. Then he may cover his privities with a piece of cloth.

A naked monk who perseveres in this conduct, sustains repeatedly these and other various painful feelings: the grass pricks him, heat and cold attack him, flies and mosquitos sting him. A naked monk should be aspiring to freedom from bonds. Penance suits him. Knowing what the Revered One has declared, one should thoroughly and in all respects conform to it.

A monk who has come to any of the following resolutions,—having collected food, etc., I shall give of it to other monks, and I shall eat what they have brought; or having collected food, etc., I shall give of it to other monks, but I shall not eat what they have brought; or having collected food, etc., I shall not give of it to other monks, but I shall eat what they have brought; or having collected food, etc., I shall not give of it to other monks, nor eat what they have brought; or I shall assist a fellow-ascetic with the remnants of my dinner, which is acceptable and remained in the same state in which it was received, and I shall accept the assistance of fellow-ascetics as regards the remnants of their dinner, which is acceptable and remained in the same state in which it was received;—that monk should keep these vows even if he should run the risk of his life—aspiring to freedom from bonds. Penance suits him. Knowing what the Revered One has declared, one should thoroughly conform to it.

Entering Nirvana

The wise ones who attain in due order to one of the unerring states in which suicide is prescribed, those who are rich in control and endowed with knowledge, knowing the incomparable religious death, should continue their contemplation.

Knowing the twofold obstacles, i.e., bodily and mental, the wise ones, having thoroughly learned the law, perceiving in due order that the time for their death has come, get rid of Karman.

Subduing the passions and living on little food, he should endure hardships. If a mendicant falls sick, let him again take food.

He should not long for life, nor wish for death; he should

yearn after neither, life or death.

He who is indifferent and wishes for the destruction of Karman, should continue his contemplation. Becoming unattached internally and externally, he should strive after absolute purity.

Whatever means one knows for calming one's own life, that a wise man should practise in order to gain time for continuing penance.

In a village or in a forest, examining the ground and recognising it as free from living beings, the sage should spread the straw.

Without food he should lie down and bear the pains which attack him. He should not for too long time give way to worldly feelings which overcome him.

When crawling animals or such as live on high or below, feed on his flesh and blood, he should neither kill them nor rub the wound.

Though these animals destroy the body, he should not stir from his position.

After the Asravas have ceased, he should bear pains as if he rejoiced in them.

When the bonds fall off, then he has accomplished his life.

We shall now describe a more exalted method for a well-controlled and instructed monk.

This other law has been proclaimed by Jnatriputra:

He should give up all motions except his own in the thrice-threefold way.

He should not lie on sprouts of grass, but inspecting the bare ground he should lie on it.

Without any comfort and food, he should there bear pain.

When the sage becomes weak in his limbs, he should strive after calmness.

For he is blameless, who is well fixed and immovable in his intention to die.

He should move to and fro on his ground, contract and

stretch his limbs for the benefit of the whole body; or he should remain quiet as if he were lifeless.

He should walk about, when tired of lying, or stand with passive limbs; when tired of standing, he should sit down.

Intent on such an uncommon death, he should regulate the motions of his organs.

Having attained a place swarming with insects, he should search for a clean spot.

He should not remain there whence sin would rise.

He should raise himself above sinfulness, and bear all pains.

And this is a still more difficult method, when one lives according to it: not to stir from one's place, while checking all motions of the body.

This is the highest law, exalted above the preceding method:

Having examined a spot of bare ground he should remain there.

Having attained a place free from living beings, he should there fix himself.

He should thoroughly mortify his flesh, thinking: There are no obstacles in my body.

Knowing as long as he lives the dangers and troubles, the wise and restrained ascetic should bear them as being instrumental to the dissolution of the body.

He should not be attached to the transitory pleasures, nor to the greater ones; he should not nourish desire and greed, looking only for eternal praise.

He should be enlightened with eternal objects, and not trust in the delusive power of the gods; a Brahmin should know of this and cast off all inferiority.

Not devoted to any of the external objects he reaches the end of his life; thinking that patience is the highest good, he should choose one of the described three good methods of entering Nirvana. Thus I say.

3

Uttaradhyayana Sutra

On Living Beings and Things Without Life

Now learn from me with attentive minds the division of Living Beings and Things without life, which a monk must know who is to exert himself in self-control.

The Living Beings and the Things Without Life make up this world; but the space where only Things Without Life are found is called the Non-world

The Living Beings and the Things Without Life will be described with reference to 1. substance, 2. place, 3. time, and 4. development.

Things Without Life

Things Without Life are: 1. possessing form, 2. formless; the formless things are of ten kinds, those possessing form are of four kinds.

The ten kinds of formless things are: 1. Dharma, 2. its divisions, 3. its indivisible parts; 4. Adharma, 5. its divisions, 6. its indivisible parts; 7. Space, 8. its divisions, 9. its indivisible parts, and 10. Time.

Dharma and Adharma are co-extensive with the World; space fills the World and the Non-world; time exists in what is called the place of time.

Dharma, Adharma, and Space are ever without beginning and end.

And Time also, if regarded as a continuous flow, is called so; but with regard to an individual thing it has a beginning and an end.

The four kinds of things possessing form are 1. compound things, 2. their divisions, 3. their indivisible parts, and 4. atoms.

Compound things and atoms occur as individual things and apart or different from others, in the whole world and in parts of the world; this is their distribution with regard to place.

Subtle things occur all over the world, gross things only in a part of it.

I shall now give their fourfold division with regard to Time.

With regard to the continuous flow or development of a thing it is without beginning and without end; but with regard to its existence as an individual thing it has both a beginning and an end.

The longest duration of Things Without Life possessing form is an immeasurable period; the shortest one Samaya.

The longest interruption in the existence of things without life possessing form is an endless Time; the shortest one Samaya.

Their development is fivefold: with regard to 1. colour, 2. smell, 3. taste, 4. touch, and 5. figure.

Those which develop with regard to colour are of five kinds: 1. black, 2. blue, 3. red, 4. yellow, and 5. white.

Those which develop with regard to smell are of two kinds: 1. sweet-smelling substances, and 2. of bad smell.

Those which develop with regard to touch are of five kinds: 1. bitter, 2. pungent, 3. astringent, 4. sour, and 5. sweet.

Those which develop with regard to touch are of eight kinds: 1. hard, 2. soft, 3. heavy, 4. light, 5. cold, 6. hot, 7. smooth, and 8. rough.

In this way the substances have been declared, which develop with regard to touch.

Those which develop with regard to figure are of five kinds: 1. globular, 2. circular, 3. triangular, 4. square, and 5. long.

Things of black colour are subdivided with regard to smell, taste, touch, and figure.

The same subdivision holds good with blue, red, yellow, and white things.

Things of sweet smell are subdivided with regard to colour, taste, touch, and figure; things of bad smell are similarly subdivided.

Things of bitter taste are subdivided with regard to colour, smell, touch, and figure.

The same subdivision holds good with pungent, astringent, sour, and sweet things.

Things of hard touch are subdivided with regard to colour, smell, taste, and figure.

The same subdivision holds good with soft, heavy, light, cold, hot, smooth, and rough things.

Things of globular figure are subdivided with regard to colour, smell, taste, and touch.

The same subdivision holds good with circular, triangular, square, and long things.

Thus the division of Things Without Life has briefly been told.

Living Beings

I shall now, in due order, deliver the division of Living Beings.

Living Beings are of two kinds: 1. those still belonging to the Samsara, and 2. the perfected souls (siddhas). The latter are of many kinds; hear me explain them.

(1) The perfected souls are those of women, men, hermaphrodites, of orthodox, heterodox, and householders.

Perfection is reached by people of the greatest, smallest, and middle size, on high places, underground, on the surface of the earth, in the ocean, and in water.

Ten hermaphrodites reach, at the same time, perfection, twenty women, one hundred and eight men; four householders, ten heterodox, and one hundred and eight orthodox monks.

Two individuals of the greatest size reach perfection simultaneously, four of the smallest size, and one hundred and eight of the middle size.

Four individuals reach perfection simultaneously on high places, two in the ocean, three in water, twenty underground, and one hundred and eight on the surface of the earth.

From where are the perfected souls debarred? Where do the perfected souls reside? Where do they leave their bodies, and where do they go, on reaching perfection?

Perfected souls are debarred from the non-world; they reside on the top of the world; they leave their bodies here, and go there, on reaching perfection.

Twelve Yojanas above the Sarvartha Vimana is the place called Ishatpragbhara, which has the form of an umbrella; there the perfected souls go.

It is forty-five hundred thousand Yojanas long, and as many broad, and it is somewhat more than three times as many in circumference.

Its thickness is eight Yojanas, it is greatest in the middle, and decreases toward the margin, till it is thinner than the wing of a fly.

This place, by nature pure, consisting of white gold, resembles in form an open umbrella, as has been said by the best of Jinas.

Above it is a pure blessed place called Shita, which is white like a conch-shell, the anka-stone, and Kunda-flowers; a Yojana thence is the end of the world.

The perfected souls penetrate the sixth part of the uppermost Krosha of the above-mentioned Yojana.

There at the top of the world reside the blessed perfected souls, rid of all transmigration, and arrived at the excellent state of perfection.

The dimension of a perfected soul is two-thirds of the height which the individual had in his last existence.

The perfected souls, considered singly, as individuals have a beginning but no end; considered collectively they have neither a beginning nor an end.

They have no visible form, they consist of Life throughout, they are developed into knowledge and faith, and they possess paramount happiness which admits of no comparison.

They all dwell in one part of the world, and have developed into knowledge and faith, they have crossed the boundary of the Samsara, and reached the excellent state of perfection.

(2) Living Beings which still belong to the Samsara, are of two kinds : movable, and immovable ones: the immovable ones are of three kinds:

Earth Lives, Water Lives, and plants; these are the three kinds of immovable living beings; now learn from me their subdivision.

The Earth Lives are of two kinds: subtle and gross; and both of them are either fully developed or undeveloped.

The gross and fully developed are of two kinds: smooth or rough. The smooth ones are of seven kinds:

Black, blue, red, yellow, white, pale dust, and clay.

The rough ones are of thirty-six kinds:

Earth, gravel, sand, stones, rocks, rock-salt, iron, copper, tin, lead, silver, gold, and diamond;

Orpiment, vermilion, realgar, Shasaka, antimony, coral, Abhrapatala, Abhravaluka; these are varieties of gross Earth-bodies and kinds of precious stones.

Hyacinth, natron, Anka, crystal, Lohitaksha, emerald, Masaragalla, Bhujamochaka, and sapphire;

Chandana, red chalk, Hamsagarbha, Pulaka, and sulphur, Chandraprabha, lapis lazuli, Jalakanta, and Suryakanta.

These thirty-six kinds of `rough earth' have been enumerated. The 'subtle earth' is but of one kind, as there is no variety.

The subtle species is distributed all over the world, but the gross one is found in a part of the world only.

I shall now give their fourfold division with regard to Time.

With regard to the continuous flow or development of an Earth-body it is without a beginning and end; but with regard to its existence in its present form it has both a beginning and end.

Twenty-two thousand years is the longest duration of the Earth Lives; its shortest is less than a Muhurta.

The longest duration of the body of Earth Lives, if they do not leave that kind of body, is an immeasurable Time; the shortest is less than one Muhurta.

The longest interval between an Earth Life's leaving its body till its return to it, is an endless Time; the shortest less than one Muhurta.

Their varieties, caused by difference of colour, smell, taste, touch, figure, and place, are counted by thousands.

The Water Lives are of two kinds: subtle and gross ones; and both of them are either fully developed or undeveloped.

The gross fully developed ones are of five kinds: pure water, dew, exudations, fog, and ice.

The subtle water is of one kind, as there is no variety. The subtle species is distributed all over the world, but the gross one is found in a part of the world only.

With regard to the continuous flow or development of an Earth-body it is without a beginning and end; but with regard to its existence in its present form it has both a beginning and end.

Seven thousand years is the longest duration of the life of Water Lives, its shortest is less than a Muhurta. (All that has been said of Earth Lives is repeated here).

Plants are of two kinds: subtle and gross ones; and both of them are either fully developed or undeveloped.

The gross and fully developed plants are of two kinds: either many have one body in common, or each has its own body.

Those who severally have their own body are of many kinds: trees, shrubby plants, shrubs, big plants, creeping plants, grass;

Palms, plants of knotty stems or stalks, mushrooms, water-plants, annual plants, and herbs. These are called plants possessing severally their own body.

Those plants of which many have one body in common are of many kinds: Aluya, Mulaya, ginger;

Harili, Sirili, Sassirili, Javai, Keyakandali, onion, garlic, plantain-tree, Kuduvvaya;

Lohinthuya, Thihuya, Tuhaga, Kanha, Vajjakanda, Suranaya;

Assakanni, Sihakanni, Musundhi, turmeric, and many others besides.

The subtle plants are of one kind, as there is no variety. Subtle plants are distributed all over the world, gross plants are found in a part of the world only.

Ten thousand years is the longest duration of the life of plants.

Thus the three kinds of immovable living beings have briefly been told. I shall now explain in due order the three kinds of movable living beings.

The movable beings are the Fire Lives, the Wind Lives, and those with an organic body; these are the three kinds of movable beings. Learn from me their subdivision.

The Fire Lives are of two kinds: subtle and gross ones; and both of them are either fully developed or undeveloped.

The gross and fully developed ones are of many kinds: coal, burning chaff, fire, and flame of fire;

Meteors, and lightning, and many other kinds besides.

The subtle Fire Lives are but of one kind, as there is no variety.

The Wind Lives are of two kinds. The gross and fully developed ones are of five kinds: squalls, whirlwinds, thick winds, high winds, and low winds;

And the Samvartaka wind, etc.; thus they are of many kinds.

The subtle Wind Lives are but of one kind, as there is no variety.

Movable being with organic bodies, i.e., animals are of four kinds: those possessing two organs of sense, those with three organs, those with four organs, those with five organs.

Beings with two organs of sense are of two kinds: subtle and gross ones. Both are either fully developed or undeveloped. Learn from me their subdivision.

Worms, Somangala, Alasa, Maivahaya, Vasimuha, shells, conches, Sankhanaga;

Palloya, Anullaya, cowries, leeches, Jalaga, and Chandana.

These and others are the many kinds of beings with two organs of sense. All of them live in a part of the world only, they do not live everywhere.

The duration of the life of beings with two organs of sense is twelve years at the utmost; the shortest is less than a Muhurta.

The longest duration of the body of beings with two organs of sense is a Samkhyeya or measurable Time if they do not leave that kind of body; the shortest is less than one Muhurta.

Beings with three organs of sense are of two kinds: subtle and gross ones. Both are either fully developed or undeveloped. Learn from me their subdivision.

Kunthu, ants, bugs, Ukkala, white ants, Tanahara, Katthahara, Maluga, Pattaharaga;

Duga shining like lead, which originate in the kernel of the cotton-seed, Sadavari, centipedes, Indagaiya:

Cochineal, etc. Thus they are of many kinds.

All of them live in a part of the world only, they do not live everywhere.

Beings with four organs of sense are of two kinds: subtle and gross ones. Both are either developed or undeveloped. Learn from me their subdivision.

Andhiya, Pottiya, flies, mosquitoes, bees, moths, Dhinkana, and Kankana;

Kukkuda, Singiridi, Nandavatta, scorpions, Dola, crickets, Virali, Achhivehaya;

Achhila, Sahaya Achhirodaya, Vichitta, Vichittapattaya, Uhimjaliya, Jalakari, Niya, and Tantavagaiya.

Beings with five organs of sense are of four kinds: denizens of hell, animals, men, and gods.

Denizens of hell are of seven kinds according to the seven hells; they are called Ratnabha, Sharkarabha, Valukabha;

Pankabha, Dhumabha, Tama, and Tamatama. Thus the seven kinds of denizens of hell have been enumerated.

All the denizens of hell live in a part of the world only; they do not live everywhere.

In the first hell the longest duration of their life is one Sagaropama; the shortest is ten thousand years.

In the second hell the longest duration of their life is three Sagaropamas.

In the third hell the longest duration of their life is seven Sagaropamas; the shortest is three Sagaropamas.

In the fourth hell the longest duration of their life is ten Sagaropamas; the shortest is seven Sagaropamas.

In the fifth hell the longest duration of their life is seventeen Sagaropamas; the shortest is ten Sagaropamas.

In the sixth hell the longest duration of their life is twenty-two Sagaropamas; the shortest is seventeen Sagaropamas.

In the seventh hell the longest duration of their life is thirty-three Sagaropamas; the shortest is twenty-two Sagaropamas.

The length of the life of denizens of hell is also that of their continuance in the same kind of body, with regard both to the longest and shortest duration of it.

The animals which possess five organs of sense are of

two kinds, those which originate by *generatio aequivoca*, and those which are born from the womb.

Either of them are again of three kinds: 1. aquatic, 2. terrestrial, and 3. aerial animals. Learn from me their subdivision.

Fishes, tortoises, crocodiles, Makaras, and Gangetic porpoises are the five kinds of aquatic animals.

The longest duration of the life of aquatic animals is one crore of former years; the shortest is less than one Muhurta.

The longest duration of the aquatic animals' continuance in the same kind of body is from two to nine crore of former years.

Quadrupeds and reptiles are the two kinds of terrestrial animals. The quadrupeds are of four kinds; listen to my description of them:

(1) Solidungular animals, as horses, etc.

(2) Biungular animals, as cows, etc.;

(3) Multiungular animals, as elephants, etc;

(4) Animals having toes with nails, as lions, etc.

The reptiles are of two kinds: those which walk on their arms, as lizards, etc., and those which move on their breast, as snakes etc. Both are again of many kinds.

The longest duration of the life of terrestrial animals is three Palyopamas; the shortest is less than one Muhurta.

The longest duration of the terrestrial animals' continuance in the same kind of body is three Palyopamas plus from two to nine crore of former years; the shortest is less than one Muhurta.

Winged animals are of four kinds: those with membranous wings, those with feathered wings, those with wings in the shape of a box, and those which sit on outspread wings.

The longest duration of the life of aerial animals is an Asamkhyeya-part of a Palyopama; the shortest is less than one Muhurta.

The longest duration of the aerial animals' continuance in the same kind of body is an Asamkhyeya-part of a

Palyopama plus from two to nine crore of former years; the shortest is less than one Muhurta.

Men are of two kinds; listen to my description of them: men originating by *generatio aequivoca*, and men born from the womb.

Those who are born from the womb are of three kinds: those living in the Karmabhumi, those living in the Akarmabhumi, and those living on the minor continents.

They have, in the same order, fifteen, thirty, and twenty-eight subdivisions. These are the numbers handed down.

Men originating by *generatio aequivoca* are of as many kinds. They all live but in a part of the world.

Gods are of four kinds; listen to my description of them: 1. Bhaumeyikas; 2. Vyantaras; 3. Jyotishkas; 4. Vaimanikas.

There are ten kinds of Bhaumeyikas eight of Vyantaras who live in woods, five of Jyotishkas, and two of Vaimanikas.

The Bhaumeyikas are: the Asura-Kumaras, Naga-Kumaras, Suvarna-Kumaras, Vidyut-Kumaras, Agni-Kumaras, Dvipa-Kumaras, Udadhi-Kumaras, Vata-Kumaras, and Ghanika-Kumaras.

The eight kinds of Vyantaras are: Pisachas, Bhutas, Yakshas, Rakshasas, Kinnaras, Kimpurushas, Mahoragas, and Gandharvas.

The moons, the suns, the Nakshatras, the planets, and the hosts of stars are the fivefold dwellings of Jyotishkas.

The Vaimanika gods are of two kinds: those who are born in the heavenly Kalpas, and those who are born in the regions above them.

The former are of twelve kinds: those who live in the following Kalpas, after which they are named: Saudharma, Isana, Sanatkumara, Mahendra, Brahmaloka, and Lantaka;

Mahashukla, Sahasrara, Anata, Pranata, Arana, and Achyuta. These are the gods who are born in Kalpas.

The gods who are born in the regions above the Kalpas are of two kinds: The Graiveyakas, and the Anuttaras. The

Graiveyakas are of nine kinds.

The lowest of the lowest, the middle of the lowest, the highest of the lowest, the lowest of the middle;

The middle of the middle, the highest of the middle, the lowest of the highest, the middle of the highest;

The highest of the highest. These are the Graiveyaka gods.

The Vijayas, the Vaijayantas, the Jayantas, the Aparajitas,

And the Sarvarthasiddhas: these are the five kinds of Anuttara gods.

These and others besides are the many kinds of Vaimanika gods.

The longest duration of the life of the Bhaumeyika gods is somewhat more than a Sagaropama, the smallest ten thousand years.

The longest duration of the life of the Vyantaras is one Palyopama, the shortest is ten thousand years.

The longest duration of the life of the Jyotishkas is one Palyopama plus one hundred thousand years, the shortest is the eighth part of a Palyopama.

The longest duration of life in the Saudharmakalpa is two Sagaropamas, the shortest is one Palyopama.

Having thus learned the nature of living beings and lifeless things which is in accordance with the principles of reasoning, and believing in it, a sage should delight in self-control.

After having lived as a Shramana many years, a sage should mortify himself by religious exercises.

The longest duration of the mortification is twelve years; the middle, one year; and the shortest, six months.

In the first four years he should abstain from dressed food, in the second four years he should keep various fasts.

During two years he should eat Achamla at the end of every second fast; in the following half year he should keep not too long fasts.

In the second half of the year he should keep long fasts.

During the whole year he should eat but small portions of Achamla.

During the last year a sage should make the ends of two consecutive fasts meet, and should break his fast after half a month or a whole month, till he dies.

Those souls who cherish heretical opinions, commit sins, and kill living beings, will not reach Bodhi at the time of death.

Those souls who cherish orthodox opinions, do not commit sins, and are enveloped in white Leshya, wil reach Bodhi at the time of death.

Those souls who cherish heretical opinions, commit sins, and are enveloped in black Leshya, will not reach Bodhi at the time of death.

The miserable men who do not know the creed of the Jinas, will many times commit unholy suicide and die against their will.

The Jaina Creed

Four Requisites

Four things of paramount value are difficult to obtain here by a living being: human birth, instruction in the Law, belief in it, and energy in self-control.

1. The universe is peopled by manifold creatures, who are, in this Samsara, born in different families and castes for having done various actions.

Sometimes they go to the world of the gods, sometimes to the hells, sometimes they become Asuras in accordance with their actions.

Sometimes they become Kshatriyas, or Chandalas and Bukkasas, or worms and moths, or insects called Kunthu and ants.

Thus living beings of sinful actions, who are born again and again in ever-recurring births, are not disgusted with the Samsara, but they are like warriors never tired of the battle of life.

Living beings bewildered through the influence of their actions, distressed and suffering pains, undergo misery in non-human births.

But by the cessation of Karman, perchance, living beings will reach in due time a pure state and be born as men.

2. And though they be born with a human body, it will be difficult for them to hear the Law, having heard which they

will do penances, combat their passions and abstain from killing living beings.

3. And though, by chance, they may hear the Law, it will be difficult for them to believe in it; many who are shown the right way, stray from it.

4. And though they have heard the Law and believe in it, it is difficult for them to fulfil it strenuously; many who approve of the religion, do not adopt it

Having been born as a man, having heard the Law, believing in it, and fulfilling it strenuously, an ascetic should restrain himself and shake off sinfulness.

The pious obtain purity, and the pure stand firmly in the Law: the soul afterwards reaches the highest Nirvana, being like unto a fire fed with ghee.

Leave off the causes of sin, acquire fame through patience! A man who acts up to this will rise to the upper regions after having left this body of clay.

The Yakshas who are gifted with various virtues, live in the heavenly regions, situated one above the other, shining forth like the great luminaries, and hoping never to descend thence.

Intent on enjoying divine pleasures and changing their form at will, they live in the upper Kalpa heavens many centuries of former years.

The Yakshas, having remained there according to their merit, descend thence at the expiration of their life and are born as men.

Men are of ten kinds.

Fields and houses, gold, cattle, slaves and servants: where these four goods, the causes of pleasure, are present, in such families he is born.

He will have friends and relations, be of good family, of fine complexion, healthy, wise, noble, famous, and powerful.

After having enjoyed, at their proper time, the unrivalled pleasures of human life, he will obtain true knowledge by his pure religious merit acquired in a former life.

Perceiving that the four requisites are difficult to obtain, he will apply himself to self-control, and when by penances he has shaken off the remnant of Karman, he will become an eternal Siddha.

Thus I say.

Impurity

You cannot prolong your life, therefore be not careless; you are past help when old age approaches. Consider this: what protection will careless people get, who kill living beings and do not exert themselves?

Men who adhering to wrong principles acquire wealth by evil deeds, will lose it, falling into the snares of their passions and being held captive by their hatred.

As the burglar caught in the breach of the wall perishes by the work the sinner himself had executed, thus people in this life and the next cannot escape the effect of their own actions.

If a man living in the Samsara does an action for the sake of somebody else, or one by which he himself also profits, then, at the time of reaping the fruit of his actions, his relations will not act as true relations (i.e., will not come to his help).

Wealth will not protect a careless man in this world and the next. Though he had seen the right way, he does not see it, even as one in the dark whose lamp has suddenly been put out.

Though others sleep, be thou awake! Like awise man, trust nobody, but be always on the alert; for dangerous is the time and weak the body. Be always watchful like a Bharunda bird!

A monk should step carefully in his walk, i.e., in his life, supposing everthing to be a snare for him. First he must bestow care on his life till he wins the stake, viz., enlightenment, and afterwards he should despise it, annihilating his sins.

By conquering his will, a monk reaches liberation, as a well-broken horse which is clad in harness goes to battle. Be watchful in your young years; for thereby a monk quickly obtains liberation.

If he does not get victory over his will early, he will get it afterwards; such reasoning presupposes the eternity of human life. But such a man despairs when his life draws to its close, and the dissolution of his body approaches.

One cannot quickly arrive at discernment; therefore one should exert one's self, abstain from pleasures, understand the world, be impartial like a sage, and guard one's self: thus never be careless.

A Shramana who again and again suppresses the effects of delusion, and controls himself, will be affected in a rough way by external things; but a monk should not hate them in his mind.

External things weaken the intellect and allure many; therefore keep them out of your mind. Keep off delusion, remove pride, do not practise deceit, leave off greed.

Heretics who are impure and vain, are always subject to love and hate, and are wholly under the influence of their passions. Despising them as unholy men, desire virtues till the end of your life.

Thus I say.

Death against One's Will

In this ocean of life with its currents, births, difficult to cross, one man has reached the opposite shore; one wise man has given an answer to the following question.

These two ways of life ending with death have been declared: death with one's will, and death against one's will.

Death against one's will is that of ignorant men, and it happens to the same individual many times. Death with one's will is that of wise men, and at best it happens but once.

Mahavira has thus described the first kind in which an ignorant man, being attached to pleasures, does very cruel actions.

A man attached to pleasures and amusements will be caught in the trap of deceit. He thinks: 'I never saw the next world, but I have seen with my own eyes the pleasures of this life.'

'The pleasures of this life are in your hand, but the future ones are uncertain. Who knows whether there is a next world or not?'

The fool boasts: 'I shall have the company of most men.' But by his love of pleasures and amusements he will come to grief.

Then he begins to act cruelly against movable and immovable beings, and he kills living beings with a purpose or without.

An ignorant man kills, lies, deceives, calumniates, dissembles, drinks liquor, and eats meat, thinking that this is the right thing to do.

Overbearing in acts and words, desirous for wealth and women, he accumulates sins in two ways, just as a young snake gathers dust both on and in its body.

Then he suffers ill and is attacked by disease; and he is in dread of the next world when he reflects on his deeds.

I have heard of the places in hell, and of the destination of the sinner, where the fools who do cruel deeds will suffer violently.

Then going to the place where he is to be born again according to his deeds, he feels remorse, as I have heard from my teacher.

As a charioteer, who against his better judgment leaves the smooth highway and gets on a rugged road, repents when the axle breaks; so the fool, who transgresses the Law and embraces unrighteousness, repents in the hour of death, like the charioteer over the broken axle.

Then when death comes at last, the fool trembles in fear; he dies the 'death against one's will,' having lost his chance like a gambler vanquished by Kali.

Thus has been explained the fools' 'death against one's will;' now hear from me the wise men's `death with one's will!'

Full of peace and without injury to any one is, as I have heard from my teachers, the death of the virtuous who control themselves and subdue their senses.

Such a death does not fall to the lot of every monk, nor of every householder; for the morality of householders is of various character, and that of monks is not always good throughout.

Some householders are superior to some monks in self-control; but the saints are superior to all householders in self-control.

Bark and skin of a goat, nakedness, twisted hair, baldness—these outward tokens will not save a sinful ascetic.

A sinner, though he be a mendicant, will not escape hell; but a pious man, whether monk or householder, ascends to heaven.

A faithful man should practise the rules of conduct for householders; he should never neglect the Posaha fast in both fortnights, not even for a single night.

When under such discipline he lives piously even as a householder, he will, on quitting flesh and bones, share the world of the Yakshas.

Now a restrained monk will become one of the two: either one free from all misery or a god of great power.

To the highest regions, in due order, to those where there is no delusion, and to those which are full of light, where the glorious gods dwell—who have long life, great power, great lustre, who can change their shape at will, who are beautiful as on their first day, and have the brilliancy of many suns—to such places go those who are trained in self-control and penance, monks or householders,who have obtained liberation by absence of passion.

Having heard this from the venerable men who control themselves and subdue their senses, the virtuous and the learned do not tremble in the hour of death.

A wise man having weighted both kinds of death and

chosen the better one taught in the Law of Compassion, will become calm through patience, with an undisturbed mind at the time of death.

When the right time to prepare for death has arrived, a faithful monk should in the presence of his teacher suppress all emotions of fear or joy and wait for the dissolution of his body.

When the time for quitting the body has come, a sage dies the 'death with one's will,' according to one of the three methods.

Thus I say.

The False Ascetic

All men who are ignorant of the Truth are subject to pain; in the endless Samsara they suffer in many ways.

Therefore a wise man, who considers well the ways that lead to bondage and birth, should himself search for the truth, and be kind towards all creatures.

'Mother, father, daughter-in-law, brother, wife, and sons will not be able to help me, when I suffer for my own deeds.'

This truth should be taken to heart by a man of pure faith; he should therefore cut off greed and love, and not hanker after his former connections.

Cows and horses, jewels and earrings, cattle, slaves and servants: all these possessions you must give up in order to obtain the power of changing your form at will.

Everything that happens to somebody, affects him personally; therefore, knowing the creatures' love of their own self, do not deprive them of their life, but cease from endangering and combating them.

Seeing that to accept presents leads to hell, one should not accept even a blade of grass; only to preserve one's life one should eat the food that is put in one's own alms-bowl.

Here some are of opinion that they will be delivered from all misery by merely attending the teacher, without abstaining from sins.

Acknowledging the truth about bondage and liberation, but talking only, not acting in accordance with these tenets, they seek comfort for themselves in mighty words.

Clever talking will not work salvation; how should philosophical instruction do it? Fools, though sinking lower and lower through their sins, believe themselves to be wise men.

They are going a long way in the endless Samsara; therefore looking out carefully one should wander about carefully.

Choosing what is beyond and above this world, viz., liberation, one should never desire worldly objects, but sustain one's body only to be able to annihilate one's Karman.

Those will reap pains who, in thoughts, words, or acts, are attached to their body, to colours, and to forms.

Recognising the casue of Karman, one should wander about waiting for one's death; knowing the permitted quantity of food and drink, one should eat such food as has been prepared by the householders for their own consumption.

An ascetic should not lay by any store, not even so little as the grease sticking to his alms-bowl; but as a bird with its plumage, so he with his alms-bowl should wander about without desires.

Receiving alms in a manner to avoid faults, and controlling one's self, one should wander about in a village without a fixed residence; careful among the careless one should beg one's food.

Thus has spoken the Arhat Jnatriputra, the venerable native of Vaisali, who possesses the highest knowledge and who possessess the highest faith, who possesses at the same time the highest knowledge and the highest faith.

Thus I say.

The Ten Conditions of Perfect Chastity

O long-lived Jambusvamin! I Sudharman have heard the following discourse from the Venerable Mahavira:

Here, indeed, the venerable Sthaviras have declared ten conditions for the realisation of celibacy, by hearing and understanding which the monks will reach a high degree of self-discipline, of Samvara, and of contemplation, will be well protected by the three Guptis, will guard their senses, guard their chastity, and will thus never be remiss in the attendance on their religious duties.

What, then, are those ten conditions for the realisation of celibacy as declared by the venerable Sthaviras, by hearing and understanding which the monks will reach a high degree of self-discipline, of Samvara, and of contemplation, will be protected by the three Guptis, will guard their senses, guard their chastity, and will thus never be remiss in the attendance on their religious duties?

These, then, are the ten conditions for the realisation of celibacy.

1. A Nirgrantha may occupy various places for sleep or rest; but a Nirgrantha should not occupy places, for sleep or rest, frequented by women, cattle, or eunuchs. The preceptor has explained the reason for this. If a Nirgrantha occupies places for sleep or rest, frequented by women, cattle, or eunuchs, then, though he be chaste, there may arise a doubt with regard to his chastity, or a sensual desire, or a feeling of remorse, or he will break the rules, or he will become a slave to passion, or he will acquire a dangerous illness of long duration, or he will desert the faith which the Kevalin has proclaimed. Therefore, a Nirgrantha should not occupy places, for sleep or rest, frequented by women, cattle, or eunuchs.

2. A Nirgrantha should not converse with women. The preceptor has explained the reason for this.

3. A Nirgrantha should not sit together with women on the same seat. The preceptor has explained the reason for this.

4. A Nirgrantha should not look at, or contemplate, the charms and beauties of women.

5. A Nirgrantha should not, behind a screen, or curtain, or wall, listen to the screeching or crying of women.

6. A Nirgrantha should not recall to his memory the pleasure and amusements which in the past he enjoyed together with women.

7. A Nirgrantha should not eat well-dressed food.

8. A Nirgrantha should not eat or drink to excess.

9. A Nirgrantha should not wear ornaments. The preceptor has explained the reason for this. If he wears ornaments, or adorns his body, he might become an object of desire to women.

10. A Nirgrantha should not care for sounds, colours, tastes, smells, and feelings.

Thus I say.

The Bad Shramana

A Nirgrantha who has entered the order, who has learned the Law, who has received religious discipline, and who has obtained the benefit of Bodhi which is difficult to obtain, may perhaps afterwards begin to live as he likes.

He will say: I have a good bed and wherewithal to cover me; I obtain food and drink; I know everything that comes to pass, friend; why then should I study, sir?

He who, after entering the order, always sleeps, eats, and drinks as much as he likes, and lives comfortably, is called a bad Shramana.

The sinner who despises the learning and discipline which his preceptor and teachers have taught him, is called a bad Shramana.

He who does not, as he should, strive to please his preceptor and teachers, does not, in his arrogance, treat them with respect, is called a bad Shramana.

He who hurts living beings, seeds, and sprouts, who does not control himself, though he believes himself well-controlled, is called a bad Shramana.

He who uses a bed, a plank, a chair, a seat, or his duster, without having well wiped these things, is called a bad Shramana.

He who walks with great haste and without care, being overbearing and fierce, is called a bad Shramana.

He who carelessly inspects things, throwing down his duster at random, not being attentive to the inspection of things, is called a bad Shramana.

He who carelessly inspects things, his attention being absorbed by what he hears, who always slights his teachers, is called a bad Shramana.

He who is deceitful, talkative, arrogant, greedy, who does not control himself, nor share his food, etc., with those who are in want, and is not of an amiable disposition, is called a bad Shramana.

He who is a controversialist, and ill-behaved, who perverts the truth, and delights in quarrels and contentions, is called a bad Shramana.

He who sits down on a weak, shaking seat wherever he lists,and is not careful in sitting down, is called a bad Shramana.

He who sleeps with dusty feet and does not inspect his couch, being careless about his bed, is called a bad Shramana.

He who eats milk, curds, and other things produced from milk, and does not practise austerities, is called a bad Shramana.

He who eats after sunset, and when admonished, makes an angry reply, is called a bad Shramana.

He who leaves his own teacher, and follows heretical ones, who continuously changes his school, being of a bad disposition, is called a bad Shramana.

He who has left his own house, and busies himself in another's house who lives by fortune-telling, is called a bad Shramana.

He who eats the food of his relations, and does not like living by alms, who reposes on the seat of the householder, is called a bad Shramana.

Such a monk, who, like the heretics, does not protect himself from sins, who though having the appearance of a monk is the lowest among his worthy brethern, is despised in this world like poison; he is nobody in this world and in that beyond.

But he who always avoids these sins, and is pious amongst his brethren, is welcomed in this world like nectar; he conquers this world and the next.

Thus I say.

The Samitis and Guptis

The eight articles of the creed are the Samitis and the Guptis; there are five Samitis and three Guptis.

The Samitis are: 1. Irya-samiti, going by paths trodden by men, beasts, carts, etc., and looking carefully so as not to occasion the death of any living creature; 2. Bhasha-samiti gentle, salutary, sweet, righteous speech; 3. Eshana-samiti, receiving alms in a manner to avoid the forty-two faults that are laid down; 4. Adana-samiti, receiving and keeping of the things necessary for religious exercises, after having carefully examined them; 5. Uchchara-samiti, performing the operations of nature in an unfrequented place.

The three Guptis are: 1. Mano-gupti, preventing the mind from wandering in the forest of sensual pleasures by employing it in contemplation, study etc.; 2. Vag-gupti preventing the tongue from saying bad things by a vow of silence, etc.; 3. Kaya-gupti, putting the body in an immovable posture as in the case of Kayotsarga.

The Samitis are thus briefly enumerated, in which the whole creed taught by the Jinas and set forth in the twelve Angas, is comprehended.

1. The walking of a well-disciplined monk should be pure in four respects; in respect to 1. The cause; 2. the time; 3. the road; 4. the effort.

The cause is: knowledge, faith, and right conduct; the time is day-time; the road excludes bad ways.

The effort is fourfold, viz., as regards: 1. substance,

2. place, 3. time, and 4. condition of mind. Hear me explain them.

1. With regard to substance: the walking monk should look with his eyes; with regard to place: the space of a yuga (four hastas or cubits); with regard to time: as long as he walks; and with regard to condition of mind; carefully.

He walks carefully who pays attention only to his walk and his body executing it, whilst he avoids attending to the objects of sense, but minds his study, the latter in all five ways.

2. To give way to: anger, pride, deceit and greed, laughter, fear, loquacity and slander; these eight faults should a well-disciplined monk avoid; he should use blameless and concise speech at the proper time.

3. As regards begging, a monk should avoid the faults in the search, in the receiving, and in the use of the three kinds of objects, viz., food, articles of use, and lodging.

A zealous monk should avoid in the search for alms the faults occasioned either by the giver or by the receiver; in the receiving of alms the faults inherent in the receiving; and in the use of the articles received, the four faults.

4. If a monk takes up or lays down the two kinds of things belonging to his general and supplementary outfit, he should proceed in the following way.

A zealous monk should wipe the thing after having inspected it with his eyes, and then he should take it up or put it down, having the Samiti in both respects.

5. Excrements, urine, saliva,mucus, uncleanliness of the body, offals of food,waste things, his own body (when he is about to die), and everything of this description is to be disposed of in the way to be described.

In a place neither frequented nor seen by other people, which offers no obstacles to self-control, which is even, not covered with grass or leaves, and has been brought into its present condition not long ago, which is spacious, has an inanimate surface-layer, not too near the village, not perforated by holes, and is exempt from insects and seeds—

in such a place he should leave his excrements, etc.

The five Samitis are thus briefly enumerated, I shall now explain in due order the three Guptis.

1. There is, 1. truth; 2. untruth; 3. a mixture of truth and untruth; 4. a mixture of what is not true, and what is not untrue. The Gupti of mind refers to all four.

A zealous monk should prevent his mind from desires for the misfortune of somebody else, from thoughts or acts which cause misery to living beings, and from thoughts or acts which cause their destruction.

2. The Gupti of speech is also of four kinds as said above.

A zealous monk should prevent his speech from expressing desires, etc.

3. In standing, sitting, lying down, jumping, going, and in the use of his organs, a zealous monk should prevent his body from intimating obnoxious desires, from doing acts which cause misery to living beings, or which cause their destruction.

These are the five Samitis for the practice of the religious life, and the Guptis for the prevention of everything sinful.

This is the essence of the creed, which a sage should thoroughly put into practice; such a wise man will soon get beyond the Circle of Births.

Thus I say.

Should a Monk Wear or Not Wear Clothes

There was a Jina Parshva by name, an Arhat, worshipped by the people, who was thoroughly enlightened and omniscient, a prophet of the Law, and Jina.

And there was a famous disciple of this Light of the World, the young Shramana Kesh, who had completely mastered the sciences and right conduct.

He possessed the light of Shruta and Avadhi knowledge, and was surrounded by a crowd of disciples; wandering from village to village he arrived in the town of Shravasti.

In the district of that town there is a park, called Tinduka; there he took up his abode in a pure place to live and sleep in.

Now at that time there lived the Prophet of the Law, the Jina, who in the whole world is known as the venerable Vardhamana.

And there was a famous disciple of this Light of the World, the venerable Gautama by name, who had completely mastered the sciences and right conduct.

He knew the twelve Angas, was enlightened, and was surrounded by a crowd of disciples; wandering from village to village he too arrived in Shravasti.

In the district of that town there is a park Koshthaka; there he took up his abode in a pure place to live and sleep in.

The young Shramana Keshi and the famous Gautama, both lived there, protecting themselves by the Guptis and being careful.

The pupils of both, who controlled themselves, who practised austerities, who possessed virtues, and who protected their Self, made the following reflection:

'Is our Law the right one, or is the other Law the right one? Are our conduct and doctrines right, or the other?

'The Law as taught by the great sage Parshva, which recognises but four vows, or the Law taught by Vardhamana, which enjoins five vows?

'The Law which forbids clothes for a monk, or that which allows an under and upper garment? Both pursuing the same end, what has caused their difference?'

Knowing the thoughts of their pupils, both Keshi and Gautama made up their minds to meet each other.

Gautama, knowing what is proper and what is due to the older section of the church, went to the Tinduka park, accompanied by the crowd, his pupils.

When Keshi, the young monk, saw Gautama approach, he received him with all becoming attention.

He at once offered Gautama the four pure kinds of straw

and hay to sit upon.

Keshi, the young Shramana, and the famous Gautama, sitting together, shone forth with a lustre like that of sun and moon.

There assembled many heretics out of curiosity, and many thousands of laymen;

Gods, Danavas, Gandharvas, Yakshas, Rakshasas, and Kinnaras assembled there, and there came together invisible ghosts too.

Keshi said to Gautama, 'I want to ask you something, holy man.' Then to these words of Keshi Gautama made the following reply: 'Sir, ask whatever you like.' Then with his permission Keshi spoke to Gautama:

`The Law taught by the great sage Parshva, recognises but four vows, whilst that of Vardhamana enjoins five.

'Both Laws pursuing the same end, what has caused this difference? Have you no misgivings about this twofold Law, O wise man?'

Then to these words of Keshi Gautama made the following reply: `Wisdom recognises the truth of the Law and the ascertainment of true things.

`The first saints were simple but slow of understanding, the last saints prevaricating and slow of understanding, those between the two simple and wise; hence there are two forms of the Law.

`The first could but with difficulty understand the precepts of the Law, and the last could only with difficulty observe them, but those between them easily understood and observed them.'

'Well, Gautama, you possess wisdom, you have destroyed my doubt; but I have another doubt which you must explain to me, Gautama.

`The Law taught by Vardhamana forbids clothes, but that of the great sage Parshva allows an under and upper garment.

`Both Laws pursuing the same end, what has caused this difference? Have you no misgivings about this twofold Law, O wise man?'

To these words of Keshi, Gautama made the following reply: `Deciding the matter by their superior knowledge, the Tirthankaras have fixed what is necessary for carrying out the Law.

'The various outward marks of religious men have been introduced in order that people might recognise them as such; the reason for the characteristic marks is their usefulness for religious life and their distinguishing character.

'Now the opinion of the Tirthankaras is that knowledge, faith, and right conduct are the true causes of final liberation, and not the outward marks.'

'Well, Gautama, you possess wisdom, you have destroyed my doubt; but I have another doubt, which you must explain to me, Gautama.

'Gautama, you stand in the midst of many thousand foes who make an attack on you; how have you vanquished them?'

'By vanquishing one, five are vanquished; by vanquishing five, ten are vanquished; by this tenfold victory, I vanquish all foes.'

Keshi said to Gautama: 'Whom do you call a foe?' To these words of Keshi Gautama made the following reply:

'Self is the one invincible foe, together with the four cardinal passions, (anger, pride, deceit, and greed, they are five) and the five senses make ten. These foes, O great sage, I have regularly vanquished.'

'Well, Gautama, you have wisdom, you have destroyed my doubt, but I have another doubt you must explain to me.

'We see many beings in this world who are bound by fetters; how have you got rid of your fetters and are set free, O sage?'

'Having cut off all fetters, and having destroyed them by the right means, I have got rid of my fetters and am set free, O sage.'

Keshi said to Gautama: 'What do you call fetters?' To these words of Keshi Gautama made the following reply:

'Love, hatred, etc., are heavy fetters, attachment is a dangerous one; having regularly destroyed them, I live up to the rules of conduct.'

'Well, Guatama, you have wisdom, you have destroyed my doubt, but I have another doubt you must explain to me.

'O Gautama, in the innermost heart there grows a plant which brings forth poisonous fruit; how have you torn it out?'

'I have thoroughly clipped that plant, and torn it out altogether with its roots; thus I have got rid of the poisonous fruit.'

Keshi said to Gautama, 'What do you call that plant?' To these words of Keshi Gautama made the following reply:

'Love of existence is that dreadful plant which brings forth dreadful fruit; having regularly torn it out, I live pleasantly.'

'Well, Gautama, you have wisdom, you have destroyed my doubt, but I have another doubt you must explain to me.

'Gautama, there is blazing up a frightful fire which burns the embodied beings; how have you put it out?'

'Taking water, excellent water, from the river produced by the great cloud, I always pour it over my body; thus sprinkled the fire does not burn me.'

Keshi said to Gautama, 'What do you call the fire?' To these words of Keshi Gautama made the following reply:

'The passions are the fire; knowledge, a virtuous life, and penances are the water; sprinkled with the drops of knowledge the fire of the passions is extinguished and does not burn me.'

'Well, Gautama, you have wisdom, you have destroyed my doubt, but I have another doubt you must explain to me.

'The unruly, dreadful, bad horse, on which you sit, runs about, Gautama! how comes it to pass that it does not run off with you?'

'I govern it well in its course by the bridle of knowledge; it does not go astray with me, it keeps to the right path.'

Keshi said to Gautama, 'What do you call this horse?' To these words of Keshi Gautama made the follwoing reply:

'The mind is that unruly, dreadul, bad horse; I govern it by the discipline of the Law so that it becomes a well-trained Kamboja-steed.'

'Well, Gautama, you have wisdom, you have destroyed my doubt, but I have another doubt you must explain to me.

'There are many bad roads in this world, which lead men astray; how do you avoid, Gautama, going astray as you are on the road?'

'They all are known to me, those who are in the right path and those who have chosen a wrong path; therefore I do not go astray, O sage!'

Keshi said to Gautama, 'What do you call the path?' To these words of Keshi Gautama made the following reply:

'The heterodox and the heretics have all chosen a wrong path; the right path is that taught by the Jinas; it is the most excellent path.'

'Well, Gautama, you have wisdom, you have destroyed my doubt, but I have another doubt you must explain to me.

'Is there a shelter, a refuge, a firm ground for the beings carried away by the great flood of water? Do you know the island, O Gautama?'

'There is a large, great island in the midst of water, which is not inundated by the great flood of water.'

Keshi said to Gautama, `What do you call this island?' To these words of Keshi Gautama made the following reply:

'The flood is old age and death, which carry away living beings; Law is the island, the firm ground, the refuge, the most excellent shelter.'

'Well, Gautama, you have wisdom, you have destroyed my doubt, but I have another doubt you must explain to me.

'On the ocean with its many currents there drifts a boat; how will you, Gautama, on board of it reach the opposite shore?'

'A boat that leaks will not reach the opposite shore; but a boat that does not leak, will reach it.'

Keshi said to Gautama, `What do you call this boat?' To these words of Keshi Gautama made the following reply:

'The body is the boat, life is the sailor, and the Circle of Births is the ocean which is crossed by the great sages.'

'Well, Gautama, you have wisdom, you have destroyed

my doubt, but I have another doubt you must explain to me.

'In this dreadfully dark gloom there live many beings; who will bring light into the whole world of living beings?"

'The spotless sun has risen which illuminates the whole world; he will bring light into the whole world of living beings.'

Keshi said to Gautama, `What do you call this sun?' To these words of Keshi Gautama made the following reply:

'Risen has he who put an end to the Cirlce of Births, the omniscient Jina, the luminary, who brings light into the whole world of living beings.'

'Well, Gautama, you have wisdom, you have destroyed my doubt, but I have another doubt you must explain to me.

'Do you, O sage, know a safe, happy, and quiet place for living beings which suffer from pains of body and mind?

'There is a safe place in view of all, but difficult of approach, where there is no old age nor death, no pain nor disease.'

Keshi said to Gautama, `What is this place called?' To these words of Keshi Gautama made the following reply:

'It is what is called Nirvana, or freedom from pain, or perfection, which is in view of all; it is the safe, happy, and quit place which the great sages reach.

'That is the eternal place, in view of all, but difficult of approach. Those sages who reach it are free from sorrows, they have put an end to the stream of existence.'

'Well, Gautama, you possess wisdom, you have destroyed my doubt; obeisance to you, who are not troubled by doubts, who are the ocean, as it were, of all Sutras.

After his doubt had been solved, Kesi, of enormous sanctity, bowed his head to the famous Gautama.

And in the pleasant Tinduka park he sincerely adopted the Law of the five vows, which was proclaimed by the first Tirthankara, according to the teaching of the last Tirthankara.

In that meeting of Keshi and Gautama, knowledge and virtuous conduct were for ever brought to eminence, and subjects of great importance were settled.

The whole assembly was greatly pleased and fixed their thoughts on the right way, they praised Keshi and Gautama: May the Venerable ones show us favour!

Thus I say.

The Leaf of the Tree

Sermon delivered by Mahavira to his disciple Indrabhuti.

As the fallow leaf of the tree falls to the ground, when its days are gone, even so the life of men will come to its close; Gautama, be careful all the while!

As a dew-drop dangling on the top of a blade of Kusa-grass lasts but a short time, even so the life of men; Gautama, be careful all the while!

As life is so fleet and existence so percarious, wipe off the sins you ever committed; Gautama, be careful all the while.

A rare chance, in the long course of time, is human birth for a living being; hard are the consequences of actions; Gautama, be careful all the while.

When the soul has once got into an earth-body, it may remain in the same state as long as an Asamkhya period; Gautama, be careful all the while.

When the soul has once got into a water-body, it may remain in the same state as long as an Asamkhya period; Gautama, be careful all the while.

When a soul has once got into a fire-body, it may remain in the same state as long as an Asamkhya period; Gautama, be careful all the while.

When the soul has once got into a wind-body, it may remain in the same state as long as an Asamkhya period; Gautama, be careful all the while.

When the soul has once got into a vegetable-body, it remains long in that state, for an endless time, after which its lot is not much bettered; Gautama, be careful all the while.

When the soul has once got into a body of a Dvindriya

i.e., a being possessing two organs of sense, it may remain in the same state as long as a period called Samkheya; Gautama, be careful all the while.

When the soul has once got into a body of a Trindriya, i.e., a being possessing three organs of sense, it may remain in the same state as long as a period called Samkheya; Gautama, be careful all the while.

When the soul has once got into a body of a Caturindriya, i.e., a being possessing four organs of sense, it may remain in the same state as long as a period called Samkheya; Gautama, be careful all the while.

When the soul has once got into a body of a Panchendriya, i.e., a being possessing five organs of sense, it may remain in the same state as long as seven or eight births; Gautama, be careful all the while.

When the soul has once got into the body of a god or of a denizen of hell, it may remain in that state one whole life; Gautama, be careful all the while.

Thus the soul which suffers for its carelessness, is driven about in the Samsara by its good and bad Karman; Gautama, be careful all the while.

Though one be born as a man, it is a rare chance to become an Arya; for many are the Dasyus and Mlechchhas; Gautama, be careful all the while.

Though one be born as an Arya, it is a rare chance to possess all five organs of sense; for we see many who lack one organ or other; Gautama, be careful all the while.

Though he may possess all five organs of sense, still it is a rare chance to be instructed in the best Law; for people follow heretical teachers; Gautama, be careful all the while.

Though he may have been instructed in the right Law, still it is a rare chance to believe in it; for many people are heretics; Gautama, be careful all the while.

Though one believe in the Law, he will rarely practise it; for people are engrossed by pleasures; Gautama, be careful all the while.

When your body grows old, and your hair turns white, the power of your ears decreases; Gautama, be careful all the while.

When your body grows old, and your hair turns white, the power of your eyes decreases.

When your body grows old, and your hair turns white, the power of your nose decreases.

When your body grows old, and your hair turns white, the power of your tongue decreases.

When your body grows old, and your hair turns white, the power of your touch decreases.

When your body grows old, and your hair turns white, all your powers decrease.

Despondency, the kings's evil, cholera, mortal diseases of many kinds befall you; your body wastes and decays; Gautama, be careful all the while.

Cast aside from you all attachments, as the leaves of a lotus let drop off the autumnal water, exampt from every attachment; Gautama, be careful all the while!

Give up your wealth and your wife; you have entered the state of the houselessness; do not, as it were, return to your vomit; Gautama, be careful all the while.

Leave your friends and relations, the large fortune you have amassed; do not desire them a second time; Gautama, be careful all the while.

There is now no Jina, but there is a highly esteemed guide to show the way; now being on the right path; Gautama, be careful all the while!

Now you have entered on the path from which the thorns have been cleared, the great path; walk in the right path; Gautama, be careful all the while.

Do not get into an uneven road like a weak burden-bearer; for you will repent of it afterwards; Gautama, be careful all the while.

You have crossed the great ocean; why do you halt so near the shore? make haste to get on the other side; Gautama, be careful all the while.

Going through the same religious practices as perfected saints, you will reach the world of perfection, Gautama, where there is safety and perfect happiness; Gautama, be careful all the while.

The enlightened and liberated monk should control himself, whether he be in a village or a town, and he should preach to all the road of peace; Gautama, be careful all the while.

Having heard the Buddha's well-delivered sermon, adorned by illustrations, Gautama cut off love and hatred and reached perfection.

Thus I say.

Karman, Leshyas and their Destruction

I shall now in due order explain the eight kinds of Karman, bound by which the soul turns round and round in the Circle of Births.

The eight kinds of Karman are the following:

1. Jnanavaraniya, which acts as an obstruction to right knowledge;
2. Darshanavaraniya, which acts as an obstruction to right faith;
3. Vedaniya, which leads to experiencing pain or pleasure;
4. Mohaniya, which leads to delusion;
5. Ayushkarman, which determines the length of life;
6. Naman, which determines the name or individuality of the embodied soul.
7. Gotra, which determines his Gotra;
8. Antaraya, which prevents one's entrance on the path that leads to eternal bliss.

I. Obstruction of knowledge is fivefold:

a. Shruta, knowledge derived from the sacred books;
b. Abhinibodhika, perception;
c. Avadhijnana, supernatural knowledge;
d. Manahparyaya, knowledge of the thoughts of other people;
e. Kevala, the highest, unlimited knowledge.

2. The kinds of obstruction to right faith are: 1. sleep; 2. activity; 3. very deep sleep; 4. a high degree of activity; 5. a state of deep-rooted greed, etc.

3. Vedaniya is twcfold, pleasure and pain; there are many subdivisions of pleasure and so there are of pain also.

4. Mohaniya is twofold, as referring to faith and to conduct; the first is threefold, the second twofold.

The three kinds of Mohaniya referring to faith are: 1. right faith; 2. wrong faith; 3. faith partly right and partly wrong.

The two kinds of Mohaniya referring to conduct are: 1. what is experienced in the form of the four cardinal passions; 2. what is experienced in the form of feelings different from them.

The first kind of this Karman is sixteenfold, the second sevenfold or ninefold.

5. Ayushkarman is fourfold as referring to 1. denizens of hell; 2. brute creation; 3. men; 4. gods.

6. Naman is twofold, good and bad; there are many subdivisions of the good variety, and so there are of the bad one also.

7. Gotra is twofold, high and low; the first is eightfold, and so is the second also.

8. Antaraya is fivefold, as preventing: 1. gifts; 2. profit; 3. momentary enjoyment; 4. continuous enjoyment; and 5. power.

Thus the division of Karman and the subdivisions have been told.

Now hear their number of atoms, place, time, and development.

The number of atoms of every Karman is infinite; it is infinitely greater than the number of fettered souls, but less than that of the perfected ones.

The Karman in the six directions of space binds all souls, and it binds the whole soul in all its parts in every possible way.

The longest duration of Karman is thirty Crores of Crores of Sagaropamas (3,000,000,000,000,000 Sagaropamas), and the shortest a part of a Muhurta.

The holds good with both Avaraniyas, with Vedaniya and Antaraya.

The longest duration of Mohaniya is seventy Crores of Crores of Sagaropamas, and the shortest a part of a Muhurta.

The longest duration of Ayushka is thirty-three Crores of Crores of Sagaropamas, and the shortest a part of a Muhurta.

The longest duration of Naman and Gotra is twenty Crores of Crores of Sagaropamas. and the shortest eight Muhurtas.

The number of perfected souls is infinite, and that of the subdivisions of Karman is also infinite; the number of atoms in all these sub-divisions exceeds the number of all souls.

Therefore, a wise man should know the different subdivisions of these Karmans, and should exert himself to prevent and to destroy them.

Thus I say.

Leshyas Produced by Karman

I shall deliver in due order the lecture on Leshya; hear the nature of the six Leshyas produced by Karman.

Hear 1. the names, 2. colours, 3. tastes, 4. smells,

5. touches, 6. degrees, 7. character, 8. variety, 9. duration, 10. result, and 11. life of the Leshyas.

1. They are named in the following order: black, blue, grey, red, yellow, and white.

2. The black Leshya has the colour of a rain-cloud, a buffalos horn, the fruit of Rishtaka, or the eye of the wagtail.

The blue Leshya has the colour of the blue Ashoka, the tail of the Chasha, or of lapis lazuli.

The grey Leshya has the colour of the flower of Atasi, the feathers of the Kokila, or the collar of pigeons.

The red Leshya has the colour of vermilion, the rising sun, or the bill of a parrot.

The yellow Leshya has the colour of orpiment, turmeric, or the flowers of Shana and Asana.

The white Leshya has the colour of a conch-shell, the anka-stone, Kunda-flowers, flowing milk, silver, or a necklace of pearls.

3. The taste of the black Leshya is infinitely more bitter than that of Tumbaka, the fruit of the Nimb-tree, or of Rohini.

The taste of the blue Leshya is infinitely more pungent than Trikatuka and Hastipippali.

The taste of grey Leshya is infinitely sourer than that of unripe Mango and Kapittha.

The taste of red Leshya is infinitely more pleasant than that of ripe Mango and Kapittha.

The taste of yellow Leshya is infinitely better than that of excellent wine and various liquors, honey and Maireyaka.

The taste of white Leshya is infinitely better than that of dates, grapes, milk, candied and pounded sugar.

4. The smell of the bad Leshyas, the three first, is infinitely worse than that of the corpse of a cow, dog, or snake.

The smell of the three good Lesyas is infinitely more pleasant than that of fragrant flowers and of perfumes when they are pounded.

5. The touch of the bad Leshyas is infinitely worse than that of a saw, the tongue of a cow, or leaf of the teak tree.

The touch of the three good Leshyas is infinitely more pleasant than that of cotton, butter, or Sirisha-flowers.

6. The degrees of the Leshyas are three, or nine, or twenty-seven, or eighty-one, or two hundred and forty-three.

7. A man who acts on the impulse of the five Asravas, does not possess the three Guptis, has not ceased to injure the six kinds of living beings, commits cruel acts, is wicked and violent, is afraid of no consequences, is mischievous and does not subdue his senses—a man of such habits develops the black Leshya.

A man of the following qualities: envy, anger, want of self-control, ignorance, deceit, want of modesty, greed, hatred, wickedness, carelessness, love of enjoyment; a man who pursues pleasures and does not abstain from sinful undertakings, who is wicked and violent—a man of such habits develops the blue Leshya.

A man who is dishonest in words and acts, who is base, not upright, a dissembler and deceiver, a heretic, a vile man, a talker of hurtful and sinful things, a thief, and full of jealousy—a man of such habits develops the grey Leshya.

A man who is humble, steadfast, free from deceit and inquisitiveness, well disciplined, restrained, attentive to his study and duties, who loves the Law and keeps it, who is afraid of forbidden things and strives after the highest good—a man of such habits develops the red Leshya.

A man who has but little anger, pride, deceit, and greed, whose mind is at ease, who controls himself, who is attentive to his study and duties, who speaks but little, is calm, and subdues his senses— a man of such habits develops the yellow Leshya.

A man who abstains from constant thinking about his misery and about sinful deeds, but engages in meditation on the Law and truth only, whose mind is at ease, who controls himself, who practises the Samitis and Guptis, whether he be still subject to passion or free from passion, is calm, and subdues his senses—a man of such habits develops the white Leshya.

8. There are as many varieties of Leshyas as there are Samayas in the innumerable Avasarpinis and Utsarpinis, and as there are countless worlds.

9. Half a Muhurta is the shortest, and thirty-three Sagaropamas plus one Muhurta is the longest duration of the black Leshya.

Half a Muhurta is the shortest, and ten Sagaropamas plus one Palyopama and a part of an Asamkhyeya is the longest duration of the blue Leshya.

Half a Muhurta is the shortest, and three Sagaropamas plus one Palyopama and a part of an Asamkhyeya is the longest duration of the grey Leshya.

Half a Muhurta is the shortest, and two Sagaropamas plus one Palyopama and a part of an Asamkhyeya is the longest duration of the red Leshya.

Half a Muhurta is the shortest, and ten Sagaropamas plus one muhurta is the longest duration of the yellow Leshya.

Half a Muhurta is the shortest, and thirty-three Sagaropamas plus one Muhurta is the longest duration of the white Leshya.

I Have described above the duration of the Leshyas generally; I shall now detail their duration in the four walks of mundane existence.

The shortest duration of the grey Leshya of a denizen of hell is ten thousand years, the longest three Sagaropamas plus one Palyopama and part of an Asamkhyeya.

The shortest duration of the blue Leshya of a denizen of hell is three Sagaropamas plus one Palyopama and a part of an Asamkhyeya, the longest ten Sagaropamas plus one Palyopama and a part of an Asamkhyeya.

The shortest duration of the black Leshya of a denizen of hell is ten Sagaropamas plus one Palyopama and a part of an Asamkhyeya, the longest thirty-three Sagaropamas.

I have described the duration of the Leshyas of denizens of hell; I shall now describe that of animals, men, and gods.

The duration of any of the Leshyas except the best (white one) is less than a Muhurta for the lowest organisms, animals, and men.

Half a Muhurta is the shortest duration of the white Leshya of animals and men, and the longest a Crore of former years less nine years.

I have described the duration of the Leshyas of animals and men, I shall now describe that of the gods.

The shortest duration of the black Leshya is ten thousand years, the longest a Palyopama and a part of an Asamkhyeya.

The shortest duration of the blue Leshya is equal to the longest of the black one plus one Samaya; the longest is one Palyopama plus a greater part of an Asamkhyeya.

The shortest duration of the grey Leshya is equal to the longest of the blue one plus one Samaya; the longest is one Palyopama plus a still greater part of an Asamkhyeya.

I shall now describe the red Leshya as it is with gods, Bhauameyikas, Vyantaras, Jyotishkas, and Vaimanikas.

The shortest duration of the red Leshya is one Palyopama, the longest two Sagaropamas plus one Palyopama and a part of an Asamkhyeya.

The shortest duration of the red Leshya is ten thousand years, the longest two Sagaropamas plus one Palyopama and a part of an Asamkhyeya.

The longest duration of the red Leshya plus one Samaya is equal to the shortest of the yellow Leshya; its longest, however, is ten Muhurtas longer.

The longest duration of the yellow Leshya plus one Samaya is equal to the shortest of the white Leshya; its longest, however, is thirty-three Muhurtas longer.

10. The black, blue and grey Leshyas are the lowest Leshyas; through them the soul is brought into miserable courses of life.

The red, yellow, and white Leshyas are the good Leshyas; through them the soul is brought into happy courses of life.

11. In the first moment of these Leshyas when they are joined with the soul, the latter is not born into a new existence.

In the last moment of all these Leshyas when they are joined with the soul, the latter is not born into a new existence.

While the last Muhurta is running and a part of it is still to come, the souls with their Leshyas developed, go to a new birth.

A wise man should, therefore, know the nature of these Leshyas; he should avoid the bad ones and obtain the good ones.

Thus I say.

4

Sutrakritanga

The Conduct

There are four heretical creeds which the disputants severally uphold: I. the Kriyavada, 2. the Akriyavada, 3. the Vinayavada, and 4. the Ajnanavada.

The agnostics, though they pretend to be clever, reason incoherently, and do not get beyond the confusion of their ideas. Ignorant teachers speak to ignorant pupils, and without reflection they speak untruth.

Believing truth to be untruth, and calling a bad man good, the various upholders of Vinaya, asked about it, explain their tenet.

Without perceiving the truth they speak thus: this Moksha is realised by us by Vinaya. The Akriyavadins who deny Karman, do not admit that the action of the soul is transmitted to the future moments.

They become involved in contradiction in their own assertions; they falter in their speech and are unable to repeat what is said to them. This their opinion has a valiant counter-opinion, this our opinion has no valiant counter-opinion; and Karman has six sources.

The Akriyavadins who do not understand the truth, bring forward various opinions; many men believing in them will whirl round in the endless Circle of Births.

'There rises no sun, nor does it set; there waxes no moon, nor does it wane; there are no rivers running, nor any winds blowing; the whole world is ascertained to be unreal.'

As a blind man, though he have a light, does not see colours etc., because he is deprived of his eyesight, so the

Akriyavadin, having a perverted intellect, does not recognise the action of the soul, though it does exist.

Many men in this world who have studied astrology, the art of interpreting dreams, divination from diagrams, augury, divination from bodily marks, and from portents, and the eight branches of divination from omens, know the future.

The opponents say that some forecasts are true, and the prophecies of others prove wrong; therefore they do not study those sciences, but they profess to know the world, fools though they be.

The Kriyavadin Shramanas and Brahmins understanding the world according to their lights, speak thus: misery is produced by one's own works, not by those of somebody else, fate, creator, etc. But right knowledge and conduct lead to liberation.

The Tirthankaras, being the eyes of the world and its leaders, teach the path which is salutary to men; they have declared that the world is eternal inasmuch as creatures are for ever living in it, O ye men!

The Rakshasas and the dwellers in Yama's world, the troops of Asuras and Gandharvas, and the spirits that walk the air, and individual beings: they will all be born again and again.

The Samsara which is compared to the boundless flood of water, know it to be impassable and of very long duration on account of repeated births. Men therein, seduced by their senses and by women, are born again and again both as movable and immovable beings.

The sinners cannot annihilate their works by new works; the pious annihilate their works by abstention from works; the wise and happy men who got rid of the effects of greed, do not commit sins.

They know the past, present, and future ways of the world; they are leaders of other men, but follow no leader; they are awakened, and put an end to mundane existence.

Averse to injury of living beings, they do not act, nor cause others to act. Always restraining themselves, those pious men practise control, and some become heroes through their knowledge.

He regards small beings and large beings, the whole world as equal to himself; he comprehends the immense world, and being awakened he controls himself among the careless.

Those who have learned the truth by themselves or from others, are able to save themselves and others. One should always honour a man, who is like a light and makes manifest the Law after having well considered it.

He who know himself and the world; who knows where the creatures go, and whence they will not return; who knows what is eternal, and what is transient; birth and death, and the existences of men;

He who knows the tortures of beings in hell; who knows the influx of sin and its stoppage; Asrava and Samvara; who knows misery and its annihilation, he is entitled to expound the Kriyavada,

Being not attached to sounds and colours, indifferent to tastes and smells, not desiring life nor death, guarded by control, and exempt from the Circle of Births.

Thus I say.

The Real Truth

I shall now expound, in accordance with truth, the various qualities of men; I shall explain the virtus and peace of the good, the vices and the unrest of the wicked.

Having learned the Law from men who exert themselves day and night, from the Tathagatas, they neglect the conduct in which they had been instructed, and speak rudely to their teacher.

Those who explain the pure doctrine according to their individual opinion, falsify it in repeating it after their teachers; those who speak untruth from pride of knowledge, are not capable of many virtues.

Those who on being questioned conceal the truth, defraud themselves of the real good. These bad men who believe themselves good and are full of deceit, will go to endless punishment.

He who is of a wrathful disposition and calls everything by its true name, who renews a composed quarrel, will, like a blind man groping his way with a stick, do harm to himself, being still subject to passion and possessing evil Karman.

He who is quarrelsome and talks improperly, is not impartial nor beyond the reach of deceit; but he who executes the commands of his teacher and controls himself, sees nothing but the truth and is exempt from deceit.

He who conforms to admonitions however many he receives, is kindly spoken, subtle, manly, noble, and a well-doer; such a man is impartial and beyond the reach of deceit.

He who believes himself rich in control, or inconsiderately vaunts his knowledge, or fancies himself purified by austerities, will look upon other men as shadows.

He is always turned round by delusion, and has no place in the Gotra where Vow Silence is practised in the Jaina temple, who not being awakened puts himself forward in order to gain honours through something different from control.

A Brahmin or Kshathriya by birth, a scion of the Ugra race or a Lichchhvi, who enters the order eating alms given him by others, is not stuck up on account of his renowned Gotra.

His pedigree on his mother's and on his father's side will be of no use to him, nothing will but right knowledge and conduct: when after becoming a monk he acts like a householder, he will not succeed in obtaining final liberation.

If a poor monk subsisting on the meanest food is attached to vanities, desires fame, and not being awakened, makes his monkhood a means of subsistence, he will suffer again and again in the Circle of Births.

A monk, who is eloquent, speaks very well, has bright ideas, is clever, possesses a fine intellect, and has purified his soul, may perhaps despise other men on account of his intellect.

Thus an intelligent monk who puts himself forward, has not yet realised carefulness; or rather he is a weak-minded man who elated by his success blames other men.

A monk should combat pride of genius, pride of sanctity, pride of birth, and pride of good living, which is enumerated as the fourth; such a man is wise and of the right stuff.

The wise leave off these kinds of pride, the pious do not cultivate them; the great sages are above all such things as Gotra, and they ascend to the place where there is no Gotra at all to Moksha.

A monk who looks upon his body as on a corpse and fully understands the Law, will on entering a village or a town distinguish between what may be accepted and what may not, and will not be greedy of food or drink.

A monk having conquered aversion to control and delight in sensual objects, living in company with many brethren or leading a single life, should silently repeat to himself: 'A man must come and go according to his Karman alone', i.e., without deriving any help from others.

Knowing it by intuition or having learned it from others, one should teach the Law which is a benefit to men; the pious are not given to blameable sinful practices.

If a monk preaches the Law to some one whose disposition he has not ascertained, that man, not believing what he is taught, will become angry, and may wound him in a way that will shorten or end his life. When he knows their disposition, he may teach others the truth.

A wise man by suppressing his Karman and his will should renounce his interest in everything else. For through the objects of sight, i.e., senses, which are causes of danger, men come to harm. Knowing the truth with regard to movable and immovable beings a monk should exert himself.

Not desiring honour or fame, he should say nothing to anybody either to please or to irritate him. Avoiding all evils, a monk should without embarrassment and passion preach the Law.

Well considering his duties in accordance with truth,

abstaining from doing injury to living beings, not desiring life nor death, he should wander about released from the Circle of Births.

Thus I say.

The Nirgrantha

He who has given up all wordly ties and is instructed in our creed, should practise chastity, exerting himself; obeying the commands of his teacher he should make himself well acquainted with conduct; a clever monk should avoid carelessness.

As birds of prey, e.g., Dhankas, carry off a fluttering young bird whose wings are not yet grown, when it attempts to fly from the nest, but is not able to do so, because it is too young and its wings are not yet grown;

Just as they carry off a young bird whose wings are not yet grown, so many unprincipled men will seduce a novice who has not yet mastered the Law, thinking that they can get him in their power, when they have made him leave the Gachchha.

A good man should long to live with his teacher in order to perform his duties, knowing that he who does not live with his teacher will not put an end to his mundane existence. Making manifest the conduct of the virtuous, an intelligent monk should not leave the company of his teacher.

A monk who complies with the rules for Yatis as regards postures, lying down, sitting, and exerting, who is thoroughly acquainted with the Samitis and Guptis, should in teaching others explain each single point of conduct.

Whether he hears pleasant sounds or dreadful ones, he should not allow himself to be influenced by them, and persevere in control; nor should a monk be sleepy or careless, but by every means he should get rid of doubts.

If admonished by a young or an old monk, by one above him or one of equal age, he should not retort against him, being perfectly free from passion; for one who is carried away by the stream of the Samsara, will not get to its opposite shore.

He should not become angry if doing anything wrong his own creed is quoted against him by a heretic, or if he is corrected by somebody else be he young or old, or by a female slave engaged in low work or carring a jar, or by some householder.

He should not be angry with them nor do them any harm, nor say a single hard word to them, but he should promise not to commit the same sin again; for this is better than to do wrong.

As to one who has lost his way in the wood, others who have not, show it, thus some teach the path which is salutary to men. Therefore he should think: this is for my good that those who know put me right.

Now he who has lost his way should treat with all honour him who has not. This simile has been explained by the Prophet. Having learned what is right one should practise it.

As a guide in a dark night does not find the way since he cannot see it, but recognises the way when it has become light by the rising of the sun;

So a novice who has not mastered the Law, does not know the Law, not being awakened; but afterwards he knows it well through the words of the Jinas, as with his eye the wanderer sees the way after sunrise.

Always restrained with regard to movable and immovable beings which are on high, below, and on earth, a monk should wander about entertaining no hostile thoughts towards them and being steadfast in control.

At the right time he may put a question about living beings to a well-conducted monk, who will explain the conduct of the virtuous; and what he hears he should follow and treasure up in his heart, thinking that it is the doctrine of the Kevalins.

Living in this company of the teacher and protecting himself or other beings in the three ways in thoughts, words, and acts, he gets peace and the annihilation of sins as they say. Thus speak those who know the three worlds, and they do not again commit faults.

A monk by hearing the desired Truth gets bright ideas and becomes a clever teacher; desiring the highest good and practising austerities and silence, he will obtain final Liberation living on pure food.

Those who having investigated the Law expound it, are awakened and put an end to mundane existence; able to liberate both themselves and others, they answer the well-deliberated questions.

He does not conceal the truth nor falsify it; he should not indulge his pride and desire for fame; being wise he should not joke, nor pronounce benedictions.

Averse to injury of living beings, he does not disgrace his calling by the use of spells; a good man does not desire anything from other people, and he does not give utterance to heretical doctrines.

A monk living single should not ridicule heretical doctrines, and should avoid hard words though they be true; he should not be vain, nor brag, but he should without embarrassment and passion preach the Law.

A monk should be modest though he be of a fearless mind; he should expound the Syadvada; he should use the two permitted kinds of speech, living among virtuous men, impartial and wise.

He who follows the instruction may believe something untrue; one should kindly tell him 'It is thus or thus.' One should never hurt him by outrageous language, nor give long-winded explanations of difficult passages.

If the pupil does not understand his short explanation, he should explain at greater length. When the pupil has heard it, he will correctly understand the Truth. A monk should utter pure speech, which is in accordance with the creed of the Jinas, and should declare the distinction of sin.

Thus I say.

The Destruction of Karman

Rishabha said to his sons:

Acquire perfect knowledge of the Law! why do you not study it? It is difficult to obtain instruction in it after this life. The days that are gone by will never return, nor is it easy a second time to obtain human birth.

See, young and old men, even children in the mother's womb die. As a hawk catches a quail, so life will end when its time is spent.

A man may suffer for the sake of his parents; he will not easily obtain happiness after this life. A pious man should consider these causes of danger and cease to act.

For in this world living beings suffer individually for their deeds; for the deed they have done themselves, they obtain punishment, and will not get over it before they have felt it.

Even gods, Gandharvas, Rakshasas, and Asuras; animals who live on earth, and snakes; kings, common people, merchants, and Brahmins: they all must leave their rank and suffer.

Notwithstanding their pleasures and relations, all men must suffer in due time the fruit of their works; as a coco-nut detaching itself from its stalk falls down, so life will end when its time is spent.

Even a very learned or virtuous man, or a Brahmin or an ascetic, will be severely punished for his deeds when he is given to actions of deceit.

See, those heretics who search for the knowledge of truth, but who do not cross the Samsara, talk only about the highest good without reaching it.

How will you understand what is near you and what is beyond? In the meanwhile you suffer for your deeds.

He who walks about naked and lean, he who eats only once after a month, if he is filled with deceit, will be born an endless number of times.

Man, cease from sins! For the life of men will come to an end. Men who are drowned in lust, and addicted to pleasure will, for want of control, be deluded.

Exert and control yourself! For it is not easy to walk on ways where there are minutely small animals. Follow the commandments which Arhats have well proclaimed.

Heroes of faith who desist from sins and exert themselves aright, who subdue wrath, fear, etc., will never kill living beings; they desist from sins and are entirely happy.

It is not myself alone who suffers, all creatures in the world suffer; this a wise man should consider, and he should patiently bear such calamities as befall him, without giving way to his passions.

As a wall covered with a plastering of dried cowdung is by a shock made thin, so a monk should make his body lean by fasting, etc. He should abstain from slaughter of living beings. This is the Law proclaimed by the Sage.

As a bird covered with dust removes the grey powder by shaking itself, so a worthy and austere Brahmin, who does penance, annihilates his Karman.

Young and old people claim a houseless Shramana as their own, though he begs according to the Law, observes the rules of conduct, and performs austerities. People will even cry themselves hoarse, but they will not captivate him.

Whatever they will do to move his pity, however they will cry about their son, they will not captivate a worthy and virtuous monk or make him return to domestic life.

Though they tempt him with pleasures, and though they should bind him and carry him home, if he does not care for a worldly life, they will not captivate him or make him return to domestic life.

His father and mother, his children and wife who claim him, will admonish him: 'See, you are our supporter; care not for the next world in order to support us.'

Some people are foolishly attached to others, and are thereby deluded; the unrighteous make them adopt unrighteousness, and they exult in their wickedness.

Therefore, a worthy and wise man should be careful,

ceasing from sin and being entirely happy. The virtuous heroes of faith have chosen the great road, the right and certain path to perfection.

He who has entered the road leading to the destruction of Karman, who controls his mind, speech, and body, who has given up his possessions and relations and all undertakings, should walk about subduing his senses.

A sage thinks that he should leave off sins just as a snake leaves its slough; and he is not proud of his Gotra and other advantages; or is there any use in blaming others?

A man who insults another will long whirl in the Circle of Births; to blame others is not good. Considering this a sage is not conceited.

He who is independent, and he who is the servant of a servant, if they but observe the Vow of Silence, they have no reason to be ashamed; therefore a monk should behave equally towards all.

Indifferent and pure with regard to every kind of control, a Shramana should walk about; he who entertains pure thoughts during his whole life, dies as a worthy and wise man.

The sage who sees the far-off goal, liberation, past and future things, will practise indifference, though he suffer corporal punishment and be beaten.

Possessing perfect wisdom, a sage always vanquishes his passions; he correctly expounds the Law; he never neglects even the smallest duty; he is neither angry nor proud.

A man who controls himself according to the Law, which is praised by many people, and is not bound by any worldly ties, who is always pure like a lake, proclaims the Law of Kasyapa.

Seeing that numerous living beings lead an individual life, and that every one feels pleasure and pain just as the others, a wise man who observes the Vow of Silence, leaves off injuring them.

A sage has completely mastered the Law, and has ceased to do actions; but the selfish grieve, they will not thereby

recover their lost property.

Know that property entails pains in this world, and very great pains in the next. Who will lead a domestic life when he knows that everything must perish?

One should know and renounce the great attachment to the world, and respect and honours on earth; for conceit is a very thin thorn difficult to pull out. A wise man, therefore, should abandon worldliness.

A monk should perform postures as Kayotsarga, etc. alone on his seat, and alone on his couch he should meditate; excelling in the performance of austerities, guarded in words, and restrained in thoughts.

An ascetic does not shut the door of a deserted house where he puts up, nor does he open it; when asked he returns no rude answer; he cuts no grass, nor does he strew it on the ground for a couch.

Where he is at sunset, there he calmly performs his duties; a sage bears pleasant and unpleasant things, be there insects, or wild beasts, or snakes.

He bears the three kinds of calamities arising from beasts, men, and gods. A great sage will not be seized with a shivering, etc., when he stays in a deserted house.

He should not fear for his life, nor should he desire to be praised for his courage. Fearful things will frighten the mind of a monk who stays in a deserted house.

They say that he who is very well disciplined, who protects others, who lives in a place removed from other people, who is not frightened by dangers, possesses right conduct, etc.

A monk who uses warm or hot water, who follows the Law, and loathes wrong conduct, will by intercourse with bad kings become deficient in his devotion though he be ever so virtuous.

When a monk quarrels and uses very bad language, he will suffer great spiritual loss; therefore a wise man should not quarrel.

He who abstains from cold water, who plans or

undertakes nothing, and has ceased from even the smallest actions, who does not eat food out of the dish of a householder, possesses right conduct.

Though life cannot be prolonged, as the saying is, still foolish people sin recklessly; a foolish man is filled to the brim with sins. Considering this a sage is not conceited.

By self-invented rites common people seek holiness, they are full of deceit and shrouded in delusion. But a monk is holy through his innocence, he allows no troubles to influence his words, thoughts, and acts.

As a clever gambler, playing at dice, is not vanquished, since he casts the Krita, but not Kali, nor Treta, nor Dvapra;

So adopt for your welfare the best and highest Law which has been proclaimed in this world by the Saviour, as the clever gambler casts the Krita, and avoids the other casts.

I have heard that sensual pleasures are said to have the strongest hold on men; but those who abstain from them follow the Law of Kashyapa.

Those who follow the Law that has been proclaimed by Jnatrika, the great seer, are virtuous and righteous; they confirm each other in the Law.

Take no heed of the seductive pleasures, endeavour to shake off delusion. Those who are not subdued by the wicked pleasures, know meditation to be their duty.

A monk should not tell stories, nor ask idle questions, nor gossip. But, knowing the highest Law, he should perform his religious duties, and regard nothing his own.

A monk should not indulge deceit, greed, pride, and wrath. Those are virtuous who have arrived at the right understanding of these passions, and who have well practised control.

A monk should be free from attachment, wise, controlling himself, seeking the Law, earnest in the performance of austerities, and subduing his senses. It is difficult to obtain the soul's benefit.

Right conduct, etc., which has been taught by the Jnatrika, the sage who knew everything in the whole world, has either not been learned or not been truly practised by creatures now in distress.

Many men who thought this Law to be the highest good and conducive to their spiritual welfare, obeyed their preceptors, ceased from works, and have crossed the great flood of worldly existence.

Thus I say.

If a monk who abstains from actions, suffers pain for acts done through ignorance, that Karman will be annihilated through control. The wise reach perfection getting rid of death.

Those who resist the seductions are placed on a line with those who have crossed the Samsara. Therefore, look up at beatitude as the end in view. Those virtuous men regard pleasures as equal to diseases.

Men of princely rank wear precious things imported by merchants; likened to these precious things are the excellent great vows together with the prohibition of eating at night.

Pleasure-seeking men who are greedy and are absorbed by amusements, are reckless and like the wretched; they do not know that meditation has been enjoined as a duty.

As a bullock which is hurt and urged on by the driver becomes weak, and at last, when its strength is exhausted and it is unable to move, sinks down;

So he who knows the pursuit of pleasures, must sooner or later give up their enjoyment lest they drag him down. He who is still surrounded by pleasant things, should not love pleasures, whether he obtains them, or for some reason or other does not obtain them.

Lest the lot of the wicked should fall to you, escape the influence of the senses, and discipline yourself! The wicked will much and strongly grieve, groan, and wail.

See, life in this world is transient; though your life lasts a hundred years, you die as a short-lived man; mind that your years swiftly pass. Nevertheless, greedy men are attached to pleasures.

Those who engage in undertakings, who work the

perdition of their souls, and who kill living beings, will go to the world of the wicked, to the abode of the Asuras for a long time to dwell there.

Though life cannot be prolonged, as the saying is, still foolish people sin recklessly thinking: 'We are only concerned with the present time; who has seen the next world and returned thence?'

Believe in the words of him who sees everything, you who are blind, as it were, you whose sight is blinded, ah, whose sight is obstructed by your works which result in delusion!

The unhappy again and again suffer from delusion; therefore have done with praise and honours! A wise ascetic should consider that living beings are like himself as regards love of life, aversion to pain, etc.

The man also who still lives in the house, should, in accordance with his creed, be merciful to living beings; we are bidden to be fair and equal with all; thereby even a householders goes to the world of the gods.

Being instructed in the creed of the Lord, exert yourself in the truth, i.e., in control! A monk who has thoroughly subdued his selfishness should collect pure alms.

Knowing the truth, one should live up to it, seeking the Law, earnest in the performance of austerities, possessing the Guptis, being accomplished, one should always exert oneself, intent on the soul's benefit, and desiring the highest good, liberation.

The fool thinks that his wealth, cattle, and relations will save him; they him, or he them. but they are no help, no protection.

When calamity befalls him, or the end of his life draws near, he must go and come alone; the wise believe that there is nothing to protect him.

All living beings owe their present form of existence to their own Karman; timid, wicked, suffering latent misery, they err about in the Circle of Births, subject to birth, old age, and death.

He should know that the present time is the best opportunity to mend, and that an awakening is difficult to obtain. A wise man should be aware of this. The first Jina has said this, and so the remaining ones will say it.

O ye monks, the virtuous Jinas that have been and will be, the followers of the Law of Kashyapa, they all have commended these virtues.

Do not kill living beings in the threefold way, being intent on your spiritual welfare and abstaining from sins. In this way numberless men have reached perfection, and others, who live now, and are to come, will reach it.

Thus I say.

Keep Away from Women

A monk who has left his mother and father and all worldly ties, determines to walk about alone and wise, to abstain from sexual pleasures, and to ask for a secluded place where to lodge.

With clever pretences women make up to him, however foolish they be; they know how to contrive that some monks will become intimate with them.

They will often sit down at his side; they always put on fine clothes; they will show him the lower part of their body, and the armpit, when lifting up their arms, so that he will follow them about.

And occasionally a woman will tempt him to a comfortable couch or bed. But he should know these things to be as many traps under various disguises.

He should not look at them, nor should he consent to anything inconsiderate, nor walk together with them; thus he will well guard himself.

Inviting a monk and winning his confidence, they offer themselves to him. But he should know, and fly from these temptations in their various forms.

Meekly and politely they approach him with their manifold arts to win his heart; and talking sweetly in confidential conversatoin they make him do what they like.

As men by baiting with a piece of flesh a fearless single lion get him into a trap, so women may capture an ascetic though he be careful.

And then they make him do what they like, even as a wheelwright gradually turns the felly of a wheel. As an antelope caught in a snare, so he does not get out of it, however he struggles.

Afterwards he will feel remorse like one who has drunk milk mixed with poison; considering the consequences, a worthy monk should have no intercourse with women.

Therefore, he should avoid women, knowing them to be like a poisoned thorn. He is no Nirgrantha who without companion goes into houses, being a slave to passion and preaches his religion.

Those who are attached to this sinful intercourse must be recknoned among the wicked. Even a monk who practises severe austerities should avoid the company of women.

A monk should have no intercourse with his daughters and daughters-in-law, with nurses or female slaves, or with grown-up girls.

When the relations and friends see the intimacy of a monk with a girl, they become angry saying: All creatures love pleasures; you are a man, protect and support her.

But some become angry even when they see an innocent Shramana, and suspect the fidelity of their wives because of the dishes they serve up.

Those who have intercourse with women have already ceased to practise meditation; Shramanas, therefore, for the benefit of their souls, do not go to the apartments of women.

Though many leave the house, some of them arrive but at a middling position, between householder and monk; they merely talk of the path to perfection. The force of sinners is talking.

In the assembly he pronounces holy words, yet secretly he commits sins; but the wise know him to be a deceiver and great rogue.

The sinner does not confess his wrong, but rather boasts of it when reprimanded. Though he is admonished not to act as most men do, he becomes weak again and again.

Some men of great intelligence who perform their duties as supporters of women, get into their power, though they be well acquainted with the Striveda, Kamasastra.

The adulterers' hands and feet are cut off, their skin and flesh are torn off, they are roasted alive, and acid is poured into their wounds.

Their ears and nose are cut off, and their throats cut; all this they will suffer, but though suffering there for their sins they will not promise not to do the same again.

All this some have learned, and it has been well demonstrated in the Striveda. Though people know it, they do wrong impelled by Karman.

One man women have in their heart, another in their words, and another still in their actions. Therefore, a monk should not trust women, knowing that they are full of deceit.

A young woman, putting on fine ornaments and clothes, will say to a Shramana: 'I shall give up my former way of life and practise control. Reverend sir, teach me the Law!'

Or by professing herself a lay-disciple and coreligionist of the Shramanas, she will try to make a friend of him. As a pot filled with lac will melt near the fire, so even a wise monk will fall through intercourse with women.

A pot filled with lac thrown into the fire melts quickly and is destroyed; so monks are lost through intercourse with women.

Some commit sins with a girl, but when questioned about it, they say: 'I have done no sin; she only slept in my lap like my daughter.'

This is a second folly of the sinner that he obstinately denies what he has done. He commits a twofold sin, since, for the sake of his reputation, he falls again.

Some women will say, by way of invitation, to a good-looking, self-knowing monk: 'Holy man, accept a robe, an alms bowl, food or drink at our house!'

He should regard their words like wild rice, and should not desire to call at their house; for a fool who is bound in the fetters of sensuality will be subject to delusion again and again.

Thus I say.

A monk, living single, should not fall in love; if he loves pleasures, he should again become indifferent. Now hear the pleasures of Shramanas, which some monks enjoy.

When a monk breaks the law, dotes on a woman, and is absorbed by that passion, she afterwards scolds him, lifts her foot, and tramples on his head.

'O monk, if your will not live with me as a woman who has still her hair, I shall tear it out; but do not live separated from me.'

But when they have captured him, they send him on all sorts of errand: 'Look for the bodkin to carve the bottle-gourd, fetch some nice fruit.

'Bring wood to cook the vegetables, or that we may light a fire at night; paint my feet, come and meanwhile rub my back!

'Look after my clothes, bring food and drink, get me some perfume, a broom, a barber to shave my head!

'Give me the collyrium-box, my ornaments, the lute, Lodhra-powder, a Lodhra-flower, the Venupalasika-lute, a pill!

'A Utpalakushta, Tagara-powder, and aloe pounded together with Ushira, oil for anointing the face, baskets of bamboo wickerwork to put my things in!

'Reach me the lip-salve, fetch the umbrella and slippers, the knife to cut the string, have my robe dyed bluish!

'Give me the pot to cook the vegetables in Myrobalans, the jar to fetch water in, the stick to paint the mark upon the forehead, the pin to apply collyrium to the eyelids, or the fan when it is hot!

'Fetch me the pincers, the comb, the ribbon to bind up the hair, reach me the looking-glass, put the tooth-brush near me!

'Fetch me areca-nut and betel, needle and thread, the chamber-pot, the winnowing basket, the mortar, the pot for liquefying soap!

'Give me the vessel used in worshipping the gods, the water-pot. Friend, dig a privy. Fetch the bow for our son, the bullock for the Shramanera!

'The small pot, the drum, and the ball of cloth for the boy to play with. Shramana, the rainy season is at hand, look after the house and the stores!

'Fetch the chair with woven twine seat, the wooden shoes to walk on!' Pregnant women order their husbands about like slaves to fulfil their craving.

When a son, the reward of their wedded life, is born, the mother bids the father to hold the baby, or to give it to her. Thus some supporters of their sons have to carry burdens like camels.

Getting up in the night they lull the baby asleep like nurses; and though they are ashamed of themselves, they wash the clothes like washermen.

This has been done by many men who for the sake of pleasures have stooped so low; they become the equals of slaves, animals, servants, beasts of burden—mere nobodies.

One should not mind the entreaties of women, but abstain from their friendship and company. These pleasures which are derived therefrom are called causes of blamable actions.

Restraining himself by the thought that these dangerous pleasures will not be to his benefit, a monk should abstain from women, and commit no unnatural crime.

A wise and learned monk whose soul is in a pure condition (Leshya), will abstain from doing work for others; in thoughts, words, and actions he will bear all troubles.

The hero of faith who has vanquished sin and delusion, has said all this. A monk, therefore, whose soul is pure and free from sins should wander about till he reaches final liberation. Thus I say.

5

Life, Food, Liberation

Activity, Merit, Demerit, Sin, Hell, etc.

O long-lived Jambusvamin! I Sudharman have heard the following discourse from the Venerable Mahavira. We now come to the Lecture called 'On Activity.' The contents of it are as follows:

It treats, briefly, of two subjects: merit and demerit. The former is when the Self is at rest, the latter, when it is in disturbance,

Now the explanation of the first subject, demerit, is as follows.

As regards committing of sin, among denizens of hell, brute animals, gods, men, and whatever other suchike beings there be, the sentient beings feel the pain.

And these beings practise the following thirteen kinds of activity—

1. sinning for one's interest;
2. sinning without a personal interest;
3. sinning by slaying;
4. sinning through accident;
5. sinning by an error of sight;
6. sinning by lying;
7. sinning by taking what is not freely given;
8. sinning by a mere conceit;
9. sinning through pride;
10. sinning through bad treatment of one's friends;
11. sinning through deceit;
12. sinning through greed;
13. actions referring to a religious life.

1. The first kind of committing sins is that prompted by a motive. This is the case when a man for his own sake, for the sake of his relations, his house, his family, his friends, for the sake of Nagas, Bhutas, or Yakshas does injury to movable or immovable beings, or has it done by another person, or consents to another's doing it. Thereby the bad Karman accrues to him. This is the first kind of committing sins, that prompted by a motive.

2. We now treat of the second kind of committing sins, that which is not prompted by personal interest. This is the case when a man slays, kills, cuts, pierces, hacks, mangles, or puts to death movable living beings, not because he wants their body, skin, flesh, blood, heart, bile, feathers of their tail, tail, big or small horns, teeth, tusks, nails, sinews, bones, or marrow; nor because he has been wounded by them, or is wounded, or will be wounded; nor in order to support his children, or to feed his cattle, or to enlarge his houses, nor for the maintenance of Shramanas and Brahmins, nor for the benefit of his body; setting aside reason a fool acquires the habit of cruelty, being a wanton killer.

This is the case when a man slays, etc., immovable living beings as Ikkata-reed, Kathina, Jantuka-grass, Para-grass, Moksha-trees, grass, Kusa-grass, Kuchchhaka, Pappaka, or straw, not in order to support his children, etc.

Or when a man on a marsh, a lake, a sheet of water, a pasture-ground, a place surrounded by a ditch, a moat, a thicket, stronghold in a thicket, forest, stronghold in a forest, mountain, stronghold on a mountain, piles up grass and lights a fire, or has it lighted by another person, or consents to another's lighting it. Thereby the bad Karman accrues to him. This is the second kind of committing sins, that prompted by no personal interest.

3. We now treat of the third kind of committing sins, called slaying. This is the case when a man thinking that some one has hurt, hurts, or will hurt him, or one of his people, or somebody else, or one of that person's people, kills movable and immovable beings, has them killed by another person, or

consents to another's killing them. Thereby the bad Karman accrues to him. This is the third kind of committing sins, called slaying.

4. We now treat of the fourth kind of committing sins, called accidental. This is the case when in marshes etc., a man who lives on deer, who likes deer, who dotes on deer, goes a hunting deer. Fancying to see deer, he takes aim with his arrow to kill the deer. Thinking that he will kill the deer, he kills a partridge, or a duck, or a quail, or a pigeon, or a monkey, or a francoline partridge. Here instead of one being he hurts another, therefore he is called an accidental killer.

This is the case when a man weeding rice, Kodrava, panic seed, Paraka, or Ralaka, uses his knife to cut some weeds. Fancying that he is cutting some weed-grasses, he cuts rice etc. Here instead of one plant he hurts another; therefore he is called an accidental killer. Thereby the bad Karman accrues to him. This is the fourth kind of committing sins, called accidental.

5. We now treat of the fifth kind of committing sins, by an error of sight. This is the case when a man living together with his mother, father, brothers, sisters, wives, sons, daughters, or daughters-in-law, and mistaking a friend for an enemy, kills the friend by mistake.

This is the case when during a riot in a village, or a scot-free town, or a town with an earth wall, or a poor town, or an isolated town, or a large town, or a sea-town, or a mine, or a hermitage, or a halting-place of processions or caravans, or a capital, a man mistaking for a robber one who is not, kills him by mistake. Thereby the bad Karman accrues to him. This is the fifth kind of committing sins, by an error of sight.

6. We now treat of the sixth kind of committing sins, by lying. This is the case when a man for his own sake, or for the sake of his relations, his house, or his servants tells lies, causes another person to tell lies, or consents to another's telling lies. Thereby the bad Karman accrues to him. This is the sixth kind of committing sins, by lying.

7. Now we treat of the seventh kind of committing sins,

by taking what is not freely given. This is the case when a man for his own sake takes himself what is not freely given, has it taken by another person, or consents to another's taking it. Thereby the bad Karman accrues to him. This is the seventh kind of committing sins, by taking what is not freely given.

8. Now we treat of the eighth kind of committing sins, by mere conceit. This is the case when a man, without being disappointed by anybody in any way, meditates, melancholy, sorry, angry, downcast, anxious in thoughts and ideas, plunged in a sea of sorrow and misery, reposing his head on the palm of his hand, overcome by painful reflections, and casting his eyes on the ground. There are four mental, but real, conditions of this kind, wrath, pride, deceit, and greed; for wrath, pride, deceit, and greed are mental conditions. Thereby the bad Karman accrues to him. This is the eighth kind of committing sins, by a mere conceit.

9. Now we treat of the ninth kind of committing sins, through pride. This is the case when a man drunk as it were with pride of caste, family, beauty, piety, knowledge, success, power, intelligence, or any other kind of pride, slights, blames, abuses, reviles, despises somebody else and extols himself, thinking: 'he is my inferior, I am of better caste or family, and possess greater power and other advantages.' When he leaves this body and is only accompanied by his Karman, he, without a will of his own, goes forth from womb to womb, from birth to birth, from death to death, from hell to hell. He is cruel, stubborn, fickle, and proud. Thereby the bad Karman accrues to him. This is the ninth kind of committing sins, through pride.

10. We now treat of the tenth kind of committing sins, consisting in bad treatment of one's friends. This is the case when a man living together with his mother, father, brothers, sisters, wives, sons, daughters, or daughters-in-law, severely punishes even the smallest offence of theirs; e.g., he ducks the offender in cold water, or pours hot water over him, or scalds him with fire, or lashes his sides sore with a halter, reed, rope, strap of leather, whip, or thong of a whip, or he beats the

offender with a stick, bone, fist, clod, or potsherd. When such a man is at home, his people are miserable; but when he is abroad, they rejoice. Such a man, who is for ever punishing, severely punishing, is hateful in this world and the next, irritable, passionate, an extortioner. Thereby the bad Karman accrues to him. This is the tenth kind of committing sins, consisting in bad treatment of one's friends.

11. We now treat of the eleventh kind of committing sins, through deceit. Those who conceal their thoughts, who are shrouded in darkness, who are light as the feather of an owl or heavy like a mountain, use unworthy speech though they be Aryas. They believe themselves different from what they really are; asked one thing, they answer another, they speak different from what is to be spoken.

As a man in whose body sticks an arrow, does not extricate it fearing the pain, nor has it extricated by somebody else, nor destroys it, but hides it; and the arrow, being not removed, goes deeper and deeper in the flesh; so a deceitful man, having practised deception, does not confess it, expiate it, blame the deed to himself or others, does not remove it, annihilate it, and endeavous not to do it again, does not practise the prescribed austerities and penance. A deceitful man is generally not trusted in this world, a deceitful man is not trusted in the next world. He blames and reviles the person whom he has deceived, he praises himself, and rejoices, and does not desist from his vile practices; he conceals the wrong he has done to others, and does not acquire a pure Leshya. Thereby the bad-Karman accrues to him. This is the eleventh kind of committing sins, through deceit.

12. We now treat of the twelfth kind of committing sins, through greed. Those heretical monks who live in woods, in huts, about villages, or practise some secret rites, are not well controlled, nor do they well abstain from slaying all sorts of living beings. They employ speech that is true and untrue at the same time: 'do not beat me, beat others; do not abuse me, abuse others; do not capture me, capture others; do not torment me, torment others; do not deprive me of life, deprive

others of life.' And thus they are given to sensual pleasures, desire them, are held captive by them, passionately love them for four or five years, for six or ten years—the period may be shorter or longer. After having enjoyed these pleasures, and having died at their allotted time, they will be born in some places inhabited by Asuras and evildoers. And when they are released therefrom, they will be born deaf and dumb, or blind, or dumb by birth. Thereby the bad Karman accrues to him. This is the twelfth kind of committing sins, through greed.

These twelve kinds of committing sins should be well understood by a pious Sramana or Brahmin.

13. We now treat of the thirteenth kind of acquiring Karman, that having reference to religious life. A monk who controls himself for the benefit of his soul, who in walking carefully avoids to cause the death of any living creature, who uses gentle and righteous speech, who receives alms in a manner to avoid the forty-two faults, who is careful in receiving and keeping of things necessary for religious exercises, who performs the operations of nature, excrements, urine, saliva, corporal impurities and mucus in an unfrequented place, who is careful with regard to mind, speech, and body, who guards his mind, speech, and body so as to protect his soul from passions, who guards his senses, who leads a chaste life regulated by the three Guptis, who carefully walks, stands, sits down, lies down, and speaks, who carefully takes up and lays down his cloth, alms-bowl, blanket, broom,—even such a monk performs various subtle actions called Iryapathika if it did but consist in moving an eyelash. This Karman is acquired and comes in contact with the soul in the first moment, in the second moment it is experienced, in the third it is destroyed; thus it is acquired, comes in contact with the soul, takes rise, and is destroyed. For all time to come the person in question is exempt from Karman. Thereby the bad Karman accrues to him. This is the thirteenth kind of acquiring Karman, that inseparable from a religious life.

All the Arhats and Bhagavats of the past, present, and future have told, tell, and will tell, have declared, declare, and will declare the above thirteen kinds of acquiring Karman. They have practised, practise, and will practise the thirteenth kind of acquiring Karman.

•

As a supplement to the above discussion will now be told the subject of men's success by occult sciences. Some men differing in intellect, will, character, opinions, taste, undertakings, and plans, study various evil sciences; viz., the divination from terrestrial accidents, from strange phenomena from dreams, from phenomena in the air, from changes in the body, from sounds, from mystical signs, from seeds; the interpretation of the marks of women, men, elephants, cows, partridges, cocks, ducks, quails, of wheels, parasols, shields, sticks, swords, precious stones, jewels; the art to make one happy or miserable, to make a woman pregnant, to deprive one of his wits; incantations, conjuring; oblations of substances; the martial arts; the course of the moon, sun, Venus, and Jupiter; the falling of meteors; great conflagration; divination from wild animals, the flight of crows, showers of dust, rain of blood, the Vaitali and Ardhavaitali arts, the art of casting people asleep, of opening doors, the art of Chandalas, of Sabaras, of Dravidas, of Kalingas, of Gaudas, of Gandharas; the spells for making somebody fall down, rise, yawn; for making him immovable, or cling to something; for making him sick, or sound; for making somebody go forth, disappear, or come. These and similar sciences are practised by some men for the sake of food, drink, clothes, a lodging, a bed, and various objects of pleasure. They practise a wrong science, the unworthy, the mistaken men. After having died at their allotted time, they will be born in some places inhabited by Asuras and evildoers. And when they are released therefrom, they will again be born deaf and dumb, or night-blind.

Some man for his own sake or for the sake of his relations, family, or servants, or entering the service of an acquaintance or neighbour of his, becomes his companion or his helpmate, or he goes to meet him, or he becomes a burglar, or a cut-purse, or he tends sheep, or he becomes a hunter, or he catches birds, or he uses nets for catching deer, or he becomes a fisherman or a cowherd or a slayer of cows or a dog-keeper or he hunts with dogs.

A man, becoming the companion of another man, will follow him everywhere, and having inspired him with confidence beats, cuts, pierces, tears, thrashes, or puts him to death, and thereby gets his food. By these very evil deeds he degrades himself.

A man, becoming the helpmate of another man, always attends on him, and having inspired him with confidence beats, etc., degrades himself.

A man, going to meet somebody, on the road, beats, etc., degrades himself.

A man, becoming a burglar, breaks into a house and beats, etc., degrades himself.

A man, becoming a cut-purse, cuts the purse and beats, etc., degrades himself.

A man, becoming a tender of sheep, beats, cuts, pierces, tears, thrashes, or puts to death a ram or some other animal.

A man, becoming a hunter, beats, or puts to death a buffalo or some other animal.

A man, using nets for catching deer, beats, etc., an antelope or some other animal.

A man, catching birds, beats, etc., a bird or some other animal.

A man, becoming a fisherman, beats, etc., a fish or some other animal.

A man, becoming a cowherd, beats, etc., a cow or some other animal.

A man, becoming a dog-keeper, beats, etc., a dog or some other animal.

A man, becoming the helpmate of a dog-keeper, beats, etc., a dog or some other animal.

A man, rising in an assembly, may promise to kill some

animal and he will beat, etc., a partridge, duck, quail, pigeon, monkey, a francoline partridge, or some other animal.

A man, being angry for some reason, e.g., because his granary or his liquor-cask runs short, sets fire to the cornfields of the householders or their sons, has the fire set by another person, or consents to another's setting fire to them.

A man, being angry for some reason, e.g., because his granary or liquor-cask runs short, makes a deep cut in the strong limbs of the camels, cows, horses, or donkeys of the householders or their sons, has it made by another person, or consents to another's making the cut.

A man, being angry for some reason, e.g., because his granary or his liquor-cask runs short, covers with brambles or twigs the householders', or their sons', stable for the camels, cows, horses, or donkeys, and burns them, or has them burnt by another person, or consents to another's burning them.

A man, being angry for some reason, etc. as above, steals a householder's or his sons' earrings or girdle, or jewels, or pearls, has them stolen by another person, or consents to another's stealing them.

A man, being angry, etc., robs Shramanas or Brahmins of their umbrella, stick, staff, small property, pot, chair, clothes, blanket, leather boots, knife, or scabbard, has it done by another person, or consents to another's robbing them.

A man, without consideration and without any provocation, sets fire to the cornfields of the householders.

A man, without consideration, makes a deep cut in the strong limbs of the camels.

A man, without consideration, covers with brambles and twigs the stables for the camels, and burns them.

A man, without consideration, steals the earrings, etc.

A man, on seeing Shramanas or Brahmins whom he detests, degrades himself by various evil deeds. Either he gives them a slap with the open hand to turn them away, or he abuses them. And when the monk at the proper time calls at his house on the begging-tour, he does not give him alms but says: those who become Shramanas are the meanest workmen, men unable to support their family, low-caste men, wretches, idlers!

Such men praise this life, this miserable life; they do nothing on behalf of the next world; they suffer, grieve, blame themselves, grow feeble, are afflicted, and undergo great pain; they do not cease to cause others to suffer, grieve, etc., to slay and to put men in fetters; and while they make suffer or kill, or make suffer and kill beings, and do various evil deeds, they enjoy the excellent pleasures of human life; viz., such a man eats at dinner-time, he drinks at drinking-time, he dresses himself at dressing-time, he goes to bed at the proper time, and sleeps at sleeping-time. Doing everything in its turn, he bathes, makes the offering to the house-gods, performs auspicious rites and expiatory acts, washes his head, hangs a wreath round his neck, adorns himself with precious stones and golden trinkets, puts on his head a chaplet of flowers; with his body strengthened, with a wreath hanging down to the girdle of his loins, dressed in new clothes, his limbs and body anointed with sandal, sitting on a large throne in a lofty upper room of his house, surrounded by women and a troop of followers, in the light of torches burning the whole night, under the great din of uninterrupted story-telling, dramatical plays, singing, and music, as beating of time, performing on the Vina, Turya, the great drum, and Patupataha, he enjoys the excellent pleasures of human life.

When he gives an order to one man, even four or five men will, without being asked, go up to him and say: ' Speak, beloved of the gods, what shall we do? what shall we fetch? what shall we give you? what trinket shall we put on you? what is your heart's desire? what relishes your mouth?'

Unworthy men who see him will say: 'Forsooth, this man is a god; this man is the anointed of the gods, this man will support us, as he supports others.' But noble men who see him will say: 'This man does cruel actions, and maintains himself by them. His is the southern region, the hell, the dark fortnight. In the future he will not easily obtain enlightenment.'

The conduct described in the preceding part is agreeable

to some heretical monks, to some householders, to men governed by love of life. This conduct is unworthy, impure, void of virtues, not holy, not right, not eradicating sins; it is not the road to perfection, liberation, Nirvana, final delivery, not the road of those who are freed from all misery; it is thoroughly untrue, and bad.

This is the explanation of the first subject, demerit.

•

Now the explanation of the second subject, merit, is as follows:

Here in the East, West, North, and South there are some men, Aryas, non-Aryas, ugly men. They own fields and houses, etc.

The conduct described in this part is holy, right, all just the reverse of what was said, thoroughly true, and good. This is the explanation of the second subject, merit.

Now the explanation of the third subject, the mixed state, is as follows:

Those who live in woods, in huts, near villages, etc. The conduct described in this part is not holy, thoroughly untrue, and bad.

This is the explanation of the third subject, the mixed state.

•

Now the explanation of the first subject, demerit, is as follows:

Here in the East, West, North, and South live some men; they are householders, men of great desires, great undertakings, great possessions, unrighteous men, men practising unrighteousness, very unrighteous men, men speaking unrighteously, living unrighteously, thinking unrighteously, given to unrighteousness, men of unrighteous character and conduct, men gaining an unrighteous livelihood.

They beat, cut, pierce, skin, are bloody-handed, violent, cruel, wicked, rash; they habitually practise bribery, fraud, deceit, imposture, dishonesty, and trickery; they are of bad character and morals, they are difficult to please, they do not abstain from killing living beings; as long as they live they do not abstain from wrath, the sin of wrong belief; nor from bathing, rubbing, painting, anointing themselves; from sounds, touches, tastes, colours, smells; from wreaths and ornaments; from cars, carriages, vehicles, litters, swings, coach and pair, palanquins, beds, seats; from enjoying a ride or drive; from having many followers; from buying, selling, doing business with Mashas, half Mashas, and Rupees; from silver, gold, riches, corn, precious stones, pearls, conches, stones, and corals; from using wrong weights and measures; from undertakings and slaughter; from working and making others work; from cooking and making others cook; from cutting, pounding, threatening, beating, binding, killing, and causing pain; and whatever other suchlike wicked and sinful actions of worthless men there be, that cause pain to other beings: these men do not abstain from them as long as they live.

As some idle, cruel men wantonly injure Kalama, Masura, sesamum, Mudga, beans, Nishpava, Kulattha, Alisanda, Elamichcha, so an idle, cruel man wantonly hurts partridges, ducks, quails, pigeons, francoline partridges, deer, buffaloes, boars, iguanas, tortoises, and snakes.

A man will occasionally severely punish even the smallest offence of his domestics, viz., a slave or messenger or hired servant or vassal or parasite; e.g., punish him, pull out his hair, beat him, put him in irons, in fetters, in stocks, into prison, screw up in a pair of shackles his hands and feet and break them, cut off his hands or feet. or ears or nose or lips or head or face, pierce his feet, tear out his eyes, teeth, tongue, hang him, brush him, whirl him round, impale him, lacerate him, pour acids in his wounds, belabour him with cutting-grass, bind him to a lion's tail, or a bull's tail, burn him in a wood on fire, let him be devoured by crows and vultures, stop his food and drink, keep him a prisoner for life, let him die any of these horrid deaths.

A man will occasionally severely punish even the smallest offence of his next of kin, viz., his mother or father or brother or sister or wife or sons or daughters or daughters-in-law; e.g., he ducks the offender in cold water, etc., hateful in this world and the next. They suffer, grieve, blame themselves, grow feeble, are afflicted, and undergo great pain; they do not cease to cause others to suffer, grieve, etc., to slay and to put men in fetters.

And thus they are given to sensual pleasures, desire them, are held captive by them, passionately love them for four or five years, for six or ten years—the period may be shorter or longer. Having enjoyed pleasures, having produced the effects of iniquity, having acquired the Karman of many sinful actions which generally bear him downwards, he goes to the bottom of the hell. As a ball of iron or. stone, when thrown in the water, sinks below the surface of the water till it stops at the bottom, so a man of the sort we are treating of, who is full of Karman, full of sin, full of demerit, full of disgrace, full of iniquity, full of wicked thoughts, deceit, imposture, and fraud, and, as a rule, kills animals, having died at the allotted time, will sink below this earth, and go to the bottom of the hell.

These hells are round inside, square outside, on their floor razorlike arrows are thick-set and covered with flowers, they are filled with perpetual darkness, never lighted up by the planets, moon, sun, Nakshatras, and stars; their floor is slippery with a coating of marrow, fat, flesh, blood, and matter, and besmeared with grease; these hells are impure, smelling detestably, black, of the colour of fire, very rugged, difficult to pass, horrid. And horrid are the pains in these hells.

And those who are condemned to live in these hells, do

not sleep nor slumber, nor do they get any consolation or comfort or recreation or encouragement; but the denizens of hell there suffer exquisite, great, deep, hard, rough, violent, painful, sharp, intolerable agonies.

As a tree growing on a hill falls by its weight when its roots are cut, on a low, rugged, inaccessible place, so a man of the sort we are treating of wanders from womb to womb, from birth to birth, from death to death, from hell to hell, from pain to pain. His is the southern region, the hell, the dark fortnight. In the future he will not easily obtain enlightenment. The conduct described in the preceding part is unworthy, impure, it is thoroughly untrue, and bad. This is the explanation of the first subject, demerit.

Now the explanation of the second subject, merit, is as follows:

Here in the East, West, North, and South there are some such men as abstain from undertakings and possessions, righteous men, men practising righteousness, men gaining a righteous livelihood. They are of good character and morals, they are easy to please and good. They abstain from killing living beings as long as they live, just the reverse of whatever other suchlike wicked actions there be, that cause pain to other beings: these men abstain from them as long as they live.

There are such monks as in walking carefully avoid to occasion the death of any living creature, lead chaste lives regulated by the three Guptis, as are free from anger, pride, deceit, and greed, as are calm, tranquil, passionless, happy, free from the Asravas, and bondage, without sorrow; as water does not adhere to a copper vessel, or collyrium to mother-of-pearl so sins find no place in them; their course is unobstructed like that of Life; like the firmament they want nothing to support them; like the wind they know no obstacles; their heart is pure like the water of rivers or tanks in autumn; like the leaves of a lotus they cannot be soiled by anything; their senses are well protected like the limbs of a tortoise; they are single and alone like the horn of a rhinoceros; they are free like birds; they are always waking like the fabulous bird Bharuna; they are valorous like elephants, strong like bulls, difficult to attack like lions, steady and firm like Mount Mandara, deep like the ocean, mild like the moon, refulgent like the sun, pure like excellent gold; like the earth they patiently bear everything; like a well-kindled fire they shine in their splendour.

There are no obstacles anywhere for these reverend men. The obstacles have been declared to be of four kinds, animals born from eggs, viviparous animals, things belonging to somebody, articles necessary for religious exercises. In whichever direction they want to go, there they meet with no obstacle; but being pure and free, full of learning, control, and austerities, they purify themselves.

These reverend men practise the following mode of living which just suffices for carrying on existence; they eat but one meal in two, three, four, five, six, seven days, in half a month, in one, two, three, four, five, six months; they have vowed to live on such food only as has been taken out of the cooking-vessel, or as is still in it, or the first kind of food in one place and the second in another, or on low food, or bad food, or food collected in small bits, or food given with a dirty hand, or the reverse, or food given with a hand, etc. soiled by it; they have vowed to accept such alms only as are within sight when they beg, or are out of sight, as they are asked whether they would accept, or as they are not asked about, as are given with contempt, or the reverse; they beg in houses where they are unknown, or when food is scarce; they accept only such things as are at hand, or only a limited number of gifts, or only a fixed quantity of food; they beg according to the rules laid down for begging; they eat low food or bad food or tasteless food or badly tasting food or rough food or disagreeable food; they lead a low or mean life; they drink sour gruel, they eat nothing seasoned with ghee or similar materials; they do not drink liquors or eat meat, they do not eat highly-flavoured food; they eat standing, or supported by something, or sitting on a stool or an armchair; they lie down stretched out like a stick, or curved like a bent piece of wood; they sit in the sun, they go naked; they do not scratch themselves; they do not spit; they do not cut their beard, hair, and nails, they do not take any care of their person.

Living in this way they practise many years Shramanahood, and if then they fall sick, or even if they do not, they refuse food and omit many meals by abstaining from food. When they have attained that for whose sake they went about naked and bald-headed, did not bathe, nor clean their teeth, nor protect their head from the sun, nor wear shoes; they slept on the bare ground or a plank or a piece of wood, plucked out their hair, led a life of chastity, entered the houses of strangers, and bore, with indifference, success, failure, honour, disgrace, slights, blame, reviling, threatening, beating, all sorts of hardships, and the twenty-two calamities and troubles; when they have attained their end, they reach, while they are breathing their last, the highest knowledge and faith, called Kevala, which is infinite, supreme, unobstructed, unimpeded, complete and full; and then they obtain absolute perfection, enlightenment, deliverance, final beatitude, and put an end to all misery.

Some become liberated without assuming another body after quitting the last. But others, having died at the allotted time, are, on account of a residue of good Karman, born in one of the regions of the gods. Among very beautiful, very splendid, very excellent, very glorious, very strong, very powerful, very happy gods, they become very beautiful, very splendid, gods; their breasts shining with necklaces; their arms encumbered with bracelets and armrings; wearing ear-ornaments which play on their cheeks, and earrings which hang down to the bracelets on their upper arms; wearing various ornaments on their hands; their crowns adorned with gay wreaths; putting on highly perfumed, excellent clothes; using beautiful, excellent garlands and ointments; their splendid body ornamented with a long down-reaching garland; having divine colours, touches, constitution of the body, and rank; lighting up and illumining all ten quarters of the universe with their divine beauty, splendour, lustre, brightness, brilliance, and light; beautiful when they go, beautiful when they rest, and happy also in the time to come.

The conduct described in the preceding part is worthy, pure, it is thoroughly true, and good.

This is the explanation of the second subject, merit.

•

Now the explanation of the third subject, the mixed state, is as follows:

Here in the East, West, North, and South there are some such men as have few desires, few undertakings, few possessions, righteous men, men practising righteousness, men gaining a righteous livelihood. They are of good character and morals, easy to please, and good. They abstain, as long as they live, from one kind of killing living beings, but they do not abstain from another, similar suchlike wicked actions there be, that cause pains to other beings, from some of them these men abstain as long as they live, from others they do not abstain.

There are, for instance, followers of the Shramanas, who comprehend the doctrine about living beings and things without life, who understand the difference between virtues and sins, who are well grounded in the knowledge of the Asravas, Samvara, the realisation and annihilation of Karman, the subject of actions, bondage, and final liberation; who, without anybody to back them, cannot be seduced from the creed of the Nirgranthas by hosts of gods, Asuras, Nagas, Suvarnas, Yakshas, Rakshasas, Kinnaras, Kimpurushas, Garudas, and snake-gods; who have no doubts, scruples, or misgivings about this creed of the Nirgranthas, but have grasped its meaning, got hold of its meaning, got information about its meaning, ascertained its meaning, and understood its meaning; whose very marrow of the bones has been penetrated by their love for the Nirgrantha creed; avowing that it alone is true, and all others futile. They keep the bar of their gates raised and their door open, having no desire to enter a stranger's house or his seraglio. They strictly keep the Posaha fast on the fourteenth and eighth days of the month, on certain festivals, and on full-moon days. They provide the Nirgrantha Shramanas with pure acceptable food, drink, dainties and spices, with clothes, alms-bowls, blankets and brooms, with drugs and medicines, with stools, planks, beds, and couches. They purify themselves by practising the Silavratas and Gunavratas, the Viramana, the Pratyakhyana, the Posaha fasts, and austerities which they have vowed to perform.

Living in this way they are for many years followers of the Shramanas, and if then they fall sick, or even if they do not, they refuse food and omit many meals by abstaining from food. Having confessed their sins and expiated them, and having attained perfection, they die at their allotted time, to be born again as gods in one of the regions of the gods, it is thoroughly true, and good.

This is the explanation of the third subject, the mixed state.

•

He who does not practise cessation from sin, is called a foolish man; he who practises cessation from sin, is called a wise man; he who in one regard practises cessation from sin and in another does not, is said to be in a state partaking of that of a wise man and that of a foolish man.

The conduct of him who does not practise cessation from all sins, is that of a man who kills living creatures; it is unworthy, thoroughly untrue, and bad.

The conduct of him who practises cessation from all sins, is that of a man who does not kill living creatures; it is worthy, pure, thoroughly true, and good.

The conduct of a man who in one regard practises cessation from all sins and in another does not, is that of a man who kills some living creatures and does not kill others; it is worthy, pure, thoroughly true, and good.

Those whom we have been treating of, fall under the two heads: merit and demerit; the former is when the Self is at rest, the latter, when it is in disturbance.

Now the explanation of the first subject is as follows:

There are enumerated three hundred and sixty-three philosophical schools: those of the Kriyavada, those of the Akriyavada, those of the Ajnanikavada, and those of the Vainayikavada. These philosophers teach final beatitude, they teach final deliverance, they speak as Sravakas, they speak as teachers of Sravakas.

All these philosophers, founders of systems of their own, differing in intellect, will, character, opinions, taste, undertakings, and plans, formed one large circle, and every one of them stood in his place.

One man took hold of a vessel quite full of burning coals by an iron pair of tongs, and addressed those philosophers, founders of systems of their own, differing in intellect, undertakings and plans, in the following way: 'Heighho! ye philosophers, founders of undertakings and plans! take this vessel full of burning coals and hold it for a minute in your hands! But do not take hold of it by a pair of tongs, nor put out the fire, nor come to the help of one of your own creed or of an alien creed, by putting out the fire, etc.; but fair and honest, without using any trick, stretch out your hands.' Having thus spoken, the man took hold of the vessel quite full of burning coals by an iron pair of tongs, and offered to put it in the hands of those philosophers. But the philosophers, founders of undertakings and plans, held back their hands. On this the man addressed all the philosophers, founders of undertakings and plans, in the following way: ' Heighho, ye philosophers, why do you hold back your hands?' 'Our hand will be burned.' 'What then, if it is burned?' 'We shall suffer pain.' 'Because you are afraid of pain, you hold back your hands!' So are all creatures averse to pain. This is a maxim of general application, it is a true principle, a religious reflection; this maxim, this principle, this religious reflection holds good with regard to every living being. Therefore those Shramanas and Brahmins who say that all sorts of living beings may be beaten or treated with violence or abused or tormented or deprived of life, will in the time to come suffer cutting or piercing, will experience birth, old age, death, conception in the womb, the Circle of Births, regeneration, existence as a foetus, the whole scale of mundane existences, and suffer a variety of pains.

They will many times undergo punishment, pulling out of the hair, threatening, putting in irons, whirling round; they will witness the death of their mothers, fathers, brothers, sisters, sons, daughters, and daughters-in-law; they will experience poverty, bad luck, company of hated people, separation from those whom they love, misery, and despair; they will again and again wander about in the beginningless and endless, immense wilderness of the fourfold Samsara. They will not reach perfection, not put an end to all misery.— This is a maxim of general application, holds good with regard to every living being.

But those Shramanas and Brahmins who say that all sorts of living beings should not be beaten, etc., will in the time to come not suffer cutting, etc. They will not undergo many punishments, put an end to all misery.

Thus those beings who practise the first twelve kinds of actions, have not attained perfection, have not, nor do, nor will put an end to all misery.

But those beings who practise the thirteenth kind of action, have attained perfection, etc., all down to have put, or put, or will put an end to all misery.

Thus a monk who obtains his soul's good and benefit, who guards himself, who well directs the functions of his soul, who well exerts himself, who protects himself from evil, who is careful of himself, who saves himself from the Samsara, should withhold his soul from the twelve kinds of committing sins.

Thus I say.

Life Varieties and their Food

O long-lived Jambusvamin! I Sudharman have heard the following discourse from the Venerable Mahavira. We now come to the lecture called 'Knowledge of Food.' The contents of it are as follows:

Here in the East, West, North, and South there are, all in all, in the world four kinds of seed: seeds generated at the top of the plant, at its root, at its knots, at its stem. According to the seed and place of growth of these plants some beings—born in earth, originated in earth, and grown in earth, having in it their birth, origin, and growth, being impelled by their Karman, and coming forth in it on account of their Karman, growing there in particles of earth, the origin of various things—come forth as trees.

These living beings feed on the liquid substance of these particles of earth, the origin of various things; these beings consume earth bodies, water-bodies, fire-bodies, wind-bodies, bodies of plants; they deprive of life the bodies of manifold movable and immovable beings; the destroyed bodies which have been consumed before, or absorbed by the rind, are digested and assimilated by them. And the bodies of these trees which bring forth their different parts, are of manifold colours, smells, tastes, touches, forms, and arrangement of corporeal particles.

These beings animating trees come into existence because of their Karman; so we are taught by the Tirthankaras.

And again it has been said of old: some beings born in trees, originated by trees, sprung from trees, springing from trees that originated in earth, come forth as trees originated by trees. These beings feed on the sap of the trees originated in earth.

In the same way, and in nearly the same words, the offshoots of the trees mentioned in the preceding paragraph are treated of.

And again it has been said of old: some beings born in trees, etc., growing in trees that are originated by trees, come forth as their roots, bulb, stem, branches, twigs, leaves, flowers, fruits, and seeds. These beings feed on the sap of those trees originated by trees, the bodies of the roots, bulb, stem, etc. are of manifold colours, etc.

(The four paragraphs that come next, are identical with the preceding ones, except that 'creeper' is substituted for 'tree.'

(In the same way 'grass' is treated in four paragraphs, but is much abridged; then it is said that 'herbs' and 'plants' are to be treated in four paragraphs each.)

And again it has been said of old: some beings born in earth, growing there in particles of earth that are the origin of various things, come forth as Aya, Kaya, Kuhawa, Kandu, Uvvehaliya, Nivvehaliya, Esava, Sakkha, Khattaga, Vasaniya. The rest but substitute the words Aya, etc. for 'trees.' Here there is only one paragraph, the remaining three do not apply here.

And again it has been said of old : some beings born in water, etc., all substitute only 'water' for 'earth.' Thus we have four paragraphs for trees, four for creepers, four for grass, four for herbs, four for plants.

Now it has been said of old: some beings born in water, etc., all as above, down to growing in particles of water that are the origin of various things, come forth as Udaga, Avaga, Panaga, Sevala, Kalambuya, Kaseruya, Kachchhabhaniya, Uppala, Pauma, Kumuya, Nalina, Subhagasoniya, Pondariya, Mahapondariya, Sayavatta, Sahassavatta, Kalhara, Kokanada, Tamarasa, as stalks and fibres of lotus, as Pukkhala, and Pukkhalatthibhaga.

And again it has been said of old: some beings come forth as movable beings from trees born in earth, from trees originated by trees, from the roots, seeds produced by trees, originated by creepers born on trees, from creepers born on creepers, from the roots, etc. of creepers born on creepers, from grass, from herbs, from plants, from Aya, etc., Kura born in earth; from trees born in water similar as with trees born in earth, from Udaga, etc., Pukkhalatthibhaga born in water.

These creatures feed on the sap of the trees, creepers, grass, herbs, plants, be they born in earth or water, on trees or creepers or grass or herbs or plants; the sap of their roots, etc., seeds of Ayas, etc., of Udakas, etc. And these creatures consume earth-bodies, etc., assimilated by them. And the bodies of these beings born of trees, creepers, grass, herbs, plants, their roots, etc., of Ayas, etc., of Udagas, etc., are of manifold colours, etc.

And again it has been said of old: a man and a woman combine in cohabitation in a cunnus, which was produced by their Karman, and there they deposit their humours. Therein are born the souls of different men, viz., of those born in Karmabhumi, or in Akarmabhumi, or in the minor continents, of Aryas and barbarians, as women or men or eunuchs, according to the semen and blood of the mother and the other circumstances contingent on their coming into existence. These beings at first feed on the menses of the mother and the semen of the father, or both combined into an unclean, foul substance. And afterwards they absorb with a part of their bodies the essence of whatever food the mothers take. Gradually increasing and attaining to the proper dimensions of a foetus they come forth from the womb, some as males, some as females, some as neuters. As long as they are babies, they suck the mother's milk; but when they grow older, they eat boiled rice. Or gruel, or both movable and immovable beings. These beings consume earth-bodies, etc., all assimilated by them. And the bodies of these men, viz., those born in Karmabhumi, or Akarmabhumi, or in the minor continents, of Aryas and barbarians, are of manifold colours.

(This paragraph is nearly identical with the preceding one, but substitute 'aquatic animals of five organs of sense, viz. fishes, to porpoises,' for 'different men' in the beginning and the end. The following sentence in the middle is slightly different; it runs thus: 'as long as they are young, they feed on the mothers' humours, but when they grow older they eat plants, or both movable and immovable beings.'

(This paragraph treats of quadrupeds, terrestrial animals with five organs of sense, viz., solidungular animals, biungular animals, multiungular animals, and animals having toes with nails. All as in the last paragraph, only 'as long as they are young, they feed on their mothers' milk.'

(This paragraph treats of reptiles moving on the breast, being terrestrial animals with five organs of sense, viz., snakes, huge snakes, Asalika, and dragons. All as before, but the following passage is different. Some bring forth eggs, some bring forth living young ones; some come out of the egg as males, some as females, some as neuters. As long as they are young, they live on wind.

(This paragraph treats of terrestrial animals with five organs of sense, walking on their arms, viz., iguanas, ichneumons, porcupines, frogs, chameleons, Khoras, Gharakoillas, Vissambharas, rats, mongooses, Pailaiyas, cats, Gohas, Kauppaiyas.

(This paragraph treats of aerial animals with five organs of sense: birds with membranous wings, birds with feathered wings, birds with wings in the shape of a box, and birds which sit on outspread wings. All as before; only the following passage is different: 'As long as they are young, they are hatched by their mothers' warmth.')

And again it has been said of old: there are beings of manifold birth and origin, etc., growing there on the animate or inanimate bodies of manifold movable or immovable creatures, come forth as parasites. These beings feed on the humours of various movable and immovable creatures, etc. And the bodies of these movable and immovable parasites are of manifold colours, etc.

In the same way vermin generated in filthy substances and in the skin of living animals are to be treated of.

And again it has been said of old: there are some beings of manifold birth and origin, etc., growing thereon or in the animate or inanimate bodies of manifold movable or immovable creatures as the water-body, which is produced by wind, condensed by wind, and carried along by wind; it goes upwards, when there is an upward wind; it goes downwards, when there is a downward wind; it goes in a horizontal direction, when there is a horizontal wind; its varieties are hoar-frost, snow, mist, hailstones, dew, and rain. These beings feed on the humours of these manifold movable and immovable creatures, etc. And the bodies of these water-lives, viz., hoar-frost, etc., produced by manifold movable or immovable creatures, are of manifold colours, etc.

And again it has been said of old: some beings, born in water, etc., all similar to water-bodies in the water produced by manifold movable or immovable beings. These beings feed on the humours of the water-bodies produced by manifold movable and immovable creatures.

And again it has been said of old: some beings, born in water, etc., come forth in water-bodies produced by other water-bodies. These beings feed on the humours of those other water-bodies produced by water-bodies.

And again it has been said of old: some beings, born in water, etc., come forth as movable creatures in the water produced by water-bodies. These beings feed on the humours of the water-bodies produced by water.

And again it has been said of old: some beings, of various birth and origin, etc., come forth as fire-bodies in the manifold animate or inanimate bodies of movable or immovable creatures. These beings feed on the manifold movable or immovable creatures.

(The remaining three paragraphs are similar to those treating of water-bodies.

(This paragraph treats of wind-bodies in the same way as the preceding ones treated of fire-bodies; like it, it consists of four paragraphs.)

And again it has been said of old: some beings, of various birth and origin, etc., come forth, in the manifold animate and inanimate bodies of movable and immovable creatures, as earth, gravel, etc. Here the following verses are to be made use of:

1. Earth, gravel, sand, stones, rocks, rock-salt, iron, copper, tin, lead, silver, gold, and diamond;

2. Orpiment, vermilion, realgar, Sasaka, antimony, coral, Abhrapatala, Abhravaluka; these are varieties of gross earth-bodies, and precious stones.

3. Hyacinth, natron, Anka, crystal, Lohitaksha, emerald, Masaragalla, Bhujamochaka, and sapphire;

4. Chandana, red chalk, Hamsagarbha, Pulaka, and sulphur; Chandraprabha, lapis lazuli, Jalakanta, and Suryakanta.

These beings feed on the humours of these manifold movable and immovable beings.

(The remaining three paragraphs are similar to those treating of water-bodies.)

And again it has been said of old: all sorts of living beings, of manifold birth, origin, and growth, born in bodies, originated in bodies, grown in bodies, feeding on bodies, experience their Karman, are actuated by it, have their form and duration of life determined by Karman, and undergo changes through the influence of Karman. This you should know, and knowing it you will be careful and circumspect with regard to your food, and always exert yourself.

Thus I say.

Renunciation of Activity

O long-lived Jambusvamin! I Sudharman have heard the following discourse from the Venerable Mahavira. We now come to the Lecture called 'Renunciation of Activity,' The contents of it are as follows:

It is the Self that may not renounce activity, that may be accustomed to act, that may adhere to errors, that may be prone to sin, that may be thoroughly ignorant, that may be thoroughly stolid, that may not consider the operations of mind, speech, and body, that may not avoid and renounce sins.

The Venerable One has said, 'He, i.e., the Self is

uncontrolled, unresigned, does not avoid and renounce sins, is active, careless, prone to sin, thoroughly ignorant, thoroughly stolid. Though a fool does not consider the operations of his mind, speech, and body, nor does see even a dream; still he commits sins.

The opponent says to the teacher: 'There can be no sin, if the perpetrator of an action does not possess sinful thoughts, speech, and functions of the body, if he does not kill, if he has no internal organ, if he does not consider the operations of mind, speech, and body, if he does not see even a dream.'

What is the meaning of the opponent in making this statement? 'When there is a sinful mind, there is sin of the mind; when there is sinful speech, there is sin of the speech; when there is a sinful body, there is sin of the body. When one kills, possesses an internal organ, and considers the operations of mind, speech, and body, when one sees even a dream, then there is sin. Only he who has these qualities can commit sin.' The opponent goes on to say, 'Those who say: There is sin, though the perpetrator of an action does not possess sinful thoughts, speeches, and functions of the body, though he does not kill, though he does not possess an internal organ, though he does not consider the operations of mind, speech, and body, and though he does not see even a dream,—those who say this, are wrong.'

Here the teacher says to the opponent: ' It is true what I have just said: there is sin, though the perpetrator of the action do not possess sinful thoughts, etc. 'What is the reason thereto of?' The Acharya. says: 'The Venerable One has assigned the six classes of living beings as the reason: the earth-lives, etc. With regard to these six classes of living beings, the Self does not avoid and renounce sins, he is wicked, and does harm through cruelty: this holds good with regard to the five cardinal sins: killing of living beings, etc. and the passions: anger, etc.

The Acharya says: 'The Venerable One has illustrated this by the example of a murderer: a murderer who hates a householder or his son or the king or his servant, resolves, on an occasion offering, to enter the victim's house and to kill him when he finds an opportunity. Is not this murderer who has formed this resolution, a man who, day and night, whether sleeping or waking, is full of hostility and wrong; who is wicked and does harm through cruelty? An unbiassed opponent before whom this is laid, will answer: Indeed, he is!'

The Acharya says: 'As this murderer who has formed the above resolution is a man who does harm through cruelty—(and this holds good with regard to the five cardinal sins: killing of living beings, etc., and the passions: anger, etc., the sin of wrong belief—so it has been said of him by the Venerable One: he is uncontrolled, unresigned, he does not avoid and renounce sins, he is active, careless, prone to sin, thoroughly ignorant, thoroughly stolid. Though a fool does not consider the operations of his mind, speech, and body, nor does see even a dream, still he commits sins.

As a murderer who entertains murderous intentions towards a householder, etc., is a man who does harm through cruelty; so an ignorant man who entertains cruel intentions towards all sorts of living beings, is a man who does harm through cruelty.

An opponent might object: This is no good reasoning. For there are many living beings which one, during one's whole life, never saw, nor heard of, nor cared for, nor took notice of. Towards these beings, therefore, one cannot be said to entertain murderous intentions, nor to be one who, day and night, whether sleeping or waking, is full of hostility and wrong.

The Acharya says: The Venerable One has refuted this by two illustrations, one of a sentient being, the other of a senseless being. The first is as follows: A sentient being, possessing five organs of sense and a developed internal organ, may with regard to the six classes of living beings, movable beings, impose some restriction upon himself; e.g., that he will meet his wants, or have them met by others, by means of earth-bodies only. His intention is: I shall meet my wants, or have them met by others, by means of earth-bodies only. His intention is not to make use of this or that particular earth-body: he meets his wants, or has them met by others, by means of earth-bodies in general. With regard to them, therefore, he is uncontrolled, unrestrained, does not avoid and renounce sins. The same applies to the remaining five classes of living beings.—Some one may meet his wants, or have them met by others, by means of the six classes of living beings. His intention is: I shall meet my wants, or have them met by others, by means of the six classes of living beings; it is not: by means of some particular beings. He meets his wants, by means of living beings in general. With regard to them, therefore, he is uncontrolled. This holds good with the five cardinal sins: killing of living beings, etc., and with the passions: anger, etc. The Venerable One has said that such a creature, commits sins.

The illustration of senseless beings is as follows: Senseless beings, viz. earth-bodies, to plants, to which must be added, as a sixth item, some movable beings, which have no reason nor consciousness, nor intellect, nor mind, nor speech, in order to do something, or to have it done by others, or to consent to others' doing it; these benighted creatures are to be considered as murderers, are full of hostility and wrong against all sorts of living beings. This holds good with the five cardinal sins: killing of living beings, etc., and with the passions, to the sin of wrong belief. Know this: though these beings have neither mind nor speech, yet as they cause pain, grief, damages, harm, and injury, they must be regarded as not abstaining from causing pain, etc.

Thus even senseless beings are reckoned instrumental in bringing about slaughter of living beings, etc., to the sin of wrong belief. Beings, whatever their origin, who were sentient in one existence will become senseless ones in another and vice versa. Not getting rid of, nor shaking off, nor annihilating, nor destroying their Karman, the thoroughly wicked and ignorant wander from the body of a senseless being into that of sentient ones, or from the body of a sentient being into that of senseless ones, or from the body of a sentient being into that of another, or from the body of a senseless being into that of another. The sentient beings and the senseless ones, both are wrong in their conduct and commit sins through cruelty. The Venerable One has said that such a creature is uncontrolled, and commits sins.

The opponent asks: 'What must one do or cause to be done, in order to become controlled and restrained, to avoid and renounce sins?' The Acharya answers: The Venerable One has declared that the cause of sins are the six classes of living beings, earth-lives, etc. As I feel pain, so they do. Therefore they should not be injured or killed.

This constant, permanent, eternal, true Law has been taught by wise men who comprehend all things. Thus a monk abstains from the five cardinal sins: slaughter of living beings, etc., and of vices, the sin of wrong belief. He does not clean his teeth with a tooth-brush, he does not accept collyrium, emetics, and perfumes. Such a monk does not act nor kill, he is free from wrath, pride, deceit, and greed, he is calm and happy. The Venerable One says that such a monk is well controlled and restrained, does avoid and renounce sins, is not active, but careful and thoroughly wise.

Thus I say.

Freedom from Error

A very clever monk who practises the vow of chastity, should not adopt the following heretical doctrines, nor behave badly in this religion.

He should not believe that this world is without beginning or without end, eternal or not eternal, according to the argumentation of heretics.

From these alternatives you cannot arrive at truth; from these alternatives you are, certainly, led to error.

One should not say: that there will be an end of beings who know and teach the truth; nor that all beings are not alike, nor that they shall be in perpetual bondage, or that the prophets are eternal.

From these alternatives you cannot arrive at the truth you are led to error.

One should not say: the guilt of killing small and great animals is the same, or not the same.

From these alternatives, you cannot arrive at the truth, you are led to error.

One should know that those who accept things especially prepared for them, will be affected by demerit in some cases, or will not be affected where it is allowed by scripture.

From these alternatives, you cannot arrive at truth, you are led to error.

One should not maintain the identity of the Audarika, Aharika, and Karmana bodies, nor that everything cannot everywhere come into existence, nor that it can.

From these alternatives, you cannot arrive at truth, you are led to error.

Do not maintain that the world does not exist, maintain that it exists.

Do not maintain that Jiva, and Ajiva. do not exist, but that they exist.

Do not maintain that Dharma and Adharma do not exist, but that they exist.

Do not maintain that bondage and liberation do not exist, but that they exist.

Do not maintain that virtue and vice do not exist, but that they exist.

Do not maintain that Asrava and the stoppage of Asrava do not exist, but that they exist.

Do not maintain that the experiencing of the effect, and the annihilation of Karman do not exist, but that they exist.

Do not maintain that activity and non-activity do not exist, but that they exist.

Do not maintain that anger and pride do not exist, but that they exist

Do not maintain that deceit and greed do not exist, but that they exist.

Do not maintain that love and hate do not exist, but that they exist.

Do not maintain that the fourfold Circle of Births does not exist, but that it exists.

Do not maintain that there are no gods and goddesses, but that there are.

Do not maintain that there is no such thing as perfection and non-perfection, but that there is such a thing.

Do not maintain that there is no place exclusively reserved for those who attain to perfection, but that there is such.

Do not maintain that there are no pious and wicked men, but that there are.

Do not maintain that there is no such thing as good and bad, but that there is good and bad.

The theory will not work that a man is always good, or always bad. The wrongly instructed Shramanas do not comprehend the soul's bondage through Karman.

Do not assert that everything is imperishable, or full of pains, nor that criminals should be put to death or not be put to death; one should not speak in this way.

Do not assert that those men are well-behaved monks who lead a pure life, and that those others lead an impure life.

A wise monk should not say: we get alms from this householder or we do not; but he should improve his chances for final liberation.

A monk should conform himself to these opinions taught by the Jinas, and wander about till he reaches final liberation.

Thus I say.

A Disputation

Gosala

'Listen, Ardraka, to what Mahavlra has done. At first he wandered about as a single monk: but now he has surrounded himself by many monks, and teaches every one of them the Law at length.

'The inconstant man has decided upon this mode of life: to stand up in a crowd of men, surrounded by monks, and to teach his doctrines for the benefit of many people. Therefore, his former and his present life are not of a piece.

'Either to live as a single mendicant was right conduct or his present life; therefore both do not agree with each other.'

Ardraka

"His past, present, and future lives agree with each other; for he is really always single and alone though he be now surrounded by many followers.

"For if a Shramana or Brahmin who causes peace and security, comprehends the nature of movable and immovable living beings and explains it in a crowd numbering thousands, he realises singleness, remaining in the same mental condition as before.

"It is no sin to teach the Law, if he who teaches it is patient and resigned, subdues his senses, avoids bad speech, and uses virtuous speech.

"He who teaches the great vows of monks and the five small vows of the laity, (Anuvratas) the five Asravas and the stoppage of the Asravas, and control, who avoids Karman in this blessed life of Shramanas, him I call a Shramana."

Gosala

'As your Law makes it no sin for Mahavira to surround himself by a crowd of disciples, so according to our Law an ascetic, who lives alone and single, commits no sin if he uses cold water, eats seeds, accepts things prepared for him, and has intercourse with women.'

Ardraka

"Know this: those who use cold water, eat seeds, accept things especially prepared for them, and have intercourse with women, are no better than householders, but they are no Shramanas.

"If those who eat seeds, use cold water, and have

intercourse with women, are admitted to be Shramanas, then householders too are Shramanas; for they do the same things.

"Monks who eat seeds and use cold water, who beg alms as a means of living, will, though they leave their relations, be born again and again, and will not put an end to mundane existence."

Gosala

'In making this statement you blame all philosophers alike!'

Ardraka

"Every philosopher praises his own doctrines and makes them known.

" Shramanas and Brahmins blame one another when they teach their doctrines. The truth, they say, is all on their side; there is none on that of the opponents. But we blame only the wrong doctrines and not at all those who entertain them.

" We do not detract from anybody because of his personal qualities; but we make known the path pointed out in our creed. I have been taught the supreme, right path by worthy, good men.

"If a well-controlled man, afraid of injuring any movable or immovable living beings, above, below, or on earth, condemns evil deeds, he does not at all blame anybody in this world."

Gosala

'Out of fear your Shramana will not stay in houses for travellers or in public garden-houses; for in such places he would meet with many clever people, with lower or nobler men, with talkative or silent ones.

'He will not stay there because he fears lest some monks, wise, well instructed, learned men, who are well versed in the sacred texts and their meaning, should put questions to him.'

Ardraka

"Doing nothing without a purpose, nor without consideration, neither on the behest of the king nor from fear of anybody, he answers questions or not according to the circumstances; but he answers worthy people with a definite purpose in his mind.

"He, the wise man, impartially teaches the Law whether he goes to his pupils or not; because unworthy men have fallen from the true faith, he does not go to places frequented by them."

Gosala

'As a merchant desirous of gain shows his wares and attracts a crowd to do business, in a similar way acts the Shramana Jnatriputra. This is what I think and calculate about it.'

Ardraka

"Mahavira acquires no new Karman, he annihilates the old, avoiding wrong opinions; and thus the saviour said to others: Herein is contained the vow leading to Brahman, i.e., Moksha; this is the gain which a Shramana is desirous of. Thus I say.

"A merchant kills living beings and desires property; not leaving his kinsmen, he attracts a crowd in order to do business.

"Desiring riches and addicted to sensuality, merchants wander about to earn their living. But we say that they are passionately fond of pleasures, unworthy, and desiring the enjoyment of love.

"They do not abstain from slaughter and the acquirement of property, they are in bondage and full of wickedness; and their gain of which you spoke, will be the endless Circle of Births and pains manifold.

"They do not always make profit, nor does it last for ever; they meet with both results success and failure in their quest of gain. The profit of the teacher, however, has a beginning, but no end; the saviour and sage shares his profit with others.

"Him who kills no living beings, who has compassion on all creatures, who is well grounded in the Law, and causes the truth of the Law to be known, him you would equal to those wicked men! This is the outcome of your folly."

A Buddhist

'If a savage thrusts a spit through the side of a granary, mistaking it for a man; or through a gourd, mistaking it for a baby, and roasts it, he will be guilty of murder according to our views.

'If a savage puts a man on a spit and roasts him, mistaking him for a fragment of the granary; or a baby, mistaking him for a gourd, he will not be guilty of murder according to our views.

'If anybody thrusts a spit through a man or a baby, mistaking him for a fragment of the granary, puts him on the fire, and roasts him, that will be a meal fit for Buddhas to break fast upon.

'Those who always feed two thousand worthy monks, acquire great merit and become powerful gods in Arupa.'

Ardraka

"Well-controlled men cannot accept your denial of guilt incurred by unintentionally doing harm to living beings. It will cause error and no good to both who teach such doctrines and who believe them.

"A man who knows the nature of movable and immovable living beings, above, below, and on earth," who is afraid of injuring them and abstains from wicked deeds, may speak and act in accordance with our Law; he will not be guilty of any sin.

"It is impossible to mistake a fragment of the granary for a man; only an unworthy man can say it. How can the idea of a man be produced by a fragment of the granary? Even to utter this is an untruth.

"Do not use such speech by means of which you do evil; for such speech is incompatible with virtues. No ordained monk should speak empty words.

"Oh! you have explored this subject; you have thoroughly examined the consequences of acts of living beings; your fame reaches the Eastern and Western oceans; you view the universe as if it stood on the palm of your hands!

"Thoroughly examining the consequences of acts of living beings, our monks have found out a pure way of sustaining life. It is a maxim of the monks of our creed, that nobody who lives by secret sins, should lay down the Law.

"A man who always feeds two thousand worthy monks, does not control himself, and will be blamed in this world like a man with bloody hands.

"They kill a fattened sheep, and prepare food for the sake of a particular person; they season the meat with salt and oil, and dress it with pepper.

"You are irreligious, unworthy men, devoted to foolish pleasures, who say that partaking heartily of this meat you are not soiled by sin.

"All who partake of such food, commit sins in their ignorance; but the wise do nothing of the kind. Even to utter it is an untruth.

"In compassion to all beings, the seers, the Jnariputras, avoid what is sinful; afraid of it, they abstain from food especially prepared for them.

"They abstain from wicked deeds, afraid of injuring living beings, and do no harm to any creature; therefore they do not partake of such food. This is a maxim of the monks of our creed.

"Having reached this perfection in the Law of the Nirgranthas and standing firm in it, one should live without deceit. The awakened sage who is endowed with all virtues thereby obtained very great fame."

A Vedic Priest

'Those who always feed two thousand holy mendicants, acquire great merit and become gods. This is the teaching of the Veda.'

Ardraka

"He who always feeds two thousand holy cats, i.e., Brahmins, will have to endure great pains in hell, being surrounded by hungry beasts.

"He who despises the Law that enjoins compassion, and praises the Law that permits slaughter, and who feeds but a single unprincipled man, even if he be a king, will go to darkness, and not to the gods."

A Vedantin

'Both of us follow very much the same Law; we stood firm in it, and shall do so in the time to come; we believe that virtue consists in good conduct, and that knowledge is necessary for liberation; and with regard to the Circle of Births there is no difference between us.

'But we assume an invisible, great, eternal, imperishable, and indestructible Soul, who excels all other beings in every respect, as the moon excels the stars.'

Ardraka

"If there were but one Soul common to all beings they could not be known from one another, nor could they experience different lots; there would not be Brahmins, Kshatriyas, Vaisyas, and Sudras, insects, birds, and snakes; all would be men and gods.

"Those who do not know all things by Kevala knowledge, but who being ignorant teach a Law of their own, are lost themselves, and work the ruin of others in this dreadful, boundless Circle of Births.

"Those who know all things by the full Kevala knowledge, and who practising meditation teach the whole Law, are themselves saved and save others.

"You have, in your mind, made equal both those who lead a blameable life, and those who in this world practise right conduct. Friend, you are deluded."

A Hastitapasa

'Every year we kill one big elephant with an arrow, and live upon it in order to spare the life of other animals.'

Ardraka

"If every year you kill but one animal without abstaining from sin, though you are not guilty of the slaughter of other creatures, there is little difference between you and a householder.

"If a man kills every year but one animal, and lives in other respects as a Shramana, he is unworthy, and works his perdition. Such men will not become Kevalins."

A monk who has achieved his religious perfection through the instruction of the Awakened One, and stands firm in it, who guards himself in the threefold way, i.e., with regard to thoughts, words, and acts, and who possesses the things requisite for crossing the immense ocean of existence, may preach the Law.

Thus I say.

Beings, Movable and Immovable

At that time, at that period, there was a town of the name Rajagriha: it was rich, happy, thriving. Outside of Rajagriha, in a north-eastern direction, there was the suburb Nalanda; it contained many hundreds of buildings.

In that suburb Nalanda there was a householder called Lepa; he was prosperous, famous; rich in high and large houses, beds, seats, vehicles, and chariots; abounding in riches, gold, and silver; possessed of useful and necessary things; wasting plenty of food and drink; owning many male and female slaves, cows, buffaloes, and sheep; and inferior to nobody.

This householder Lepa, a follower of the Shramanas, comprehended the doctrine of living beings and things without life.

This householder Lepa possessed, in a northeastern direction from the suburb Nalanda, a bathing-hall, called Seshadravya; it contained many hundreds of pillars, was beautiful. In a northeastern direction from this bathing-hall Seshadravya, there was a park called Hastiyama.

And there in some house the Venerable Gautama was staying. The venerable man was in the garden, and so was Udaka, the son of Pedhala, a Nirgrantha and follower of Parsva, of the Medarya Gotra. He went there where the Venerable Gautama was, and said: 'O long-lived Gautama, I want to ask you about a point of faith; O long-lived one, please explain it to me so as it has been taught by the Tirthankara.' And the Venerable Gautama spoke thus to Udaka, the son of Pedhala: "Well, long-lived one, I shall see about it, when I have heard and understood your question." And Udaka, the son of Pedhala, spoke thus to the Venerable Gautama:

'O long-lived Gautama, there are Nirgrantha Shramanas, called Kumaraputras who profess your creed; they make a zealous householder, a follower of the Shramanas, renounce injury to movable beings except on the order from an establislied authority, as the householder caused one of the captured thieves to be set free. Those who make this renunciation, make a bad renunciation; those who cause this renunciation to be made, cause a bad renunciation to be made; in causing another to make this renunciation, they annul their own allegation. Why do I say this? Beings belong to the Circle of Births; though they be now immovable beings, they will some time become movable ones, or though they be now movable beings, they will become immovable ones; when they leave the bodies of immovable beings, they will be born in bodies of movable ones, and when they leave the bodies of movable beings, they will be born in bodies of immovable ones. When they are born in bodies of immovable beings, it is no sin to kill them.

'But if they make him renounce injury to creatures which are, for the time being, movable beings, except on the order from an established authority—as the householder caused one of the captured thieves to be set free—if they take this vow, those who make this renunciation, make a good renunciation; those who cause this renunciation to be made, cause a good renunciation to be made; in causing another to make this renunciation, they do not annul their own allegation. Though in this way a correct expression is found, some monks from anger or greed cause the householder to make the renunciation without the necessary restriction. Is not this our interpretation right? O long-lived Gautama, do you approve of it?'

And Gautama spoke thus to Udaka, the son of Pedhala: "O long-lived Udaka, we certainly do not approve of it. The Shramanas or Brahmins who say thus, speak thus, declare thus, and explain thus, do not speak as Shramanas or Nirgranthas, they speak noxious speech. They mislead laymen. They make void all vows undertaken for sparing particular living beings. Why do I say this? Beings belong to the Circle of Births; though they be now immovable beings, they will some time become movable ones, when they leave the bodies of movable beings, they will be born in the bodies of immovable ones. When they are born in the bodies of movable beings, it is a sin to kill them."

And Udaka, the son of Pedhala, spoke thus: 'Which beings do you call movable beings, movable ones or others?'

And Gautama spoke thus to Udaka, the son of Pedhala: "O long-lived Udaka, what you call beings which are, for the time being, movable ones, we call movable beings; and what we call movable beings, you call beings which are, for the time being, movable ones. Both expressions are equal, and mean the same thing. O long-lived one, why do you think it more correct to say: beings which are, for the time being, movable ones; and why do you think it incorrect to say: movable beings, that you censure the one expression, and applaud the other? This your interpretation is not right.

"And the Venerable One has spoken thus: Some men there are who say: we cannot, submitting to the tonsure, renounce the life of a householder and enter the monastic state, but we shall gradually conform to the Gotra, i.e., community of the monks. Accordingly they make known the limits fix the limits, determine the limits beyond which they will not go in the enjoyment of worldly goods; and renounce injury to movable beings, except on the order of an established authority—as the householder caused one of the captured thieves to be set free. And this turns out to their benefit.

"Movable beings are called so, when they get this character through the taking effect of the Karman relating to movable beings. But when their duration of life as movable beings comes to its close, the soul, embodied in a movable being, leaves its life as such and becomes embodied in an immovable being. Immovable beings are called so, when they get this character through the taking effect of the Karman relating to immovable beings. But when their duration of life as an immovable being comes to its close, the soul, embodied in an immovable being, leaves its life as such and takes again a new form of existence; they are then called animated beings, animals of large bodies, or of long life."

And Udaka, the son of Pedhala, spoke thus to the Venerable Gautama: 'Is there not a chance, that a follower of the Shramanas, though he has renounced slaughter of but one class of living beings, ceases altogether to injure any? Why do I say this? Beings belong to the Circle of Births, though they be now immovable beings, they will some time become movable ones, and though they be movable beings, they will become immovable ones. When they leave the. bodies of immovable beings, all are born in bodies of movable ones, and when they leave the bodies of movable beings, all will be born in bodies of immovable ones. When they are born in bodies of immovable beings, they may be killed.'

And the Venerable Gautama spoke thus to Udaka, the son of Pedhala: "O long-lived one, we do not admit what you say; that there is a chance that a follower of the Shramanas should cease to do injury to any kind of living beings. Why do we say this? Beings belong to the Circle of Births, when they are born in bodies of movable beings, it is a sin to kill them. They are called animated beings, animals of large bodies, or of long life. There are always a great many animate beings, the slaughter of which a follower of the Shramanas must renounce, there are none, the slaughter of which he need not renounce. If he ceases, or has done with, or has given up injuring the large class of movable beings, his renunciation is good. What you or somebody else says, that there is a chance of a layman's ceasing to do an injury altogether, by renouncing slaughter of one kind of beings; this interpretation of yours is not right."

The Venerable One gave an illustration: "I put a question to the Nirgranthas: O long-lived ones, suppose there be some men who have made the following declaration: ' I shall not inflict punishment on those who, submitting to the tonsure, renounce the life of a householder and enter the monastic state; but I shall inflict punishment on those who lead a domestic life.' Some Shramana., who for four or five years, or for six or ten years—the period may be shorter or longer—has wandered about in the land, returns to domestic life. Now answer me: does the man break his word when he puts to death this renegade householder? " 'Certainly not I' "It is just the same with a follower of the Shramanas, who has renounced injury to movable beings, but not to immovable ones. If he kills immovable beings, he does not transgress his vow. This you acknowledge, O Nirgranthas, this you must acknowledge!"

The Venerable One gave another illustration: "I put a question to the Nirgranthas. O long-lived Nirgranthas, suppose there be householders or sons of householders, born in respectable families, who come to you for instruction in the Law. Ought they to be instructed in the Law?" 'Yes, they should.' "When they have learned and understood this Law, will they say: this creed of the Nirgranthas is true, supreme, excellent, full of virtues, right, pure, it removes doubts, it is the road to perfection, liberation, Nirvana; it is free from error and doubts, it is the road of those who are free from all misery;

those who adopt it will reach perfection, put an end to all misery; exerting ourselves we shall control ourselves with regard to all kinds of living beings.—Will they speak thus?" ' Yes.' "Should such men be admitted to the order?" 'Yes, they should.' "Should such men be instructed in the discipline and kept to attend to religious instruction? " 'Yes, they should.' "Do they renounce injury to every living being?" 'Yes, they do.' "Now suppose one of these men who lead such a life, after wandering about in the land for four or five years, or for six or ten years—the period may be shorter or longer—returns to domestic life. Will this man still abstain from doing injury to every living being? " ' No.' " The same man who at first as a householder had not renounced injury to every living being, who afterwards has renounced, and who now does not renounce injury to every living being, did at first not control himself, did so afterwards, and does not so now. As long as he does not control himself, he does not renounce injury to every living being. This you acknowledge, O Nirgranthas, this you must acknowledge!"

The Venerable One gave another illustration: "I put a question to the Nirgranthas. O long-lived Nirgranthas, suppose there be monks or nuns of other sects, who come to you for instruction in the Law, all as before, down to attend to religious instruction." 'Yes, they should.' "Is it lawful to eat with such men? " 'Yes, it is.' "Now suppose some of these people lead such a life, domestic life. Is it lawful to eat with them then? " 'No, it is not.' "The same man with whom to eat was not lawful at first, was lawful afterwards, and is not lawful now, was no Shramana at first, was a Shramana afterwards, and is no Shramana now. It is not lawful for Nirgrantha Shramanas to eat together with him. This you acknowledge, O Nirgranthas; this you must acknowledge!"

And the Venerable One spoke thus: "There are some followers of the Shramanas, who have made this declaration: we cannot, submitting to the tonsure, renounce the life of a householder and enter the monastic state, but we shall strictly observe the Posaha on the fourteenth and the eighth days of each fortnight, on the new-moon, and full-moon days, we renounce gross ill-usage of living beings, grossly lying speech, gross taking of things not given, unlawful sexual intercourse, unlimited appropriation of property; we shall set limits to our desires in the two forms and in the three ways. They will also make the following renunciation: 'Neither do nor cause anything sinful to be done for my sake.'

Having on Posaha-days abstained from eating, drinking, bathing, and using beds or chairs, may they, on their decease, be said to make a righteous end of their life? " 'Certainly, they do make such an end of their life.' "They are called animated beings, this interpretation of yours is not right."

The Venerable One spoke thus: "There are some followers of the Shramanas, who have made this declaration: we cannot, submitting to the tonsure, renounce the life of a householder and enter the monastic state; we also cannot strictly observe the Posaha on the fourteenth and the eighth days of each fortnight, on the days of new-moon and full-moon; but while we are preparing ourselves for death by fasting, we shall abstain from food and drink without longing for the end; we shall renounce all ill-usage of living beings, all lying speech, all taking of things not given, all sexual intercourse, all property, saying: 'neither do nor cause anything sinful to be done for my sake.'

And the Venerable One spoke thus: "There are some men of great desires, great undertakings, etc., who do not abstain from all ill-usage of living beings, etc., During the whole time, from their taking the vows of a follower of the Shramanas till their death, they abstain from injury to living beings. Then they die; in their next existence they experience their Karman, and receive an evil lot."

And the Venerable One spoke thus: "There are some men of no desires, no undertakings, who abstain from all ill-usage of living beings, etc., During the whole time, from their taking the vows of a follower of the Shramanas till their death, they abstain from injury to living beings. Then they die; in their next existence they experience their Karman, and receive a happy lot."

And the Venerable One spoke thus: "There are some men who live in woods, in huts, near villages, or practise some secret rites, who are not well controlled, do not well abstain from slaying all sorts of living beings. They employ speech that is true and untrue at the same time: do not beat me, beat others, etc.; having died at their allotted time, they are born in some places inhabited by Asuras and evil-doers. And when they are released therefrom, they will be born deaf and dumb or blind. They are called animated beings."

And the Venerable One spoke thus: "There are some beings of a long life, which a follower of the Shramanas abstains from injuring through life. They die after him. They are called animated beings."

(The two next paragraphs treat in exactly the same way of beings of an equally long life, which die simultaneously with him, and of beings of a short life, which die before him.)

And the Venerable One spoke thus: "There are some followers of the Shramanas, who have made this declaration: We are not able to strictly observe the Posaha-days, but we are able, when preparing ourselves for death by fasting, to abstain from food and drink without longing for the end. The vow of such a man is the Samayika Desavakarika: he declares in the morning: I shall travel only thus or thus far in an eastern, western, southern, northern direction. He renounces injury to all beings: I shall cause peace and security to all sorts of living beings.

"Within those limits the movable living beings, which the follower of the Shramanas abstains from injuring till his death, will leave their life, and will then be born, within the same limits, as movable living beings, which the follower of the Shramanas abstains from injuring till his death. With regard to them the follower of the Shramanas has made a good renunciation. They are called animated beings, etc.

"The movable beings within those limits, etc., will, after

their death, be born within the same limits as immovable beings, from injuring which without a purpose the follower of the Shramanas abstains till death, but not with a purpose, etc.

"The movable beings within those limits, etc., will, after their death, be born, beyond those limits, as movable or immovable beings, etc.

"The immovable beings within those limits, etc., will, after their death, be born, within the same limits, as movable beings, etc.

"The immovable beings within those limits, etc., will, after their death, be born, within the same limits, as immovable beings, etc.

"The immovable beings within those limits, etc., will, after their death, be born, beyond those limits, as immovable beings, etc.

"The movable and immovable beings beyond those limits, etc., will, after their death, be born, within those limits, as movable beings, etc.

"The movable and immovable beings beyond those limits, etc., will, after their death, be born, within those limits, as immovable beings, etc.

"The movable and immovable beings beyond those limits, etc., will, after their death, be born, beyond those limits, as movable and immovable beings, etc."

The Venerable One spoke thus: "It has never happened, it does not happen, nor will it ever happen, that all movable beings will die out and become immovable ones, nor that all immovable beings die out and become movable ones. Since movable and immovable beings never die out, there is no chance, as you or somebody else say, that a layman ceases to do injury altogether by renouncing slaughter of one kind of beings; this interpretation of yours is not right."

And the Venerable One spoke thus: "If a man who has been instructed in right knowledge, faith, and conduct for the avoidance of sins, blames a righteous Shramana or Brahmin though he is well disposed towards them, he effects the loss of his merit for another world; but if he does not blame them, he heightens the purity of his merit for another world."

On this Udaka, the son of Pedhala, took no further notice of the Venerable Gautama and was about to return in the direction in which he had come.

And the Venerable One spoke thus: "O long-lived Udaka, he who has learned from a Shramana or Brahmin whomsoever even one noble religious truth, and considers himself thereby furthered with regard to his peace and happiness, will respect, acknowledge, praise, salute, honour, reverence, and worship him even as a blessed and holy deity or sacred shrine."

Then Udaka, the son of Pedhala, spoke thus to the Venerable Gautama: 'As I had not before known, heard, understood, and comprehended these words, I did not believe in the meaning of your words, which I had never perceived nor heard nor understood nor appreciated, and which were never explained nor defined nor delivered nor made clear to me, nor pondered over by me. But how, Reverend Sir, as I do know, etc., these words which I have perceived, heard, etc., I believe, accept, and approve of their meaning. It is just as you say!'

Then the Venerable Gautama spoke thus to Udaka, the son of Pedhala: "Believe it, sir; accept it, sir; approve of it, sir; it is just as we have said." Then Udaka, the son of Pedhala, spoke thus to the Venerable Gautama: 'I desire, Reverend Sir, in your presence to pass from the creed which enjoins four vows, to the creed which enjoins the five great vows and the Pratikramana.'

Then the Venerable Gautama went with Udaka, the son of Pedhala, to the Venerable Ascetic Mahavira. Then Udaka, the son of Pedhala, solemnly circumambulated the Venerable Ascetic Mahavira three times from the left to the right, and having done so he praised and worshipped him, and then he spoke thus: 'I desire, Reverend Sir, in your presence to pass from the creed which enjoins four vows, to the creed which enjoins the five great vows and the Pratikramana. May it so please you, beloved of the gods, do not deny me!' Then, in the presence of the Venerable Ascetic Mahavira, Udaka, the son of Pedhala, passed from the creed which enjoins four vows, to the creed which enjoins the five great vows and the Pratikramana.

Thus I say.

Getting the White Lotus

O long-lived Jambusvamin! I Sudharman have heard the following discourse from the Venerable Mahavira. We now come to the Lecture called 'the Lotus.' The contents of it are as follows:

There is a lotus-pool containing much water and mud, very full and complete, answering to the idea one has of a lotus-pool, full of white lotuses, delightful, conspicuous, magnificent, and splendid.

And everywhere all over the lotus-pool there grew many white lotuses, the best of Nymphaeas, as we are told, in beautiful array, tall, brilliant, of fine colour, smell, taste, and touch, etc., all down to splendid.

And in the very middle of this lotus-pool there grew one big white lotus, the best of Nymphaeas, as we are told, in an excellent position, tall, splendid.

Now there came a man from the Eastern quarter to the lotus-pool, and standing on the bank of it he saw that one big white lotus. Now this man spoke thus: ' I am a knowing, clever, well-informed, discerning, wise, not foolish man, who keeps the way, knows the way, and is acquainted with the direction and bent of the way. I shall fetch tliat white lotus, the best of all Nymphaeas.' Having said this the man entered the lotus-pool. And the more he proceeded, the more the water and the mud seemed to extend. He had left the shore, and he did not come up to the white lotus, the best of Nymphaeas, he could not get hack to this bank, nor to the opposite one, but in the middle of the lotus-pool he stuck in the mud.

This was the first man. Now we shall describe the second man. There came a man from the Southern quarter to the lotus-pool, and standing on the bank of it he saw that one big white lotus. There he saw one man who had left the shore, but had not come up to the white lotus, the best of Nymphaeas, who could not get back to his bank, nor to the opposite one, but stuck in the mud in the middle of the lotus-pool. Now the second man spoke of the first man thus: 'This man is not knowing, not clever, not acquainted with the direction and bent of the way.' For that man said: 'I am a knowing, clever man, I shall fetch that white lotus, the best of Nymphaeas.' But this white lotus, the best of Nymphaeas, cannot be got in the way this man tried.

'However, he stuck in the mud. This was the second man. The same thing happened to a third and a fourth man, who came from the Western and Northern quarters respectively, and saw two and three men respectively sticking in the mud.

Now a monk living on low food and desiring to get to the shore of the Samsara, knowing, clever, etc., acquainted with the direction and bent of the way, came to that lotus-pool from some one of the four quarters or from one of the intermediate points of the compass. Standing on the bank of the lotus-pool he saw the one big white lotus. And he saw there those four men who having left the shore, stuck in the mud. Then the monk said: 'These men are not knowing, not acquainted with the direction and bent of the way; for these men thought: We shall fetch that white lotus, the best of Nymphaeas. But this white lotus, the best of Nymphaeas, cannot be got in the way these men tried. I am a monk living on low food, acquainted with the direction and bent of the way. I shall fetch that white lotus, the best of Nymphaeas.' Having said this the monk did not enter the lotus-pool; but standing on the bank of it he raised his voice: 'Fly up, O white lotus, best of Nymphaeas!' And the white lotus, the best of Nymphaeas, flew up.

I have told you, O long-lived Shramanas, a simile; you must comprehend the meaning of it. The Nirgrantha monks and nuns worshipped and praised the Venerable Ascetic Mahavira, and then spoke thus: 'You have told, O long-lived Sramana, the simile, but we do not comprehend its meaning, O long-lived Sramana!' The Venerable Ascetic Mahavira addressed the crowd of Nirgrantha monks and nuns, and spoke thus: Ah, you long-lived Shramanas! I shall tell, declare, explain, expound, and demonstrate it with its meaning, reasons, and arguments. Thus I say:

O long-lived Shramanas, meaning the world I spoke of the lotus-pool. Meaning Karman I spoke of the water. Meaning pleasures and amusements I spoke of the mud. Meaning people in general I spoke of those many white lotuses, the best of Nymphaeas. Meaning the king I spoke of the one big white lotus, the best of Nymphaeas. Meaning heretical teachers I spoke of those four men. Meaning the Law I spoke of the monk. Meaning the church I spoke of the bank. Meaning the preaching of the Law I spoke of the monk's voice. Meaning Nirvana. I spoke of the lotus' flying up. Meaning these things, O long-lived Shramanas, I told this simile.

Here in the East, West, North, and South many men have been born according to their merit, as inhabitants of this our world, some as Aryas, some as non-Aryas, some in noble families, some in low families, some as big men, some as small men, some of good complexion, some of bad complexion, some as handsome men, some as ugly men. And of these men one man is king, who is strong like the great Himavat, Malaya, Mandara, and Mahendra mountains, who governs his kingdom in which all riots and mutinies have been suppressed.

And this king had an assembly of Ugras and sons of Ugras, Bhogas and sons of Bhogas, Aikshvakas and sons of Aikshvakas, Jnatris and sons of Jnatris, Kauravas and sons of Kauravas, warriors and sons of warriors, Brahmins and sons of Brahmins, Lichchhavis and sons of Lichchhavis, commanders and sons of commanders, generals and sons of generals.

And of these men some one is full of faith. Forsooth, the

Shramanas or Brahmins made up their mind to go to him. Being professors of some religion they thought: We shall teach him our religion.' And they said: 'Know this, dear sir, that we explain and teach this religion well.

'Upwards from the soles of the feet, downwards from the tips of the hair on the head, within the skin's surface is what is called Soul, or what is the same, the Atman. The whole soul lives; when this body is dead, it does not live. It lasts as long as the body lasts, it does not outlast the destruction of the body. With it the body ends life. Other men carry. the corpse away to burn it. When it has been consumed by fire, only dove-coloured bones remain, and the four bearers return with the hearse to their village. Therefore, there is and exists no soul different from the body. Those who believe that there is and exists no such soul, speak the truth. Those who maintain that the soul is something different from the body, cannot tell whether the soul as separated from the body is long or small, whether globular or circular or triangular or square or sexagonal or octagonal or long, whether black or blue or red or yellow or white, whether of sweet smell or of bad smell, whether bitter or pungent or astringent or sour or sweet, whether hard or soft or heavy or light or cold or hot or smooth or rough. Those, therefore, who believe that there is and exists no soul, speak the truth. Those who maintain that the soul is something different from the body, do not see the following objections:

'As a man draws a sword from the scabbard and shows it you, saying: "Friend, this is the sword, and that is the scabbard," so nobody can draw the soul from the body and show it you, saying: "Friend, this is the soul, and that is the body." As a man draws a fibre from a stalk of Munga grass and shows it you, saying: "Friend, this is the stalk, and that is the fibre;" or takes a bone out of the flesh, or the seed of Amalaka from the palm of his hand, or a particle of fresh butter out of coagulated milk, and shows you both things separately; or as he presses oil from the seed of Atasi, and shows the oil and oilcake separately, or as he presses the juice from the sugar-cane and shows the juice and the molasses separately, so nobody can show you the soul and the body separately. The same applies also when fire is churned from Arani-wood. Those who believe that there is and exists no soul, speak the truth. Those who say that the soul is different from the body, are wrong.'

This murderer says: 'Kill, dig, slay, burn, cook, cut or break to pieces, destroy! Life ends here; there is no world beyond.'

These Nastikas cannot inform you on the following points: whether an action is good or bad, meritorious or not, well done or not well done, whether one reaches perfection or not, whether one goes to hell or not. Thus undertaking various works they engage in various pleasures and amusements for their own enjoyment.

Thus some shameless men becoming monks propagate a Law of their own. And others believe it, put their faith in it, adopt it, saying: 'Well, you speak the truth, O Brahmin, or O Shramana! We shall present you with food, drink, spices, and sweetmeats, with a robe, a bowl, or a broom.'

Some have been induced to honour them, some have made their proselytes to honour them.

Before entering an order they were determined to become Shramanas, houseless, poor monks who would have neither sons nor cattle, to eat only what should be given them by others, and to commit no sins. After having entered their order they do not cease from sins, they themselves commit sins, they cause others to commit sins, and they assent to another's committing sins. Thus they are given to pleasures, amusements, and sensual lust; they are greedy, fettered, passionate, covetous, the slaves of love and hate; therefore they cannot free themselves from the Circle of Births, nor free anybody else from it, nor free any other of the four kinds of living beings from it. They have left their former occupations, but have not entered the noble path. They cannot return to worldly life, nor get beyond it; they stick as it were in pleasures and amusements. Thus I have treated of the first man as one who believes that soul and body are one and the same thing.

Now I shall treat of the second man as one who believes that everything consists of the five elements.

Here in the East, they teach this religion well.

'There are five elements through which we explain whether an action is good or bad, etc. Everything down to a blade of grass consists of them.

'And one should know the intermixture of the elements by an enumeration of them. Earth is the first element, water the second, fire the third, wind the fourth, and air the fifth. These five elements are not created, directly or indirectly, nor made; they are not effects nor products; they are without beginning and end; they always produce effects, are independent of a directing cause or everything else; they are eternal. Some, however, say that there is a Self besides the five elements. What is, does not perish; from nothing nothing comes.

'All living beings, all things, the whole world consists of nothing but these five elements. They are the primary cause of the world, even down to a blade of grass.

'A man buys and causes to buy, kills and causes to kill, cooks and causes to cook, he may even sell and kill a man. Know, that even in this case he does not do wrong.'

These Nastikas cannot inform you.

Thus I have treated of the second man who believes that everything consists of the five elements.

Now I shall treat of the third man who believes that the Self is the cause of everything.

Here in the East, they teach this religion well.

'Here all things have the Self for their cause and their object, they are produced by the Self, they are manifested by the Self, they are intimately connected with the Self, they are bound up in the Self.

'As, for instance, a tumour is generated in the body, grows with the body, is not separate from the body, but is bound up in the body: so all things have the Self for their cause.

'As, for instance, a feeling of indisposition is generated in the body, grows with the body, is never separate from the body, but is bound up in the body: so all things have the Self for their cause.

'As, for instance, an anthill is made of earth, grows through earth, is not separate from earth, but is bound up in earth: so all things have the Self for their cause.

'As, for instance, a tree springs up on earth, grows on earth, is not separate from earth, but is bound up in earth: so all things have the Self for their cause.

'As, for instance, a lotus springs up in earth, grows on earth, is not separate from earth, but is bound up in earth: so all things have the Self for their cause.

'As, for instance, a mass of water is produced by water, grows through water, is not separate from water, but is bound up in water: so all things have the Self for their cause.

'As, for instance, a water-bubble is produced in water, grows in water, is not separate from water, but is bound up in water: so all things have the Self for their cause.

'And the twelve Angas, the Canon of the Ganins, which has been taught, produced, and declared by the Shramanas, the Nirgranthas, viz., the Aharanga all down to the Drishtivada, is wrong, not true, not a representation of the truth; but this our doctrine is correct, is true, is a representation of the truth.'

The heretics in question make this assertion, they uphold this assertion, they try to establish this assertion.

Therefore they cannot get out of the misery produced by this error, even as a bird cannot get out of its cage.

These heretics cannot inform you.

Thus I have treated of the third man who believes that the Self is the cause of everything.

Now I shall treat of the fourth man who believes that Fate is the cause of everything.

Here in the East, they teach this religion well.

'There are two kinds of men. One man admits action, another man does not admit action. Both men, he who admits action, and he who does not admit action, are alike, their case is the same, because they are actuated by the same force.

'An ignorant man thinks about the cause as follows: "When I suffer, grieve, blame myself, grow feeble, am afflicted, or undergo great pain, I have caused it; or when another man suffers, he has caused it." Thus an ignorant man thinks himself or another man to be the cause of what he or the other man experiences.

'A wise man thinks about the cause as follows: "When I suffer, I did not cause it; and when another man suffers, he did not cause it."

'A wise man thinks thus about the cause of what he himself or another man experiences. I say this: "Movable or immovable beings in all the four quarters, by the will of Fate come to have a body, to undergo the vicissitudes of life, to lose their body, to arrive at some state of existence, to experience pleasure and pain." '

Entertaining such opinions these heretics cannot inform you.

These worthless men entertain such opinions, and believe in them till they cannot return.

I have treated of the fourth man who believes that Fate is the cause of everything.

These four men, differing in intellect, will, character, opinions, taste, undertakings, and plans, have left their former occupations, but have not entered the noble path. They cannot return to worldly life nor get beyond it; they stick as it were in pleasures and amusements.

I say: here in the East, West, North, and South there are some men, Aryas, non-Aryas, etc., all down to ugly men. They own small or large houses and fields, they own few or many servants and peasants. Being born in such-like families, they renounce their possessions and lead a mendicant's life. Some leave their kinsmen and their property to lead a mendicant's life; others, who have no kinsmen nor property, lead a mendicant's life. Whether they have kinsmen and property or not, they renounce them and lead a mendicant's life.

Previously, however, they thought thus: 'Here, indeed, a man, who is on the point of turning monk, makes the following reflections with regard to different things: I possess fields, houses, silver, gold, riches, corn, copper, clothes, real valuable property, riches, gold, precious stones, jewels, pearls, conches, stones, corals, rubies. I enjoy sounds, colours, smells, tastes, and feelings of touch. These pleasures and amusements belong to me, and I belong to them.'

A wise man, previously, should thus think to himself: 'Here, indeed, some painful illness or disease might befall me, unwished for, unpleasant, disagreeable, nasty, painful and not at all pleasant. O ye dear pleasures, take upon you this painful illness or disease, unwished for, unpleasant, disagreeable, nasty, painful and not at all pleasant, that I may not suffer, grieve, blame myself, grow feeble, be afflicted, and undergo great pain. Deliver me from this painful illness or disease. But this desire of his has never yet been fulfilled.

Here, in this life, pleasures and amusements are not able to help or to save one. Sometimes a man first forsakes pleasures and amusements, sometimes they first forsake him. Pleasures and amusements are one thing, and I am another. Why then should we be infatuated with pleasures and amusements which are alien to our being? Taking this into consideration, we shall give up pleasures and amusements. A wise man thinks them alien to himself.

There are things more intimately connected with me, my mother, father, brother, sister, wife, children, grandchildren, daughters-in-law, servants, friends, kinsmen, companions, and acquaintances. These my relations belong to me, and I belong to them. A wise man, previously, should think thus to himself: 'Here, indeed, some painful illness or disease might befall me".

'Or some painful illness or disease, unwished for, might befall my dear relations. I will take upon me this painful illness or disease, that they may not suffer, undergo great pain. I will deliver them from this painful illness or disease.' But this desire of his has never yet been fulfilled. For one man cannot take upon himself the pains of another; one man cannot experience what another has done.

Individually a man is born, individually he dies, individually he falls from this state of existence, individually he rises to another. His passions, consciousness, intellect, perceptions, and impressions belong to the individual exclusively. Here, indeed, the bonds of relationship are not able to help nor save one.'

There are things more intimately connected with me, my hands, feet, arms, legs, head, belly, character, life, strength, colour, skin, complexion, ear, eye, nose, tongue, and touch; they are part and parcel of me. But I grow old. The strong joints become loose, the body is furrowed with wrinkles, the black hair turns white, even this dear body which has grown with food, must be relinquished in due time.

Making such reflections, a monk should lead a mendicant's life and know that all things are divided into living beings and things without life, and living beings again into movable and immovable ones.

Here, indeed, householders are killers of beings and acquirers of property, and so are even some Shramanas and Brahmins. They themselves kill movable and immovable living beings, have them killed by another person, or consent to another's killing them.

Here, indeed, householders are killers of beings and acquirers of property, and so are even some Shramanas and Brahmins. They themselves acquire sentient or senseless objects of pleasure, have them acquired by another person, or consent to another's acquiring them.

Here, indeed, householders are killers of beings and acquirers of property, and so are even some Shramanas and Brahmins. But I am no killer of beings nor an acquirer of property. Relying upon householders and such Shramanas and Brahmins as are killers of beings and acquirers of property, we shall lead a life of chastity. He should, however, part company with them. The pupil asks: What is the reason thereof? The teacher answers: As before their ordination they were killers of beings, so they will be afterwards, and vice versa,. It is evident that householders do not abstain from sins nor exert themselves in control; and as monks they will relapse into the same bad habits.

The householders and those Shramanas and Brahmins, who are killers of beings and acquirers of property, commit sins both from love and hatred. But a monk who takes this into consideration, should lead a life subject to neither love nor hatred.

I say: in the East, West, North, and South a true monk will have renounced works, be exempt from works, will have put an end to them. This has been taught by the prophets.

The Venerable One has declared that the cause of sins are the six classes of living beings, earth-lives, etc. As is my pain when I am knocked or struck with a stick, bone, fist, clod, or potsherd; or menaced, beaten, burned, tormented, or deprived of life; and as I feel every pain and agony from death down to the pulling out of a hair: in the same way, be sure of this, all kinds of living beings feel the same pain and agony, as I, when they are ill-treated in the same way. For this reason all sorts of living beings should not be beaten, nor treated with violence, nor abused, nor tormented, nor deprived of life.

I say: the Arhats and Bhagavats of the past, present, and future, all say thus, speak thus, declare thus, explain thus: all sorts of living beings should not be slain, nor treated with violence, nor abused, nor tormented, nor driven away. This constant, permanent, eternal, true Law has been taught by wise men who comprehend all things. Thus a monk abstains from the five cardinal sins: slaughter of living beings, etc. He does not clean his teeth with a tooth-brush, he does not accept collyrium, emetics, and perfumes.

A monk who does not act, nor kill, who is free from

wrath, pride, deceit, and greed, who is calm and happy, should not entertain the following wish: May I, after my departure from this world, by dint of my intellect, knowledge, memory, learning, or of the performance of austerities, religious duties, chastity, or of this habit to eat no more than is necessary to sustain life, become a god at whose command are all objects of pleasure, or a perfected saint who is exempt from pain and misery. Through his austerities he may obtain his object, or he may not obtain it.

A monk should not be infatuated with sounds, colours, smells, tastes, and feelings of touch; he should abstain from wrath, pride, deceit, and greed, from love, hate, quarrel, calumny, reviling of others, aversion to control and delight in sensual things, deceit and untruth, and the sin of wrong belief. In this way a monk ceases to acquire gross Karman, controls himself, and abstains from sins.

He does not kill movable or immovable beings, nor has them killed by another person, nor does he consent to another's killing them. In this way a monk ceases to acquire gross Karman, controls himself, and abstains from sins.

He does not acquire sentient or senseless objects of pleasure, nor has them acquired by another person, nor does he consent to another's acquiring them.

He does no actions arising from sinful causes, nor has them done by another person, nor does he consent to another's doing them.

A monk should not take food, drink, dainties, and spices when he knows that the householder to satisfy him, or for the sake of a co-religionist, has bought or stolen or taken it, though it was not given nor to be taken, but was taken by force, by acting sinfully towards all sorts of living beings; nor does he cause another person to eat it, nor does he consent to another's eating it.

A monk may think as follows: The householders have the means to procure food for those for whose sake it is prepared; viz. for himself, his sons, daughters, daughters-in-law, nurses, relations, chiefs, male and female slaves, male and female servants; for a treat of sweetmeats, for a supper, for a breakfast the collation has been prepared. This food is to be eaten by some people, it is prepared by some one else, it is destined for some one else, it is free from the faults occasioned either by the giver or by the receiver or by the act of receiving it, rendered pure, rendered free from living matter, wholly free from living things, it has been begged, has been given to the monk on account of his profession, it has been collected in small bits, it is food fit for a learned monk, it is lawful to eat it at the presenrt occasion, it is of the prescribed quantity, it greases, as it were, the axle of the carriage and anoints the sore, being just sufficient to enable one to practise control and to carry the burden of it; he should consume that food without delay even as the snake returning to its hole; that is to say: one should eat when it is time for eating, drink when it is time for drinking, dress when it is time for dressing, seek cover when it is time for seeking cover, and sleep when it is time for sleeping.

When a monk preaches the Law, he should preach it not for food, drink, clothes, resting-place, or lodging, nor for any objects of pleasure; but he should preach the Law indefatigably, for no other motive than the annihilation of Karman.

Those heroes of faith who are instructed in the Law by such a monk and exert themselves well, are possessed of all virtues, abstain from all sins, cease from all passions, conduct themselves well in every way, and reach final beatitude.

Such a monk searches the Law, knows the Law, and endeavours to gain Liberation; as it has been said: 'He may get the white lotus, the best of Nymphaeus, or he may not get it.' Such a monk knows and renounces actions, worldly occupations, and the life of a householder; he is free from passions, possesses the Samitis, is wise, always exerts himself; he is to be called: a Sramana, a Brahmin, calm, a subduer of his senses, guarding himself, liberated, a seer, a sage, virtuous, wise, a monk, living on low food, desiring to get to the shore of the Samsara, fulfilling the general and particular virtues.

Thus I say.

6

Kalpa Sutra

Lives of Tirthankaras
Mahavira

Obeisance to the Arhats!
Obeisance to the Liberated Ones!
Obeisance to the Religious Guides!
Obeisance to the Religious Instructors!
Obeisance to all Saints in the World!

This fivefold obeisance, destroying all sins, is of all benedictions the principal benediction.

In that period, in that age lived the Venerable Ascetic Mahavira, the five most important moments of whose life happened when the moon was in conjunction with the asterism Uttaraphalguni; in Uttaraphalguni he descended from heaven and having descended, he entered the womb of Devananda; in Uttaraphalguni he was removed from the womb of Devananda to the womb of Trishala; in Uttaraphalguni he was born; in Uttaraphalguni, tearing out his hair, he left the house and entered the state of houselessness; in Uttaraphalguni he obtained the highest knowledge and intuition, called Kevala, which is infinite, supreme, unobstructed, unimpeded, complete, and perfect. But in Svati the Venerable One obtained final liberation.

•

In that period, in that age the Venerable Ascetic Mahavira, having on the sixth day of the fourth month of summer, in the eighth fortnight, the light fortnight of Ashadha, descended from the great Vimana, the all-victorious and all-prosperous Pushpottara, which is like the lotus amongst the best things, where he had lived for twenty Sagaropamas till the termination of his allotted length of life, of his divine nature, and of his existence among gods; here in the continent of Jambudvipa, in Bharatavarsha—when of this Avasarpini era the Sushama-sushama, the Sushama, and Sushamaduhshama periods, and the greater part of the Duhshamasushama period, containing a Kodakodi of Sagaropamas, less forty-two thousand years, had elapsed, and only seventy-two years, eight and a half months were left, after twenty-one Tirthankaras of the race of Ikshvaku and of the Kashyapa gotra, and two of the race of Hari and of the Gautama gotra, on the whole twenty-three Tirthankaras had appeared,—the Venerable Ascetic Mahavira, the last of the Tirthakaras, took the form of an embryo in the womb of Devananda of the Jalandharayana gotra, the wife of the Brahmin Rishabhadatta, of the gotra of Kodala, in the brahmanical part of the town Kundagrama in the middle of the night, when the moon was in conjunction with the asterism Uttaraphalguni, after his alotted length of life, of his divine nature, and of his existence amongst gods had come to their termination.

The knowledge of the Venerable Ascetic Mahavira about this was threefold; he knew that he was to descend, he knew that he had descended, he knew not when he was descending.

In that night in which the Venerable Ascetic Mahavira took the form of an embryo in the womb of the Brahmini Devananda of the Jalandharayana gotra, the Brahmini Devananda was on her couch, taking fits of sleep, in a state between sleeping and waking, and having seen the following fourteen illustrious, beautiful, lucky, blest, auspicious, fortunate great dreams, she woke up. To wit:

An elephant, a bull, a lion, the anointing of the goddess Sri, a garland, the moon, the sun, a flag, a vase, a lotus lake, the ocean, a celestial abode, a heap of jewels, and a flame.

When the Brahmini Devananda, having seen these dreams, woke up, she—glad, pleased, and joyful in her mind, delighted, extremely enraptured, with a heart widening under the influence of happiness, with the hair of her body all erect in their pores like the flowers of the Kadamba touched by rain-drops—firmly fixed the dreams in her mind, and rose from her couch. Neither hasty nor trembling, with a quick and even gait, like that of the royal swan, she went to the Brahmin Rishabhadatta, and gave him the greeting of victory. Then she comfortably sat down in an excellent chair of state; calm and composed, joining the palms of her hands so as to bring the ten nails together, she laid the folded hands on her head, and spoke thus:

'O beloved of the gods, I was just now on my couch taking fits of sleep, in a state between sleeping and waking, when I saw the following fourteen illustrious, etc., great dreams; to wit, an elephant, etc.

'O beloved of the gods, what, to be sure, will be the happy, result portended by these fourteen illustrious, etc., great dreams?'

When the Brahmin Rishabhadatta had heard and perceived this news from the Brahmini Devananda, he, glad, pleased, and joyful firmly fixed the dreams in his mind, and entered upon considering them. He grasped the meaning of those dreams with his own innate intellect and intuition, which were preceded by reflection, and thus spoke to the Brahmini Devananda:

'O beloved of the gods, you have seen illustrious dreams; O beloved of the gods, you have seen beautiful, lucky, blest, auspicious, fortunate dreams, which will bring health, joy, long life, bliss, and fortune! We shall have success, O beloved of the gods, we shall have pleasure; we shall have happiness, O beloved of the gods, we shall have a son! Indeed, O beloved of the gods, after the lapse of nine complete months and seven and a half days you will give birth to a lovely and handsome boy with tender hands and feet, with a body containing the entire and complete five organs of sense, with the lucky signs, marks, and good qualities; a boy on whose body all limbs will be well formed, and of full volume, weight, and length, of a lovely figure like that of the moon! And this boy, after having passed his childhood, and, with just ripened intellect, having reached the state of youth, will repeat, fully understand, and well retain in his mind the four Vedas: the Rig-veda, Yajur-veda, Sama-veda, Atharva-veda—to which the Itihasa is added as a fifth, and the Nigghantu as a sixth—together with their Angas and Upangas, and the Rahasya; he will know the six Angas, he will be versed in the philosophy of the sixty categories, and well grounded in arithmetic, in phonetics, ceremonial, grammar, metre, etymology, and astronomy, and in many other brahmanical and monastic sciences besides. Therefore, O beloved of the gods, you have seen illustrious dreams, etc.

In this way he repeatedly expressed his extreme satisfaction.

When the Brahmini Devananda had heard and perceived this news from the Brahmin Rishabhadatta, she—glad, pleased, and joyful, etc. joining the palms of her hands, spoke thus:

'That is so, O beloved of the gods; that is exactly so, O beloved of the gods; that is true, O beloved of the gods; that is beyond doubt, O beloved of the gods; that is what I desire, O beloved of the gods; that is what I accept, O beloved of the gods; that's what I desire and accept, O beloved of the gods; that matter is really such as you have pronounced it.'

Thus saying, she accepted the true meaning of the dreams, and enjoyed together with Rishabhadatta the noble permitted pleasures of human nature.

In that period, in that age, Shakra,—the chief and king of the gods, the wielder of the thunderbolt, the destroyer of towns, the performer of a hundred sacrifices, the thousand-eyed one, Maghavan, the punisher of the Daitya Paka, the lord of the southern half of the earth, the lord of the thirty-two thousand celestial abodes, the bestrider of the elephant

Airavata, the chief of the Suras, who wears spotless clothes and robes, and puts on garlands and the diadem, whose cheeks were stroked by fine, bright, and trembling earrings of fresh gold, the most prosperous, the most brilliant, the most mighty, the most glorious, the most powerful, and the most happy one, with a splendid body, ornamented with a long down-reaching garland,—this Shakra was in the Saudharma Kalpa, in the celestial abode Saudharma Avatamshaka, in the council-hall Sudharman, on his throne Shakra; he who exercises and maintains the supreme command, government, management, guidance, direction, and sovereign power and generalship over the thirty-two thousand gods of the celestial abodes, the eighty-four thousand gods of a rank equal with that of himself, the thirty-two chief gods, the four guardians of the world, the eight principal queens with their trains, the three courts, the seven armies, and the seven commanders of these armies. He was then enjoying the permitted pleasures of divine nature under the great din of uninterrupted story-telling, dramatical plays, singing, and music, as beating of time, performance on the Vina, the Turya, the great drum, and the Patupataha.

And he viewed this whole continent Jambudvipa with his extensive knowledge called Avadhi. There he saw in the continent Jambudvipa, in Bharatavarsha, in the southern half of Bharata, in the Brahminical part of the town Kundagrama, the Venerable Ascetic Mahavira taking the form of an embryo in the womb of the Brahmin Devananda of the Jalandharayana gotra, wife of the Brahmin Rishabhadatta of the gotra of Kodala; and—glad, pleased, and joyful in his mind, delighted, extremely enraptured, with a heart widening under the influence of happiness, with the hair of his body bristling and erect in their pores like the fragrant flowers of Nipa when touched by rain-drops, with his eyes and mouth open like fullblown lotuses, with his excellent, various, trembling bracelets, with diadem and earrings, his breast lighted up by necklaces, wearing long and swinging ornaments with a pearl pendant—the chief of the gods rose with confusion, hasty and trembling from his throne, descended from the footstool, took off his shoes which were by a clever artist set with Vaidurya and excellent Rishta and Angana, and ornamented with glittering jewels and precious stones, threw his seamless robe over his left shoulder, and, arranging the fingers of his hands in the shape of a bud, he advanced seven or eight steps towards the Tirthankara. Bending his left knee and reposing on the right one, he three times placed his head on the ground and lifted it a little; then he raised his bracelet-encumbered arms, and joining the palms of his hands so as to bring the ten nails together, laid the hands on his head and spoke thus:

'Reverence to the Arhats and Bhagavats; to the Adikaras, the Tirthankaras, the perfectly-enlightened ones; to the highest of men, the lions among men, the flowers among mankind the Gandhahastins among men; to the highest in the world, the guides of the world, the benefactors of the world, the lights of the world, the enlighteners of the world; to the givers of safety, to the givers of sight, to the givers of the road, to the givers of shelter, to the givers of life, to the givers of knowledge; to the givers of the law, the preachers of the law, the lords of the law, the leaders of the law, the universal emperors of the best law; to the light, the help, the shelter, the refuge, the resting-place, the possessors of unchecked knowledge and intuition who have got rid of unrighteousness; to the conquerors and the granters of conquest, the saved and the saviours, the enlightened and the enlighteners, the liberated and the liberators, to the all-knowing ones, the all-seeing ones, to those who have reached the happy, stable, unstained, infinite, imperishable, undecaying place, called the path of perfection, whence there is no return; reverence to the Jinas who have conquered fear.

'Reverence to the Venerable Ascetic Mahavira, the Adikara, the last of the Tirthankaras who was predicted by the former Tirthankaras, etc. I here adore the Revered One yonder, see me here!' With these words he adored, he worshipped the Venerable Ascetic Mahavira, and sat down on his excellent throne facing the east. Then the following internal, reflectional, desirable idea occurred to the mind of Sakra, the chief of kings and gods:

'It never has happened, nor does it happen, nor will it happen, that Arhats, Chakravartins, Baladevas, or Vasudevas, in the past, present, or future, should be born in low families, mean families, degraded families, poor families, indigent families, beggars' families, or brahminical families. For indeed Arhats, Chakravartins, Baladevas, and Vasudevas, in the past, present, and future, are born in high families, noble families, royal families, noblemen's families, in families belonging to the race of Ikshvaku, or of Hari, or in other such-like families of pure descent on both sides.

Now this is something which moves the wonder of the world: it happens in the lapse of numberless Avasarpinis and Utsarpinis, because the imperishable, indescribable, and undestroyable Karman relating to name and gotra must take effect, that Arhats, etc., in the past, present, and future, descend in, i.e., take the form of an embryo in the womb of a woman belonging to low families, etc.; but they are never brought forth by birth from such a womb. This Venerable Ascetic Mahavira, now, in the continent Jambudvipa, in Bharatavarsha, in the brahminical part of the town Kundagrama, has taken the form of an embryo in the womb of the Brahmini Devananda of the Jalandharayana gotra, wife of the Brahmin Rishabhadatta of the gotra of Kodala. Hence it is the established custom of all past, present, and future Sakras, chiefs and kings of the gods, to cause the Arhats and Bhagavats to be removed from such-like low, mean, families, to such-like high, noble, families. It is, therefore, better that I should cause the Venerable Ascetic Mahavira, the last of the Tirthankaras who was predicted by the former Tirthankaras, to be removed from the brahminical part of the town Kundagrama, from the womb of the Brahmini Devananda. of the Jalandharayana gotra, wife of the Brahmin Rishabhadatta of the gotra of Kodala to the Kshatriya part of the town Kundagrama, and to be placed as an embryo in the womb of the Kshatriyani Trisala of the Vasishtha gotra, wife of the Kshatriya Siddhartha of the Kashyapa gotra, belonging to the clan of the Jnatri Kshatriyas; and to cause the embryo of the Kshatriyani Trisala of the Vasishtha gotra to be placed in the womb of the Brahmini Devananda of the Jalandharayana gotra.'

Thus he reflected and called Harimegamesi, the divine commander of the foot troops; having called him, he spoke thus:

' Well, now, beloved of the gods, it never has happened. Therefore, go now and remove the Venerable Ascetic Mahavira from the brahmanical part, and place the embryo of the Kshatriyani Trisala, Having done this, return quickly to report on the execution of my orders.'

When Harinegamesi, the divine commander of the foot troops, was thus spoken to by Sakra, the chief and king of the gods, he—glad, pleased, and joyful—laid his folded hands on his head and modestly accepted the words of command, saying, 'Just as your Majesty commands.' After this he left the presence of Sakra, the chief and king of the gods, and descended towards the northeastern quarter; then he transformed himself through his magical power of transformation, and stretched himself out for numerous Yojanas like a staff, during which he seized jewels, Vajra, Vaidurya, Lohitaksha, Masaragalla, Hamsagarbha, Pulaka, Saugandhika, Jyotisara, Anjana, Anjanapulaka, Jatarupa, Subhaga, Sphatika, and Rishta; of these precious materials he rejected the gross particles, and retained the subtle particles. Then for a second time he transformed himself through his magical power of transformation, and produced the definitive form which gods adopt on entering the world of men; having done so, he passed with that excellent, hasty, trembling, active, impetuous, victorious, exalted, and quick divine motion of the gods right through numberless continents and oceans, and arrived in Jambudvipa, in Bharatavarsha, in the brahminical part of the town Kundagrama, at the house of the Brahmin Rishabhadatta, where the Brahmini Devananda dwelt. Having arrived there, he made his bow in the sight of he Venerable Ascetic Mahavira, and cast the Brahmini Davananda, together with her retinue, into a deep sleep; then he took off all unclean particles, and brought forth the clean particles, and saying, 'May the Venerable One permit me,' he took the Venerable Ascetic Mahavira in the folded palms of his hands without hurting him. Thus he went to the Kshatriya part of the town Kundagrama, to the house of the Kshatriya Siddhartha, where the Kshatriyani Trisala dwelt; he cast her and her attendants into a deep sleep, took off all unclean particles, and brought forth the clean particles, and placed the embryo of the Venerable Ascetic Mahavira in the womb of the Kshatriyani Trisala, and the embryo of the Kshatriyani Trisala he placed in the womb of the Brahmini Devananda of the Jalandharayana gotra. Having done so, he returned in that direction in which he had come. With that excellent, divine motion of the gods, he flew upwards right through numberless continents and oceans, taking thousands of Yojanas in each motion, and arrived in the Saudharma Kalpa, in the divine abode called Saudharma Avatamsaka, where Sakra, the chief and king of the gods, sat on the throne called Sakra, and reported to Sakra, the chief and king of the gods, on the execution of his orders.

In that period, in that age the knowledge of the Venerable Ascetic Mahavira was threefold; he knew that he was to be removed; he knew that he was removed; he knew not when he was being removed.

In that period, in that age, on the thirteenth day of the third month of the rainy season, in the fifth fortnight, the dark fortnight of Asvina, after the lapse of eighty-two days, on the eighty-third day current since his conception, the embryo of the Venerable Ascetic Mahavira was, on the command of Sakra, safely removed by Harinegamesi from the womb of the Brahmini Devananda to that of the Kshatriyani Trisala, in the middle of the night, when the moon was in conjunction with the asterism Uttaraphalguni.

•

In that night in which the embryo of the Venerable Ascetic Mahavira was removed from the womb of the Brahmini Devananda of the Jalandharayana gotra to that of the Kshatriyani Trisala of the Vasishtha gotra, the former was on her couch taking fits of sleep in a state between sleeping and waking; and seeing that these fourteen illustrious, beautiful, lucky, blest, auspicious, fortunate, great dreams were taken from her by the Kshatriyani Trisala, she awoke.

In that night in which the embryo of the Venerable Ascetic Mahavira was removed from the womb of the Brahmini Devananda of the Jalandharayana gotra to that of the Kshatriyani Trisala of the Vasishtha gotra, the latter was in her dwelling-place, of which the interior was ornamented with pictures, and the outside whitewashed, furbished and cleansed, the brilliant surface of the ceiling was painted, the darkness was dispelled by jewels and precious stones, the floor was perfectly level and adorned with auspicious figures; which, moreover, was furnished with offerings of heaps of delicious, fragrant, strewn flowers of all five colours, was highly delightful through curling, scented fumes of black aloe, the finest Kundurukka and Turushka, and burning frankincense; was exquisitely scented with fine perfumes, and turned as it were into a smelling-bottle; on a couch with a mattress of a man's length, with pillows at head and foot, raised on both sides and hollow in the middle, soft as if one walked on the sand of the banks of the Ganges, covered with the cloth of a robe of ornamented linen, containing a well-worked towel, and hung with red mosquito curtains, delightful, soft to the touch like fur, wadding, Pura, butter, or cotton, with all the comforts of a bed, such as fragrant, excellent flowers and sandal-powder—in such a room and on such a bed Trisala was taking fits of sleep between sleeping and waking, and having seen the following fourteen, dreams, an elephant, she awoke.

1. Then Trisala saw in her first dream a fine, enormous elephant, possessing all lucky marks, with strong thighs and

four mighty tusks; who was whiter than an empty great cloud, or a heap of pearls, or the ocean of milk, or the moon-beams, or spray of water, or the silver mountain; whose temples were perfumed with fragrant musk-fluid, which attracted the bees; equalling in dimension the best elephant of the king of the gods Airavata; uttering a fine deep sound like the thunder of a big and large rain-cloud.

2. Then she saw a tame, lucky bull, of a whiter hue than that of the mass of petals of the white lotus, illumining all around by the diffusion of a glory of light; a bull whose lovely, resplendent, beautiful hump was delightful through the collection of its charms, whose glossy skin was covered with thin, fine, soft hairs; whose body was firm, well made, muscular, compact, lovely, well proportioned, and beautiful; whose horns were large, round, excellently beautiful, greased at their tops, and pointed; whose teeth were all equal, shining, and pure. He foreboded innumerable good qualities.

3. Then she saw a handsome, handsomely shaped, playful lion, jumping from the sky towards her face; a delightful and beautiful lion whiter than a heap of pearls, who had strong and lovely forearms, and a mouth adorned with round, large, and well-set teeth; whose lovely lips, resplendent through their proportions, and soft like a noble lotus, looked as if they were artificially ornamented; whose palate was soft and tender like the petals of the red lotus, and the top of whose tongue was protruding; whose eyes were like pure lightning, and revolved like red-hot excellent gold just poured out from the crucible; a lion with broad and large thighs, and with full and excellent shoulders, who was adorned with a mane of soft, white, thin, long hair of the finest quality; whose erect, well-shaped, and well-grown tail was flapping; the tops of whose nails were deeply set and sharp; whose beautiful tongue came out of his mouth like a shoot of beauty.

4. Then she, with the face of the full moon, saw the goddess of famous beauty, Sri, on the top of Mount Himavat, reposing on a lotus in the lotus lake, anointed with the water from the strong and large trunks of the guardian elephants.

She sat on a lofty throne. Her firmly placed feet resembled golden tortoises, and her dyed, fleshy, convex, thin, red, smooth nails were set in swelling muscles. Her hands and feet were like the leaves of the lotus, and her fingers and toes soft and excellent; her round and well-formed legs were adorned with the Kuruvindavarta, and her knees with dimples. Her fleshy thighs resembled the proboscis of an excellent elephant, and her lovely broad hips were encircled by a golden zone. Her large and beautiful belly was adorned by a circular navel, and contained a lovely row of hairs black as collyrium, bees, or clouds, straight, even, continuous, tin, admirable, handsome, soft, and downy. Her waist, which contained the three folds, could be encompassed with one hand. On all parts of her body shone ornaments and trinkets, composed of many jewels and precious stones, yellow and red gold. The pure cup-like pair of her breasts sparkled, encircled by a garland of Kunda flowers, in which glittered a string of pearls. She wore strings of pearls made by diligent and clever artists, shining with wonderful strings, a necklace of jewels with a string of Dinaras and a trembling pair of earrings, touching her shoulders, diffused a brilliance; but the united beauties and charms of these ornaments were only subservient to the loveliness of her face. Her lovely eyes were large and pure like the water lily. She sprinkled about the sap from two lotus flowers which she held in her splendid hands, and gracefully fanned herself. Her glossy, black, thick, smooth hair hung down in a braid.

5. Then she saw, coming down from the firmament, a garland charmingly interwoven with fresh Mandara flowers. It spread the delicious smell of Champaka, Asoka, Naga Punnaga, Priyangu, Sirisha, Mudgara, Mallika, Jati, Yuthika, Ankolla, Korantakapatra, Damanaka, Navamalika, Bakula, Tilaka, Vasantika, Nuphar, Nymphaea, Patala, Kunda, Atimukta, and Mango; and perfumed the ten divisions of the universe with its incomparably delightful fragrance. It was white through wreaths of fragrant flowers of all seasons, and brilliant through splendid, beautiful embellishments of many

colours. Towards it came humming swarms of different kinds of bees, and filled with their sweet noise the whole neighbourhood.

6. And the moon: white as cow-milk, foam, spray of water, or a silver cup, glorious, delighting heart and eyes, full, dispelling the compact darkness of the thickest wilderness, whose crescent shines at the end of the two halves of the month, opening the blossoms of the groups of Nymphaeas, adorning the night, resembling the surface of a well-polisihed mirror. She was of a white hue, like a flamingo, the stars' head-ornament, the quiver of Cupid's arrows, raising the waters of the ocean, burning as it were disconsolate people when absent from their sweethearts, the large, glorious, wandering headmark of the celestial sphere—beloved in heart and soul by Rohini. Such was the glorious, beautiful, resplendent full moon which the queen saw.

7. Then she saw the large sun, the dispeller of the mass of darkness, him of radiant form, red like the Asoka, the open Kimsuka, the bill of a parrot, or the Gunjardha, the adorner of the lotus groups, the marker of the starry host, the lamp of the firmament, throttling as it were the mass of cold, the illustrious leader of the troop of planets, the destroyer of night, who only at his rising and setting may be well viewed, but at all other times is difficult to be regarded, who disperses evil-doers that stroll about at night, who stops the influence of cold, who always circles round Mount Meru, whose thousand rays obscure the lustre of other lights.

8. Then she saw an extremely beautiful and very large flag, a sight for all people, of a form attractive to the beholders. It was fastened to a golden staff with a tuft of many soft and waving peacock's feathers of blue, red, yellow, and white colours, and seemed as if it would pierce the brilliant, celestial sphere, with the brilliant lion on its top, who was white like crystal, pearlmother, Anka-stone, Kunda-flowers, spray of water, or a silver cup.

9. Then she saw a full vase of costly metal, splendent with fine gold, filled with pure water, excellent, of brilliant

beauty, and shining with a bouquet of water lilies. It united many excellencies and all-auspicious marks, and stood on a lotus-shaped foot, shining with excellent jewels. It delighted the eyes, glittered and illumined all about; it was the abode of happy Fortune, free from all faults, fine, splendid, exquisitely beautiful, entwined with a wreath of fragrant flowers of all seasons.

10. Then she saw a lake, called Lotus Lake, adorned with water lilies. Its yellow water was perfumed by lotuses opening in the rays of the morning sun; it abounded with swarms of aquatic animals, and fed fishes. It was large, and seemed to burn through the wide-spreading, glorious beauty of all kinds of lotuses. Its shape and beauty were pleasing. The lotuses in it were licked by whole swarms of gay bees and mad drones. Pairs of swans, cranes, Chakravakas, ducks, Indian cranes, and many other lusty birds resorted to its waters, and on the leaves of its lotuses sparkled water-drops like pearls. It was a sight, pleasing to the heart and the eye.

11. Then she whose face was splendid like the moon in autumn, saw the milk-ocean, equalling in beauty the breast of Lakshmi, which is white like the mass of moon-beams. Its waters increased in all four directions, and raged with ever-changing and moving, excessively high waves. It presented a splendid and pleasant spectacle as it rushed to and from the shore with its wind-raised, changeable, and moving billows, its tossing waves, and its rolling, splendid, transparent breakers. From it issued camphor-white foam under the lashing tails of great porpoises, fishes, whales, and other monsters of the deep. Its agitated waters were in great uproar, occasioned by the vortex Gangavarta, which the vehemence and force of the great rivers produced; they rose, rushed onwards and backwards, and eddied.

12. Then she saw a celestial abode excelling among the best of its kind, like the lotus among flowers. It shone like the morning sun's disk, and was of a dazzling beauty. Its thousand and eight excellent columns inlaid with the best gold and heaps of jewels diffused a brilliant light like a heavenly lamp, and

the pearls fastened to its curtains glittered. It was hung with brilliant divine garlands, and decorated with pictures of wolves, bulls, horses, men, dolphins, birds, snakes, Kinnaras, deer, Sarabhas, Yaks, Samsaktas, elephants, shrubs, and plants. There the Gandharvas performed their concerts, and the din of the drums of the gods, imitating the sound of big and large rain-clouds, penetrated the whole inhabited world. It was highly delightful through curling, scented fumes of black aloe, the finest Kundurukka and Turushka, burning frankincense and other perfumes. It shed continuous light, was white, of excellent lustre, delighting the best of gods, and affording joy and pleasure.

13. Then she saw an enormous heap of jewels containing Pulaka, Vajra, Indranila, Sasyaka, Karketana, Lohitaksha, Marakata, Prabala, Saugandhika, Sphatika, Hamsagarbha, Anjana, and Chandrakanta. Its base was on the level of the earth, and it illumined with its jewels even the sphere of the sky. It was high and resembled Mount Meru.

14. And a fire. She saw a fire in vehement motion, fed with much-shining and honey-coloured ghee, smokeless, crackling, and extremely beautiful with its burning flames. The mass of its flames, which rose one above the other, seemed to interpenetrate each other, and the blaze of its flames appeared to bake the firmament in some places.

After having seen these fine, beautiful, lovely, handsome dreams, the lotus-eyed queen awoke on her bed while the hair of her body bristled for joy.

Every mother of a Tirthankara sees these fourteen dreams in that night in which the famous Arhat enters her womb.

•

When the Kshatriyani Trisala, having seen these fourteen illustrious, great dreams, awoke, she was glad, pleased, and joyful, rose from her couch, and descended from the footstool.

Neither hasty nor trembling, with a quick and even gait like that of the royal swan, she went to the couch of the Kshatriya Siddhartha. There she awakened the Kshatriya Siddhartha, addressing him with kind, pleasing, amiable, tender, illustrious, beautiful, lucky, blest, auspicious, fortunate, heart-going, heart-easing, well-measured, sweet, and soft words.

Then the Kshatriyani Trisala, with the permission of king Siddhartha, sat down on a chair of state inlaid with various jewels and precious stones in the form of arabesques; calm and composed, sitting on an excellent, comfortable chair, she addressed him with kind, pleasing, words, and spoke thus:

'O beloved of the gods, I was just now on my couch and awoke after having seen the fourteen dreams; to wit, an elephant, etc. What, to be sure, O my lord, will be the happy result portended by these fourteen illustrious, great dreams?'

When the Kshatriya Siddhartha had heard and perceived this news from the Kshatriyani Trisala, he glad, pleased, and joyful, firmly fixed the dreams in his mind, and entered upon considering them; he grasped the meaning of those dreams with his own innate intelligence and intuition which were preceded by reflection, and addressing the Kshatriyani Trisala with kind, pleasing, words, spoke thus:

'O beloved of the gods, you have seen illustrious dreams, you will give birth to a lovely, handsome boy, who will be the ensign of our family, the lamp of our family, the crown of our family, the frontal ornament of our family, the maker of our family's glory, the sun of our family, the stay of our family, the maker of our family's joy and fame, the tree of our family, the exalter of our family; a boy with tender hands and feet, etc. And this boy, after having passed childhood, and, with just ripened intellect, having reached the state of youth, will become a brave, gallant, and valorous king, the lord of the realm, with a large and extensive army and train of wagons. Therefore, O beloved of the gods, you have seen illustrious, dreams.'

In this way he repeatedly expressed his extreme satisfaction. When the Kshatriyani Trisala had heard and perceived this news from king Siddhartha, she glad, pleased, and joyful, spoke thus:

'That is so, O beloved of the gods, as you have pronounced it.'

Thus saying she accepted the true meaning of the dreams, and with the permission of king Siddhartha she rose from her chair of state, inlaid with various jewels and precious stones in the form of arabesques. She then returned to her own bed, neither hasty nor trembling, with a quick and even gait like that of the royal swan, and spoke thus:

'These my excellent and pre-eminent dreams shall not be counteracted by other bad dreams.'

Accordingly she remained awake to save her dreams by means of hearing good, auspicious, pious, agreeable stories about gods and religious men.

At the time of daybreak the Kshatriya Siddhartha called his family servants and spoke thus:

'Now, beloved of the gods, quickly make ready, or have made ready, the exterior hall of audience; see that it be sprinkled with scented water, cleaned, swept, and newly smeared, furnished with offerings of fragrant, excellent flowers of all five colours, made highly delightful through curling scented fumes, and turned, as it were, into a smelling box; also erect my throne, and having done this quickly return, and report on the execution of my orders.'

When the family servants were thus spoken to by king Siddhartha, they—glad, pleased, and joyful, bowed their heads, and modestly accepted the words of command, saying, 'Yes, master!' Then they left the presence of the Kshatriya Siddhartha, and went to the exterior hall of audience, made it ready, and erected the throne. Having done this, they returned to the Kshatriya Siddhartha; joining the palms of their hands so as to bring the ten nails together, laid the folded hands on their heads, and reported on the execution of their orders.

Early at the wane of the night, when the bright morning disclosed the soft flowers of the full-blown lotuses and

Nymphaeas, rose the sun: he was red like the Asoka, the open Kimsuka, the bill of a parrot or the Gunjardha; of an intense redness like that of the Bandhujivaka, the feet and eyes of the turtle dove, the scarlet eyes of the Indian cuckoo, a mass of China roses, or vermilion. He, the thousand-rayed maker of the day, shining in his radiance, awakened the groups of lotuses. When in due time the god of the day had risen and by the blows of his rays the darkness was driven away, while the inhabited world was, as it were, dipped in saffron by the morning sun, the Kshatriya Siddhartha rose from his bed, descended from the footstool, went to the hall for gymnastic exercises, and entered it. There he applied himself to many wholesome exercises, jumped, wrestled, fenced, and fought till he got thoroughly tired: then he was anointed with hundredfold and thousandfold refined different kinds of oil, which nourished, beautified, invigorated, exhilarated, strengthened, and increased all senses and limbs. On an oiled hide he was shampooed by clever men with soft and tender palms of the hands and soles of the feet, who were well acquainted with the best qualities of the practices of anointing, kneading, and stretching; well trained, skilful, excellent, expert, intelligent, and never tiring.

When by this fourfold agreeable treatment of the body the king's bones, flesh, skin, and hair had been benefited, and his fatigue banished, he left the hall for gymnastic exercises, and entered the bathing-house. The pleasant bathing-room was very agreeable, and contained many windows, ornamented with pearls; its floor was decorated with mosaic of various jewels and precious stones. On the bathing-stool, inlaid with various jewels and precious stones in the form of arabesques, he comfortably sat down and bathed himself with water scented with flowers and perfumes, with tepid water and pure water, according to an excellent method of bathing, combined with healthy exercises.

When this healthy excellent bathing under many hundredfold pleasures was over, he dried his body with a long-haired, soft, scented, and coloured towel, put on a new and costly excellent robe, rubbed himself with fresh and fragrant Gosirsha and sandal, and ornamented himself with fine wreaths and sandal-ointment. He put on ornaments of jewels and pearls, hung round his neck fitting necklaces of eighteen, nine, and three strings of pearls, and one with a pearl pendant, and adorned himself with a zone. He put on a collar, rings, and charming ornaments of the hair, and encumbered his arms with excellent bracelets: he was of excessive beauty. His face was lighted up by earrings, and his head by a diadem; his breast was adorned and decked with necklaces, and his fingers were, as it were, gilded by his rings. His upper garment of fine cloth contained swinging pearl pendants. He put on, as an emblem of his undefeated knighthood, glittering, well-made, strong, excellent, beautiful armlets, made by clever artists of spotless and costly jewels, gold, and precious stones of many kinds.

In short, the king was like the tree granting all desires, decorated and ornamented; an umbrella, hung with wreaths and garlands of Korinta flowers, was held above him. He was fanned with white excellent chowries, while his appearance was greeted with auspicious shouts of victory. Surrounded by many chieftains, satraps, kings, princes, knights, sheriffs, heads of families, ministers, chief ministers, astrologers, counsellors, servants, dancing masters, citizens, traders, merchants, foremen of guilds, generals, leaders of caravans, messengers, and frontier-guards, he—the lord and chief of men, a bull and a lion among men, shining with excellent lustre and glory, lovely to behold like the moon emerging from a great white cloud in the midst of the flock of the planets and of brilliant stars and asterisms—left the bathing-house, entered the exterior hall of audience and sat down on his throne with the face towards the east.

On the north-eastern side he ordered eight state chairs, covered with cloth and auspiciously decorated with white mustard, to be set down. Not too far from and not too near to himself, towards the interior of the palace, he had a curtain drawn. It was adorned with different jewels and precious stones, extremely worth seeing, very costly, and manufactured in a famous town; its soft cloth was all over covered with hundreds of patterns and decorated with pictures of wolves, bulls, horses, men, dolphins, birds, snakes, Kinnaras, deer, Sarabhas, Yaks, Samsaktas. elephants, shrubs, and plants. Behind it he ordered to be placed, for the Kshatriyani Trisala, an excellent chair of state, decorated with arabesques of different jewels and precious stones, outfitted with a coverlet and a soft pillow, covered with a white cloth, very soft and agreeable to the touch. Then he called the family servants and spoke thus:

'Quickly, O beloved of the gods, call the interpreters of dreams who well know the science of prognostics with its eight branches, and are well versed in many sciences besides!'

When the family servants were thus spoken to by king Siddhartha, they—glad, pleased, and joyful, laid the folded hands on their heads and modestly accepted the words of command, saying, 'Yes, master!'

Then they left the presence of the Kshatriya Siddhartha, went right through the town Kundapura to the houses of the interpreters of dreams, and called the interpreters of dreams.

Then the interpreters of dreams, being called by the Kshatriya Siddhartha's family servants, glad, pleased, and joyful, bathed, made the offering to the house-gods, performed auspicious rites and expiatory acts, put on excellent, lucky, pure court-dress, adorned their persons with small but costly ornaments, and put, for the sake of auspiciousness, white mustard and Durva. grass on their heads. Thus they issued from their own houses and went right through the Kshatriya part of the town Kundapura to the front gate of king Siddhartha's excellent palace, a jewel of its kind.

There they assembled and went to the exterior hall of audience in the presence of the Kshatriya Siddhartha. Joining the palms of their hands so as to bring the ten nails together, they laid the folded hands on their heads and gave him the greeting of victory.

The king Siddhartha saluted and honoured the

interpreters of dreams, made them presents, and received them with respect. They sat down, one after the other, on the chairs of state which had been placed there before. Then the Kshatriya Siddhartha placed his wife Trisala behind the curtain, and taking flowers and fruits in his hands, addressed with utmost courtesy the interpreters of dreams:

'O beloved of the gods, the Kshatriyant Trisala was just on her couch. What to be sure, O beloved of the gods, will be the result portended by these fourteen illustrious great dreams?'

When the interpreters of dreams had heard and perceived this news from the Kshatriya Siddhartha, they—glad, pleased, and joyful—fixed the dreams in their minds, entered upon considering them, and conversed together.

Having found, grasped, discussed, decided upon, and clearly understood the meaning of these dreams, they recited before king Siddhartha the dream-books and spoke thus:

'O beloved of the gods, in our dream-books are enumerated forty-two common dreams and thirty great dreams. Now, O beloved of the gods, the mothers of universal monarchs or of Arhats wake up after seeing these fourteen great dreams out of the thirty great dreams, when the embryo of a universal monarch or an Arhat enters their womb; an elephant, a bull, etc. The mothers of Vasudevas wake up after seeing any seven great dreams out of these fourteen great dreams, when the embryo of a Vasudeva enters their womb. The mothers of Baladevas wake up after seeing any four great dreams out of these fourteen great dreams, when the embryo of a Baladeva enters their womb. The mother of Mandalikas wake up after seeing a single great dream out of these fourteen great dreams, when the embryo of a Mandalika enters their womb. Now, O beloved of the gods, the Kshatriyani Trisala has seen these fourteen great dreams. And this boy, will be the lord of a realm with a large and extensive army and train of wagons, a universal emperor or a Jina, the lord of the three worlds, the universal emperor of the law.'

When king Siddhartha had heard and perceived this

news from the interpreters of dreams, he—glad, pleased, and joyful, spoke to them thus:

'That is so, O beloved of the gods, as you have pronounced it.'

Thus saying he accepted the true meaning of the dreams, and honoured the interpreters of dreams with praise and plenty of food, flowers, perfumes, garlands, and ornaments. He made them a present in keeping with their station in life and dismissed them.

After this the Kshatriya Siddhartha rose from his throne, went to the Kshatriyani Trisala behind the curtain, and told her the forecast.

'When the Kshatriyani Trisala had heard and perceived this news, she—glad, pleased, and joyful—accepted the true meaning of the dreams. With the permission of king Siddhartha she rose from her chair of state which was decorated with arabesques of various jewels and precious stones, and returned to her own apartments, neither hasty nor trembling, with a quick and even gait like that of the royal swan.

From that moment in which the Venerable Ascetic Mahavira was brought into the family of the Jnatris, many demons in Vaisramana's service, belonging to the animal world, brought, on Sakra's command, to the palace of king Siddhartha, old and ancient treasures, of which the owners, deponers, and families to whom they originally belonged were dead and extinct, and which were hidden in villages, or mines, or scot-free towns, or towns with earth walls, or towns with low walls, or isolated towns, or towns accessible by land and water, or towns accessible either by land or by water only, or in natural strongholds, or in halting-places for processions or for caravans, in triangular places, or in places where three or four roads meet, or in courtyards, or squares, or high roads, or on the site of villages or towns, or in drains of villages or towns, or in bazaars, or temples, or assembling halls, or wells, or parks, or gardens, or woods, or groves, or burying-places, or empty houses, or mountain caves, or hermits' cells, or secret places between walls, or in houses on an elevation, or houses for audience, or palaces.

In the night in which the Venerable Ascetic Mahavira was brought into the family of the Jnatris their silver increased, their gold increased; their riches, corn, majesty, and kingdom increased;. their army, train, treasure, storehouse, town, seraglio, subjects, and glory increased; their real valuable property, as riches, gold, precious stones, jewels, pearls, conches, stones, corals, rubies, etc., the intensity of their popularity and liberality highly increased. At that time the following personal, reflectional, desirable idea occurred to parents of the Venerable Ascetic Mahavira:

'From the moment that this our boy has been begotten, our silver increased, our gold increased, the intensity of our liberality and popularity highly increased. Therefore when this our boy will be born, we shall give him the fit name, attributive and conformable to his quality—Vardhamana.'

Now the Venerable Ascetic Mahavira, out of compassion for his mother, did not move nor stir nor quiver, but remained quiet, stiff, and motionless. Then the following, idea occurred to the mind of the Kshatriyani Trisala: 'The fruit of my womb has been taken from me, it has died, it is fallen, it is lost. Formerly it moved, now it does not move.' Thus with anxious thoughts and ideas, plunged in a sea of sorrow and misery, reposing her head on her hand, overcome by painful reflections, and casting her eyes on the ground she meditated. And in the palace of king Siddhartha the music of drums and stringed instruments, the clapping of hands, the dramatical performances, and the amusements of the people ceased. and mournful dejection reigned there.

Then the Venerable Ascetic Mahavira, knowing that such an idea had occurred to the mind of his mother, he quivered a little.

Feeling her child quivering, trembling, moving, and stirring, the Kshatriyani Trisala—glad, pleased, and joyful—spoke thus: 'No, forsooth, the fruit of my womb has not been taken from me, it has not died, it is not fallen, it is not lost. Formerly it did not move, but now it does move.' Thus she was glad, pleased, and joyful.

Then the Venerable Ascetic Mahavira, while in her womb, formed the following resolution: ' It will not behove me, during the life of my parents, to tear out my hair, and leaving the house to enter the state of houselessness.'

Bathing, making offerings to the house-gods, performing auspicious rites and expiatory acts, and adorning herself with all ornaments, the Kshatriyani Trisala kept off sickness, sorrow, fainting, fear, and fatigue by food and clothing, perfumes and garlands, which were not too cold nor too hot, not too bitter nor too pungent, not too astringent nor too sour nor too sweet, not too smooth nor too rough, not too wet nor too dry, but all just suiting the season. In the proper place and time she ate only such food which was good, sufficient, and healthy for the nourishment of her child. She took her walks in places which were empty and agreeable as well as delightful to the mind; her desires were laudable, fulfilled, honoured, not disregarded, but complied with and executed; she most comfortably dozed, reposed, remained, sat, and laid on unobjectionable and soft beds and seats, and thus most comfortably carried her unborn child.

In that period, in that age the Venerable Ascetic Mahavira—after the lapse of nine months and seven and a half days, in the first month of summer, in the second fortnight, the dark fortnight of Chaitra, on its fourteenth day, while all planets were in their exaltations, the moon in her principal conjunction, and the sky in all its directions clear, bright, and pure; while a favourable and agreeable low wind swept the earth; at the time when the fields were green and all people glad and amusing themselves, in the middle of the night while the moon was in conjunction with the asterism Uttaraphalguni—Trisala, perfectly healthy herself, gave birth to a perfectly healthy boy.

•

In that night in which the Venerable Ascetic Mahavira was born, there was a divine lustre originated by many descending and ascending gods and goddesses, and in the universe, resplendent with one light, the conflux of gods occasioned great confusion and noise.

In that night in which the Venerable Ascetic Mahavira was born, many demons in Vaisramana's service belonging to the animal world, rained down on the palace of king Siddhartha one great shower of silver, gold, diamonds, clothes, ornaments, leaves, flowers, fruits, seeds, garlands, perfumes, sandal powder, and riches.

After the Bhavanapati, Vyantara, Jyotishka, and Vaimanika gods had celebrated the feast of the inauguration of the Tirthankara's birthday, the Kshatriya Siddhartha called, at the break of the morning, together the town policemen and addressed them thus:

'O beloved of the gods, quickly set free all prisoners in the town of Kundapura, increase measures and weights, give order that the whole town of Kundapura with its suburbs be sprinkled with water, swept, and smeared with cowdung, etc. that in triangular places, in places where three or four roads meet, in courtyards, in squares, and in thoroughfares, the middle of the road and the path along the shops be sprinkled, cleaned, and swept; that platforms be erected one above the other; that the town be decorated with variously coloured flags and banners, and adorned with painted pavilions; that the walls bear impressions in Gosirsha, fresh red sandal, and Dardara of the hand with outstretched fingers; that luck-foreboding vases be put on the floor, and pots of the same kind be disposed round every door and arch; that big, round, and long garlands, wreaths, and festoons be hung low and high; that the town be furnished with offerings, etc. to smelling box; that players, dancers, rope-dancers, wrestlers, boxers, jesters, story-tellers, ballad-singers, actors, messengers, pole-dancers, fruit-mongers, bag-pipers, lute-players, and many Talacharas be present. Erect and order to erect thousands of pillars and poles, and report on the execution of my orders.'

When the family servants were thus spoken to by king Siddhartha, they—glad, pleased, and joyful—accepted the words of command, saying, 'Yes, master!'

Then they set free all prisoners, etc. Having done this, they returned to king Siddhartha, and laying their hands on their heads, reported on the execution of his orders.

The king Siddhartha then went to the hall for gymnastic exercises. After having bathed the king accompanied by his whole seraglio, and adorned with flowers, scented robes, garlands, and ornaments, held during ten days the festival in celebration of the birth of a heir to his kingdom; it was held under the continuous din and sound of trumpets, with great state and splendour, with a great train of soldiers, vehicles, and guests, under the sound, din, and noise of conches, cymbals, drums, castanets, horns, small drums, kettle drums, Muragas, Mridangas, and Dundubhis, which were accompanied at the same time by trumpets. The customs, taxes, and confiscations were released, buying and selling prohibited, no policemen were allowed to enter houses, great and small fines were remitted, and debts cancelled. Numberless excellent actors performed and many Talacharas were present, drums sounded harmoniously, fresh garlands and wreaths were seen everywhere, and the whole population in the town and in the country rejoiced and was in full glee.

When the ten days of this festival were over, the king Siddhartha gave and ordered to be given hundreds and thousands and hundred-thousands of offerings to the gods, gifts, and portions of goods; he received and ordered to be received hundreds, thousands, and hundred-thousands of presents.

The parents of the Venerable Ascetic Mahavira celebrated the birth of their heir on the first day, on the third day they showed him the sun and the moon, on the sixth day they observed the religious vigil; after the eleventh day, when the impure operations and ceremonies connected with the birth of a child had been performed, and the twelfth day had come, they prepared plenty of food, drink, spices, and sweetmeats, invited their friends, relations, kinsmen, agnates, cognates, and followers, together with the Jnatrika Kshatriyas. Then they bathed, made offerings to the house-gods, and performed auspicious rites and expiatory acts, put on excellent, lucky, pure court-dress, and adorned their persons with small but costly ornaments. At dinner-time they sat down on excellent, comfortable chairs in the dining-hall, and together with their friends, relations, kinsmen, agnates, cognates and followers, and with the Jnatrika. Kshatriyas they partook, ate, tasted, and interchanged bits of a large collation of food, drink, spices, and sweetmeats.

After dinner they went to the meeting hall after having cleansed their mouths and washed; when perfectly clean, they regaled and honoured their friends, Jnatrika Kshatriyas with many flowers, clothes, perfumes, garlands, and ornaments. Then they spoke thus to their friends:

'Formerly, O beloved of the gods, when we had begotten this our boy, the following personal, reflectional, desirable idea occurred to our mind:

"From the moment that this our boy has been begotten, our silver increased, our gold increased. Now our wishes have been fulfilled, therefore shall the name of our boy be Vardhamana."

The Venerable Ascetic Mahavira belonged to the Kashyapa gotra. His three names have thus been recorded: by his parents he was called Vardhamana; because he is devoid of love and hate, he is called Shramana; because he stands fast in the midst of dangers and fears, patiently bears hardships and calamities, adheres to the chosen rules of penance, is wise, indifferent to pleasure and pain, rich in control, and gifted with fortitude, the name Venerable Ascetic Mahavira has been given him by the gods.

The Venerable Ascetic Mahavira's father belonged to the Kashyapa gotra; he had three names: Siddhartha, Sreyamsa and Jasamsa, and his mother Trisala, Seshavati and Yasovati.

•

The Venerable Ascetic Mahavira—clever, with the aspirations of a clever man, of great beauty, controlling his senses, lucky, and modest; a Jnatri Kshatriya, the son of a Jnatri Kshatriya; the moon of the clan of the Jnatris; Videha, the son .of Videhadatta, a native of Videha, a prince of Videha—had lived thirty years in Videha when his parents went to the world of the gods i.e. died, and he with the permission of his elder brother and the authorities of the kingdom fulfilled his promise. At that moment the Laukantika gods, following the established custom, praised and hymned him with these kind, pleasing, etc. down to sweet, and soft words:

'Victory, victory to thee, gladdener of the world! Victory, victory to thee, lucky one! Luck to thee, bull of the best Kshatriyas! Awake, reverend lord of the world! Establish the religion of the law which benefits all living beings in the whole universe! It will bring supreme benefit to all living beings in all the world!'

Thus they raised the shout of victory. Before the Venerable Ascetic Mahavira had adopted the life of a householder (i.e. before his marriage) he possessed supreme, unlimited, unimpeded knowledge and intuition. The Venerable Ascetic Mahavira perceived with this his supreme unlimited knowledge and intuition that the time for his Renunciation had come. He left his silver, he left his gold, he left his riches, corn, majesty, and kingdom; his army, grain, treasure, storehouse, town, seraglio, and subjects; he quitted and rejected his real, valuable property, such as riches, gold, precious stones, jewels, pearls, conches, stones, corals, rubles, etc.; he distributed presents through proper persons, he distributed presents among indigent persons.

In that period, in that age, in the first month of winter, in the first fortnight, in the dark fortnight of Margasiras, on its tenth day, when the shadow had turned towards the east and the first Paurushi was full and over, on the day called Suvrata, in the Muhurta called Vijaya, in the palanquin

Chandra-prabha, Mahavira was followed on his way[8] by a train of gods, men, and Asuras, and surrounded by a swarm of shell-blowers, proclaimers, Pattivallas, courtiers, men carrying others on the back, heralds, and bell bearers. They praised and hymned him with these kind, pleasing, sweet and soft words:

'Victory, victory to thee, gladdener of the world! Victory to thee, lucky one! Luck to thee! with undisturbed knowledge, intuition, and good conduct conquer the unconquered Senses; defend the conquered Law of 'the Shramanas; Majesty, conquering all obstacles, live in Perfection; put down with thy devotion Love and Hate, the dangerous wrestlers; vigorously gird thy loins with constancy and overcome the eight Karmans, our foes, with supreme, pure meditation; heedful raise the banner of content, O Hero! in the arena of the three worlds gain the supreme, best knowledge, called Kevala, which is free from obscurity; obtain the pre-eminent highest rank, i.e., final liberation on that straight road which the best Jinas have taught; beat the army of obstacles! Victory, victory to thee, bull of the best Kshatriyas! Many days, many fortnights, many months, many seasons, many half-years, many years be not afraid of hardships and calamities, patiently bear dangers and fears; be free from obstacles in the practice of the Law!'

Thus they raised the shout of victory. Then the Venerable Ascetic Mahavira—gazed on by a circle of thousands of eyes, praised by a circle of thousands of mouths, extolled by a circle of thousands of hearts, being the object of many thousands of wishes, desired because of his splendour, beauty, and virtues, pointed out by a circle of thousands of forefingers, answering with his right hand a circle of thousands of joined hands of thousands of men and women, passing along a row of thousands of palaces, greeted by sweet and delightful music, as beating of time, performance on the Vina, Turya, and the great drum, in which joined shouts of victory, and the low and pleasing murmur of the people; accompanied by all his pomp, all his splendour, all his army, all his train, by all his retinue, by all his magnificence, by all his grandeur, by all his ornaments, by all the tumult, by all the throng, by all subjects, by all actors, by all time-beaters, by the whole seraglio; adorned with flowers, scented robes, garlands, and ornaments, which were accompanied at the same time by trumpets—went right through Kundapura to a park called the Shandavana of the Jnatris and proceeded to the excellent tree Asoka.

There under the excellent tree Asoka he caused his palanquin to stop, descended from his palanquin, took off his ornaments, garlands, and finery with his own hands, and with his own hands plucked out his hair in five handfuls. When the moon was in conjunction with the asterism Uttaraphalguni, he, after fasting two and a half days without drinking water, put on a divine robe, and quite alone, nobody else being present, he tore out his hair and leaving the house entered the state of houselessness.

The Venerable Ascetic Mahavira for a year and a month wore clothes; after that time he walked about naked, and accepted the alms in the hollow of his hand. For more than twelve years the Venerable Ascetic Mahavira neglected his body and abandoned the care of it; he with equanimity bore, underwent, and suffered all pleasant or unpleasant occurrences arising from divine powers, men, or animals.

Henceforth the Venerable Ascetic Mahavira was houseless, circumspect in his walking, circumspect in his speaking, circumspect in his begging, circumspect in his accepting anything, in the carrying of his outfit and drinking vessel; circumspect in evacuating excrements, urine, saliva, mucus, and uncleanliness of the body; circumspect in his thoughts, circumspect in his words, circumspect in his acts; guarding his thoughts, guarding his words, guarding his acts, guarding his senses, guarding his chastity; without wrath, without pride, without deceit, without greed; calm, tranquil, composed, liberated, free from temptations, without egoism, without property; he had cut off all earthly ties, and was not stained by any worldliness: as water does not adhere to a copper vessel, or collyrium to mother of pearl so sins found no place in him; his course was unobstructed like that of Life; like the firmament he wanted no support; like the wind he knew no obstacles; his heart was pure like the water of rivers or tanks in autumn; nothing could soil him like the leaf of a lotus; his senses were well protected like those of a tortoise; he was single and alone like the horn of a rhinoceros; he was free like a bird; he was always waking like the fabulous bird Bharunda, valorous like an elephant, strong like a bull, difficult to attack like a lion, steady and firm like Mount Mandara, deep like the ocean, mild like the moon, refulgent like the sun, pure like excellent gold; like the earth he patiently bore everything; like a well-kindled fire he shone in his splendour.

These words have been summarised in two verses:

A vessel, mother of pearl, life, firmament, wind, water in autumn, leaf of lotus, a tortoise, a bird, a rhinoceros, and Bharunda;

An elephant, a bull, a lion, the king of the mountains, and the ocean unshaken—the moon, the sun, gold, the earth, well-kindled fire.

There were no obstacles anywhere for the Venerable One. The obstacles have been declared to be of four kinds, with regard to matter, space, time, affects. With regard to matter: in things animate, inanimate, and of a mixed state; with regard to space: in a village or a town or in a wood or in a field or a threshing-floor or a house or a courtyard; with regard to time: in a Samaya or an Avalika or in the time of a respiration or in a Stoka or in a Kshana or in a Lava or in a Muhurta or in a day or in a fortnight or in a month or in a season or in a half year or in a year or in a long space of time; with regard to affects: in wrath or in pride or in deceit or in greed or in fear or in mirth or in love or in hate or in quarrelling or in calumny or in tale-bearing or in scandal or in pleasure or pain or in deceitful falsehood, etc. all down to or in the evil of wrong belief. There was nothing of this kind in the Venerable One.

The Venerable One lived, except in the rainy season, all the eight months of summer and winter, in villages only a single night, in towns only five nights; he was indifferent alike to the smell of ordure and of sandal, to straw and jewels, dirt and gold, pleasure and pain, attached neither to this world nor to that beyond, desiring neither life nor death, arrived at the other shore of the Samsara, and he exerted himself for the suppression of the defilement of Karman.

With supreme knowledge, with supreme intuition, with supreme conduct, in blameless lodgings, in blameless wandering, with supreme valour, with supreme uprightness, with supreme mildness, with supreme dexterity, with supreme patience, with supreme freedom from passions, with supreme control, with supreme contentment, with supreme understanding, on the supreme path to final liberation, which is the fruit of veracity, control, penance, and good conduct, the Venerable One meditated on himself for twelve years.

During the thirteenth year, in the second month of summer, in the fourth fortnight, the light fortnight of Vaisakha, on its tenth day, when the shadow had turned towards the east and the first wake was over, on the day called Suvrata, in the Muhurata called Vijaya, outside of the town Jrimbhikagrama on the bank of the river Rijupalika, not far from an old temple, in the field of the householder Samaga, under a Sal tree, when the moon was in conjunction with the asterism Uttaraphalguni, the Venerable One in a squatting position with joined heels, exposing himself to the heat of the sun, after fasting two and a half days without drinking water, being engaged in deep meditation, reached the highest knowledge and intuition, called Kevala, which is infinite, supreme, unobstructed, unimpeded, complete, and full.

When the Venerable Ascetic Mahavira had become a Jina. and Arhat, he was a Kevalin, omniscient and comprehending all objects; he knew and saw all conditions of the world, of gods, men, and demons: whence they come, whither they go, whether they are bom as men or animals or become gods or hell-beings, the ideas, the thoughts of their minds, the food, doings, desires, the open and secret deeds of all the living beings in the whole world; he the Arhat, for whom there is no secret, knew and saw all conditions of all living beings in the world, what they thought, spoke, or did at any moment.

In that period, in that age the Venerable Ascetic Mahavira stayed the first rainy season in Asthikagrama, three rainy seasons in Champa and Prishtichampa, twelve in Vaisali and Vanijagrama, fourteen in Rajagriha and the suburb of Nalanda, six in Mithila, two in Bhadrika, one in Alabhika, one in Panitabhumi, one in Sravasti, one in the town of Pava in king Hastipala's office of the writers: that was his very last rainy season.

In the fourth month of that rainy season, in the seventh fortnight, in the dark fortnight of Kartika, on its fifteenth day, in the last night, in the town of Pava, in king Hastipala's office of the writers, the Venerable Ascetic Mahavira died, went off, quitted the world, cut asunder the ties of birth, old age, and death; became a Siddha, a Buddha, a Mukta, a maker of the end to all misery, finally liberated, freed from all pains.

This occurred in the year called Chandra, the second of the lustrum; in the month called Pritivardana; in the fortnight Nandivardhana; on the day Suvratagni, surnamed Upasama; in the night called Devananda, surnamed Niriti; the Lava called Archya; in the respiration called Mukta; in the Stoka called Siddha; in the Karana called Naga; in the Muhurta called Sarvarthasiddha; while the moon was in conjunction with the asterism Svati he died, freed from all pains.

That night in which the Venerable Ascetic Mahavira died, freed from all pains, was lighted up by many descending and ascending gods.

In that night in which the Venerable Ascetic Mahavira died, freed from all pains, a great confusion and noise was originated by many descending and ascending gods.

In that night in which the Venerable Ascetic Mahavira died, freed from all pains, his oldest disciple, the monk Indrabhuti of the Gautama gotra, cut asunder the tie of friendship which he had for his master, and obtained the highest knowledge and intuition, called Kevala, which is infinite, supreme, complete, and full.

In that night in which the Venerable Ascetic Mahavira died, freed from all pains, the eighteen confederate kings of Kahi and Kosala, the nine Mallakis and nine Lichchavis, on the day of new moon, instituted an illumination on the Posadha, which was a fasting day; for they said: 'Since the light of intelligence is gone, let us make an illumination of material matter!'

In that night in which the Venerable Ascetic Mahavira died, freed from all pains, the great Graha called Kshudratma, resembling a heap of ashes, which remains for two thousand years in one asterism, entered the natal asterism of the Venerable Ascetic Mahavira. From the moment in which the great Graha, entered the natal asterism of the Venerable Ascetic Mahavira, there will not be paid much respect and honour to the Shramanas, the Nirgrantha monks and nuns. But when the great Graha, leaves that natal asterism, there will be paid much respect and honour to the Shramanas, the Nirgrantha monks and nuns.

In that night in which the Venerable Ascetic Mahavira died, freed from all pains, the animalcule called Anuddhari was originated: which when at rest and not moving, is not easily seen by Nirgrantha monks and nuns who have not yet reached the state of perfection, but which when moving and not at rest, is easily seen by Nirgrantha monks and nuns who have not yet reached the state of perfection. On seeing this animalcule many Nirgrantha monks and nuns must refuse to accept the offered alms.

'Master, why has this been said?' 'After this time the observance of control will be difficult 'In that period, in that age the Venerable Ascetic Mahavira had an excellent community of fourteen thousand Shramanas with Indrabhuti at their head; thirty-six thousand nuns with Chandana at their head; one hundred and fifty-nine thousand lay votaries with Sankhasataka at their head; three hundred and eighteen thousand female lay votaries with Sulasa and Revati at their head; three hundred sages who knew the fourteen Purvas, who though no Jinas came very near them, who knew the combination of all letters, and like Jina. preached according to the truth; thirteen hundred sages who were possessed of the Avadhi-knowledge and superior qualities; seven hundred Kevalins who possessed the combined best knowledge and intuition; seven hundred who could transform themselves, and, though no gods, had obtained the powers of gods; five hundred sages of mighty intellect who know the mental conditions of all developed beings possessed of intellect and five senses in the two and a half continents and two oceans; four hundred professors who were never vanquished in the disputes occurring in the assemblies of gods, men, and Asuras; seven hundred male and fourteen hundred female disciples who reached perfection, freed from all pains; eight hundred sages in their last birth who were happy as regards their station, happy as regards their existence, lucky as regards their future.

The Venerable Ascetic Mahavira instituted two epochs in his capacity of a Maker of an end: the epoch relating to generations, and the epoch relating to psychical condition; in the third generation ended the former epoch, and in the fourth year of his Kevaliship the latter.

In that period, in that age the Venerable Ascetic Mahavira lived thirty years as a householder, more than full twelve years in a state inferior to perfection, something less than thirty years as a Kevalin. forty-two years as a monk, and seventy-two years on the whole. When his Karman which produces Vedaniya, or what one has to experience in this world, Ayus, length of life, name, and family, had been exhausted, when in this Avasarpini era the greater part of the Duhshama-sushama period had elapsed and only three years and eight and a half months were left, when the moon was in conjunction with the asterism Svati, at the time of early morning, in the town of Pava, and in king Hastipala's office of the writers, Mahavira single and alone, sitting in the Samparyanka posture, reciting the fifty-five lectures which detail the results of Karman, and the thirty-six unasked questions, when he just explained the chief lecture that of Marudeva he died, freed from all pains.

Since the time that the Venerable Ascetic Mahavira died, freed from all pains, nine centuries have elapsed, and of the tenth century this is the eightieth year. Another redaction has ninety-third year instead of eightieth.

Parsva

In that period, in that age lived the Arhat Parsva, the people's favourite, the five most important moments of whose life happened when the moon was in conjunction with the asterism Visakha: in Visakha he descended from heaven, and having descended thence, entered the womb of his mother; in Visakha he was born; in Visakha, tearing out his hair, he left the house and entered the state of houselessness; in Visakha he obtained the highest knowledge and intuition, called Kevala, which is infinite, supreme, unobstructed, unimpeded, complete, and full; in Visakha he obtained final liberation.

In that period, in that age, in the first month of summer, in the first fortnight, the dark fortnight of Chaitra, on its fourth day, the Arhat Parsva, the people's favourite, descended from the Pranata Kalpa, where he had lived for twenty Sagaropamas, here on the continent Jambudvipa, in Bharatavarsha, in the town of Benares; and in the middle of the night when the moon was in conjunction with the asterism Visakha, after the termination of his allotted length of life, divine nature, and existence among the gods, he took the form of an embryo in the womb of the queen Vama, wife of

Asvasena king of Benares.

In that period, in that age the Arhat Parsva, the people's favourite—after the lapse of nine months and seven and a half days, in the second month of winter, in the third fortnight, the dark fortnight of Paushya, on its tenth day, in the middle of the night when the moon was in conjunction with the asterism Visakha—Vama, perfectly healthy herself, gave birth to a perfectly healthy boy.

The Arhat Parsva, the people's favourite, clever, with the aspirations of a clever man, of great beauty, controlling his senses, lucky, and modest, lived thirty years as a householder. Then the Laukantika gods, following the established custom, addressed him with these kind, pleasing, sweet, and soft words:

'Victory, victory to thee, gladdener of the world!' Thus they raised the shout of victory, Before the Arhat Parsva, the people's favourite, had adopted the life of a householder, etc. down to indigent persons.

In the second month of winter, in the third fortnight, the dark fortnight of Paushya, on its eleventh day, in the middle of the night, riding in his palanquin called Virala, followed on his way by a train of gods, men, and Asuras, Parsva went right through the town of Benares to the park called Asramapada, and proceeded to the excellent tree Asoka. There, etc. down to five handfuls.

When the moon was in conjunction with the asterism Visakha, he, after fasting three and a half days without drinking water, put on a divine robe, and together with three hundred men he tore out his hair, and leaving the house entered the state of houselessness.

The Arhat Parsva, the people's favourite, for eighty-three days neglected his body.

Thereafter the Arhat Parsva, the people's favourite, was houseless, circumspect, meditated upon himself for eighty-three days.

During the eighty-fourth day—it was in the first month of summer, in the first fortnight, the dark fortnight of Chaitra, on its fourth day, in the early part of the day, when the moon was in conjunction with the asterism Visakha—Parsva, under a Dhataki tree, after fasting two and a half days without drinking water, being engaged in deep meditation, reached the infinite, highest knowledge and intuition called Kevala.

The Arhat Parsva, the people's favourite, had eight Ganas and eight Ganadharas, enumerated in a Sloka:

Subha and Aryaghosha, Vasishtha and Brahmacharin Saumya and Sridhara, Virabhadra and Yasas.

The Arhat Parsva, the people's favourite, had an excellent community of sixteen thousand Shramanas with Aryadatta at their head; thirty-eight thousand nuns with Pushpakula at their head; one hundred and sixty-four thousand lay votaries with Suvrata at their head; three hundred and twenty-seven thousand female lay votaries with Sunanda at their head; three hundred and fifty sages who knew the fourteen Purvas; fourteen hundred sages who were possessed of the Avadhi knowledge; one thousand Kevalins; eleven hundred sages who could transform themselves, six hundred sages of correct knowledge, one thousand male and two thousand female disciples who had reached perfection, seven hundred and fifty sages of vast intellect, six hundred professors, and twelve hundred sages in their last birth.

The Arhat Parsva, the people's favourite, instituted two epochs in his capacity of a Maker of an end: the epoch relating to generations and the epoch relating to psychical condition; the former ended in the fourth generation, the latter in the third year of his Kevaliship.

In that period, in that age the Arhat Parsva, the people's favourite, lived thirty years as a householder, eighty-three days in a state inferior to perfection, something less than seventy years as a Kevalin, full seventy years as a Shramana, and a hundred years on the whole.

When his fourfold Karman was exhausted and in this Avasarpini era the greater part of the Duhshama-sushama period had elapsed, in the first month of the rainy season, in the second fortnight, the light fortnight of Shravana, on its eighth day, in the early part of the day when the moon was in conjunction with the asterism Visakha, Parsva, after fasting a month without drinking water, on the summit of mount Sammeta, in the company of eighty-three persons, stretching out his hands, died, freed from all pains.

Since the time that the Arhat Parsva, the people's favourite, died, freed from all pains, twelve centuries have elapsed, and of the thirteenth century this is the thirtieth year.

Arishtanemi

In that period, in that age lived the Arhat Arishtanemi, the five most important moments of whose life happened when the moon was in conjunction with the asterism Chitra. In Chitra he descended from heaven, and passing through all the states, in Chitra, he obtained final liberation.

In that period, in that age, in the fourth month of the rainy season, in the seventh fortnight, the dark fortnight of Kartika, on its twelfth day, the Arhat Arishtanemi descended from the great Vimana, called Aparajita, where he had lived for thirty-six Sagaropamas, here on the continent Jambudvipa, in Bharatavarsha, in the town of Sauripura, and in the middle of the night when the moon was in conjunction with the asterism Chitra, he took the form of an embryo in the womb of the queen Siva, wife of the king Samudravijaya.

In that period, in that age the Arhat Arishtanemi—after the lapse of nine months and seven and a half days, in the first month of the rainy season, in the second fortnight, the light fortnight of Sravana, on its fifth day, perfectly healthy herself, gave birth to a perfectly healthy boy. The name the boy was given was Arishtanemi.

The Arhat Arishtanemi, clever, etc. indigent persons. In the first month of the rainy season, in the second fortnight, the light fortnight of Sravana, on its sixth day riding in his palanquin called Uttarakura, and followed on his way by a train of gods, men, and Asuras, Arishtanemi went right through the town of Dvaravati to the park called Revatika, and proceeded to the excellent Asoka tree. There, when the moon was in conjunction with the asterism Chitra, after fasting two and a half days without drinking water, he put on a divine robe, and together with a thousand persons he tore out his hair, and leaving the house entered the state of houselessness.

The Arhat Arishtanemi for fifty-four days neglected his body, During the fifty-fifth day—it was in the third month of the rainy season, in the fifth fortnight, the dark fortnight of Asvina, on its fifteenth day, in the last part of the day, when the moon was in conjunction with the asterism Chitra—Arishtanemi under a Vetasa tree on the summit of mount Girnar, after fasting three and a half.days without drinking water, obtained infinite, highest knowledge and intuition called Kevala.

The Arhat Arishtanemi had eighteen Ganas and eighteen Ganadharas.

The Arhat Arishtanemi had an excellent community of eighteen thousand Shramanas with Varadatta at their head; forty thousand nuns with Arya Yakshini at their head; one hundred and sixty-nine thousand lay votaries with Nanda at their head; three hundred and thirty-six thousand female lay votaries with Mahasuvrata at their head; four hundred sages who knew the fourteen Purvas; fifteen hundred sages who were possessed of the Avadhi knowledge; fifteen hundred Kevalins; fifteen hundred sages who could transform themselves; one thousand sages of vast intellect; eight hundred professors; sixteen hundred sages in their last birth; fifteen hundred male and three thousand female disciples who had reached perfection.

The Arhat Arishtanemi instituted two epochs in his capacity as Maker of an end; the former ended in the eighth generation, the latter in the twelfth year of his Kevaliship.

In that period, in that age the Arhat Arishtanemi lived three centuries as a prince, fifty-four days in a state inferior to perfection, something less than seven centuries as a Kevalin, full seven centuries as a Shramana, a thousand years on the whole. When his fourfold Karman was exhausted and in this Avasarpini era a great part of the Duhshama-sushama period had elapsed, in the fourth month of summer, in the eighth fortnight, the light fortnight of Ashadha, on its eighth day, in the middle of the night when the moon was in conjunction with the asterism Chitra, Arishtanemi, after fasting a month without drinking water, on the summit of mount Girnar, in the company of five hundred and thirty-six monks, in a squatting position, died, freed from all pains.

Since the time that the Arhat Arishtanemi died, freed from all pains, eighty-four thousand years have elapsed, of the eighty-fifth millennium nine centuries have elapsed, of the tenth century this is the eightieth year.

Epochs of the Intermediate Tirthankaras

Since the time that the Arhat Nemi died, freed from all pains, 584,979 years have elapsed, this is the eightieth year. Since the death of Munisuvrata this is the year 1,184,980. Since Malli this is the year 6,584,980. Ara died 10,000,000 years before Malli; Kunthu a quarter of a Palyopama before Malli; Shanti three-quarters of a Palyopama; Dharma three Sagaropamas before Malli; Ananta seven Sagaropamas before Malli; Vimala sixteen Sagaropamas before Malli; Vasupujya forty Sagaropamas before Malli; Sreyansa a hundred Sagaropamas before Malli. Sitala died a crore of Sagaropamas, less 42,003 years and eight and a half months, before the death of Vira. Suvidhi, surnamed Pushpadanta, died ten crores of Sagaropamas before Sitala; Chandraprabha a hundred crores of Sagaropamas before Sitala; Suparsva a thousand crores of Sagaropamas before Sitala; Padmaprabha ten thousand krores of Sagaropamas before Sitala; Sumati one hundred thousand crores of Sagaropamas before Sitala; Abhinandana one million crores of Sagaropamas before Sitala; Sambhava two million crores of Sagaropamas before Sitala; Agita five million xrores of Sagaropamas before Sitala.

Rishabha

In that period, in that age lived the Arhat Rishabha, the Kosalian, four important moments of whose life happened when the moon was in conjunction with the asterism Uttarashadha; the fifth, when in conjunction with Abhijit: in Uttarashadha he descended from heaven, in Abhijit he obtained final liberation.

In that period, in that age, in the fourth month of summer, in the seventh fortnight, the dark fortnight of Ashadha on its fourth day, the Arhat Rishabha, the Kosalian, descended from the great Vimana called Sarvarthasiddha, where he had lived for thirty-three Sagaropamas, here on the continent Jambudvipa, in Bharatavarsha, in Ikshvakubhumi, and in the middle of the night, he took the form of an embryo in the womb of Marudevi, wife of the patriarch Nabhi.

In that period, in that age the Arhat Rishabha, the Kosalian,—in the first month of summer, in the first fortnight, the dark fortnight of Chaitra, on its eighth day—Marudevi, perfectly healthy herself, gave birth to a perfectly healthy boy.

(The circumstances connected with the birth of Rishabha are the same as in the case of that of Mahavira.)

The Arhat Rishabha, the Kosalian, belonged to the Kashyapa gotra, and he had five names: Rishabha, First King, First Mendicant, First Jina, and First Tirthankara.

The Arhat Rishabha, the Kosalian, clever, with the aspirations of a clever man, of great beauty, controlling his senses, lucky, and modest, lived two millions of former years as a prince, and six millions three hundred thousand former years as a king. During his reign he taught, for the benefit of the people, the seventy-two sciences, of which writing is the first, arithmetic the most important, and the knowledge of omens the last, the sixty-four accomplishments of women, the hundred arts, and the three occupations of men. At last he anointed his hundred sons as kings, and gave each a kingdom. In the first month of summer, in the first fortnight, the dark fortnight of Chaitra, on its eighth day, in the latter part of the day, riding in his palanquin called Sudarsana, followed on his way by a train of gods, men, and Asuras, Rishabha went right through the town Vinita to the park called Siddhartha Vana, and proceeded to the excellent tree Asoka. When the moon was in conjunction with the asterism Ashadha, he, after fasting two and a half days without drinking water, put on a divine robe, and together with four thousand of high, noble, royal persons, and Kshatriyas, he tore out his hair, and leaving the house entered the state of houselessness.

The Arhat Rishabha, the Kosalian, for one thousand years neglected his body, meditated upon himself for one thousand years. Thereupon—it was in the fourth month of winter, the seventh fortnight, the dark fortnight of Phalguna, on its eleventh day, in the early part of the day, when the moon was in conjunction with the asterism Ashadha, outside of the town Purimatala, in the park called Sakatamukha, under the excellent tree Nyagrodha—Rishabha after fasting three and a half days without drinking water, being engaged in deep meditation, reached the infinite, highest knowledge and intuition called Kevala.

The Arhat Rishabha, the Kosalian, had eighty-four Ganas and eighty-four Ganadharas.

The Arhat Rishabha, the Kosalian, had an excellent community of eighty-four thousand Shramanas with Rishabhasena at their head; three hundred thousand nuns with Brahmasundari at their head; three hundred and five thousand lay votaries with Sreyamsa at their head; five hundred and fifty-four thousand female lay votaries with Subhadra at their head; four thousand seven hundred and fifty sages who knew the fourteen Purvas; nine thousand sages who were possessed of the Avadhi knowledge; twenty thousand Kevalins; twenty thousand six hundred sages who could transform themselves; twelve thousand six hundred and fifty sages of vast intellect; twelve thousand six hundred and fifty professors; twenty thousand male and forty thousand female disciples who had reached perfection; twenty-two thousand nine hundred sages in their last birth.

The Arhat Rishabha, the Kosalian, instituted two epochs in his capacity as a Maker of an end; the former ended after numberless generations, the latter from the next Muhurta after his Kevaliship.

In that period, in that age the Arhat Rishabha, the Kosalian, lived two millions of former years as a prince, six millions three hundred thousand former years as a king, together eight millions three hundred thousand former years as a householder; a thousand former years in a state inferior to perfection, nine-and-ninety thousand former years as a Kevalin, together a hundred thousand former years as a Shramana., and eight millions four hundred thousand years on the whole. When his fourfold Karman was exhausted, and in this Avasarpini era the Sushama-duhshama period had nearly elapsed, only three years and eight and a half months being left, in the third month of winter, in the fifth fortnight, the dark fortnight of Magha, on its thirteenth day, in the early part of the day when the moon was in conjunction with the asterism Abhijit, Rishabha, after fasting six and a half days without drinking water, on the summit of mount Ashtapada, in the company of ten thousand monks in the Samparyanka position, died, freed from all pains.

Since the time that the Arhat Rishabha, the Kosalian, died, freed from all pains, three years and eight and a half months elapsed; thereupon one koti of kotis of Sagaropamas, less forty-two thousand and three years and eight and a half months, elapsed. At that time the Venerable Ascetic Mahavira died; after his Nirvana nine centuries elapsed, of the tenth century this is the eightieth year.

7

There Is No God

Based on Adi Purana

The world is eternal. It is also ephemeral. It has its own basic laws which remain unchanged in all situations and circumstances, though its parts keep changing according to needs and requirements. These laws have not been created by any god, and no god either rules these or can destroy them. The concept of a creator or destroyer is unjustified and self-contradictory; it is illogical as also not moral.

The concept that the world must have a creator has its roots in the idea that it is a product. If that were so, then god must also be a product, for the simple reason that his action of creating and destroying must also take place in him. We shall then have to look for the cause of god himself, leading to an endless search backwards in the cause of cause of cause of cause....

Then if it is supposed that the world had a cause, then it would not mean that the cause was a thinking entity. The maker of a product in the world can never be perfect. In that case god should also have a body, because a material object in this world can never be produced without a body having a material base with the activity of thinking, volition and will to produce something.

Everything in this world which is made of matter is changeable and therefore it must suffer. In that case god could neither be unchangeable nor blissful.

If one supposes that god has created the world without a body, by merely his abstract entity, then one cannot depend in any way on the analogies of the world of experience, the practical realities.

If god has produced the world, from what he has done it? Has be produced it from nothing? If he has done so, and if it will also disappear in nothing, then god himself must also arise from nothing and dissolve into nothing. If being (*sat*) and non being (*asat*) are absolute opposites, then one cannot arise from the other. If they are not so, then truth and falsehood, virtue and vice, etc., will also be non-existent. Then all philosophy will be meaningless.

If matter and soul are regarded to be eternal which acquire their qualities from their basic nature, and god's action is limited to managing these qualities in the world phenomenon, then one would wonder why the assistance of god was required to do so; why the matter and souls could not do these on their own, with the help of their inherent powers?

If god is the only all-powerful doer in the world, then he will have to be regarded as the cause of all evil that is the essential part of this world. One will then have to conclude that god is not good.

If god is regarded as good who permits evil to operate freely, then we shall have to accept that he is not all powerful.

If god is regarded to have created the souls, then why did he not make them good? Why has he made them evil also? Has he done so to enable him to punish them for the sins they commit in the world?

If god has called the souls to operate in the world and given it to himself to see whether they act correctly or sinfully, then he will have to be regarded as not omniscient, because if he had been omniscient, he should have foreseen it.

All this will have to be regarded as perverse, unworthy of a noble and kind entity—to let persons fall into hell and suffer horrible tortures for actions for which they have not been directly responsible.

If god has created the world, what would have been his motive? If he did it on account of his desire, was he in a state of dissatisfaction before creating the world? If so, be cannot be regarded as eternally blissful and perfect.

If god has created the world on account of his whim, then how can it be regarded as being conducted according to law?

If god has created the world out of love, to lead the unredeemed souls to salvation, then why only a very few souls reach it? Why did be conjure up the torments of the world? He could have acquired his objective in a different, better way, because he is all powerful

If god created the world to let the souls selected by him enjoy the rewards, and others rejected by him, be condemned to hell, etc., then he will have to be regarded as partial to some and enemical to others. This would question his sense of justice; he will have to be regarded as arbitrary and unjust.

If god created the world for his play, if the world is his *lila*, without a purpose and goal, just for his entertainment, then he must be regarded as a 'horrible master who finds pleasure in the sufferings of the innumerable living beings.

If god were omnipresent, he must be present in the hells. If he were omniscient, he would not have created evil beings—and 'people like the Jainas who deny him his existence.'

God's existence cannot be proved by any means of knowledge, perception, inference, revelation, or the absurd theory of Maya.

❑❑❑

Other Books on

PHILOSOPHY, RELIGION & CULTURE

No.	Title	Price
26.	The Golden Book of Upanishads	395/-
27.	Learn Rajayoga from Vivekananda	250/-
28.	Colossus Vivekananda Select	295/-
29.	Intellect India	250/-
30.	Culture India	250/-
31.	Mahatma Gandhi The Bhagavadgita	195/-
32.	Shirdi Sai Baba	80/-
33.	The Ramayana For Every Home **(New)**	125/-
34.	The Mahabharata For Every Home **(New)**	125/-
35.	Sai - The Age of Cosmic Family	80/-
36.	Sathya Sai and His Miraculous Powers	150/-
37.	To Bloom Like a Lotus	225/-
38.	The History of Sikh Gurus	225/-
39.	Indian Mythology	195/-
40.	Human Rights in Islam	395/-

Lotus PRESS

Unit No. 220, 2nd Floor, 4735/22, Prakash Deep Building,
Ansari Road, Darya Ganj, New Delhi- 110002
Ph.: 23280047, 9811594448
• E-mail : lotuspress1984@gmail.com, www.lotuspress.co.in